# Lecture Notes in Computer Science 16967

The series Lecture Notes in Computer Science (LNCS), including its subseries Lecture Notes in Artificial Intelligence (LNAI) and Lecture Notes in Bioinformatics (LNBI), has established itself as a medium for the publication of new developments in computer science and information technology research, teaching, and education.

LNCS enjoys close cooperation with the computer science R & D community, the series counts many renowned academics among its volume editors and paper authors, and collaborates with prestigious societies. Its mission is to serve this international community by providing an invaluable service, mainly focused on the publication of conference and workshop proceedings and postproceedings. LNCS commenced publication in 1973.

Peter Gorm Larsen · Kristin Yvonne Rozier
Editors

# Formal Methods for Industrial Critical Systems

## 31st International Conference, FMICS 2026
## Liverpool, UK, September 3–4, 2026
## Proceedings

Springer

*Editors*
Peter Gorm Larsen
Aarhus University
Aarhus, Denmark

Kristin Yvonne Rozier
Iowa State University
Ames, IA, USA

ISSN 0302-9743 ISSN 1611-3349 (electronic)
Lecture Notes in Computer Science
ISBN 978-3-032-36848-5 ISBN 978-3-032-36849-2 (eBook)
https://doi.org/10.1007/978-3-032-36849-2



This Springer imprint is published by the registered company Springer Nature Switzerland AG
The registered company address is: Gewerbestrasse 11, 6330 Cham, Switzerland

If disposing of this product, please recycle the paper.

# Preface

This publication contains the proceedings of the 31st ERCIM Working Group conference on Formal Methods for Industrial Critical Systems (FMICS 2026), which was held 3–4 September 2026 at the University of Liverpool in Liverpool, UK. ERCIM is the European Research Consortium for Informatics and Mathematics. FMICS was held in conjunction with CONFEST, an umbrella event consisting of three main conferences, of which FMICS is one.

The aim of the FMICS conference series is to provide a forum for researchers and practitioners who are interested in the development and application of formal methods in industry. FMICS brings together scientists and engineers who are active in the area of formal methods and interested in exchanging their experiences in the industrial usage of these methods. The FMICS conference series also strives to promote research and development for the improvement of formal methods and tools for industrial applications. FMICS is the key conference in the intersection of industrial applications and Formal Methods.

FMICS was created following a successful workshop bringing together ERCIM members interested in formal verification, held in Pisa in December 1992. The series of annual workshops began in 1996 and have promoted an ongoing scientific discussion focused on identifying the most efficient verification techniques, with a keen eye to their industrial applicability. Most of the members of the FMICS community have strong links with industry and have thus contributed to the slow but constant introduction of formal methods in the development cycle of industrial critical systems witnessed in the last decade. FMICS has also addressed other readily applicable verification techniques, such as static analysis by abstract interpretation and unifying formal techniques across the whole formal development lifecycle.

FMICS 2026 encouraged submissions on approaches that bring together formal methods and industrial context, including application of formal methods in standardization and industrial forums. The topics covered by FMICS include but are not limited to: formal specification, including specification elicitation, validation, debugging, sanity checking, revision, coverage, and explainability; case studies and experience reports on industrial applications of formal methods, focusing on lessons learned or identification of new research directions; methods, techniques, and tools to support automated analysis, certification, debugging, learning, optimization, and transformation of complex, distributed, real-time, embedded, mobile, and autonomous systems; verification and validation methods (model checking, theorem proving, SAT/SMT constraint solving, abstract interpretation, etc.) that address shortcomings of existing methods with respect to their industrial applicability (e.g., scalability and usability issues, tool qualification, and certification); and transfer to industry and impact of adoption of formal methods on the development process and associated costs in industry.

FMICS papers must describe original research work and results and must not have previously appeared in a journal or conference with published proceedings. Papers must clearly motivate relevance to industrial applications. Case study papers should identify lessons learned, validate theoretical results (such as scalability of methods), and provide specific motivation for further research and development. For all papers with experimental results, we strongly recommended providing reviewers with an artifact that they can use to reproduce results, e.g., via a paper website.

FMICS received 34 abstract submissions, resulting in 30 full-paper submissions. All papers went through a rigorous reviewing process, where each paper was read by at least three members of the Programme Committee, with extra reviews added as needed. The Programme Committee evaluated the submitted papers based on the novelty, soundness, and applicability of the presented ideas and results. A total of 8 papers were accepted for publication, giving an overall acceptance rate of 26.6%. FMICS received submissions from 17 countries: Australia, Austria, Belgium, Brazil, China, Denmark, France, Germany, Ireland, Italy, Japan, the Netherlands, Poland, Sweden, Tunisia, the United Kingdom, and the United States.

In addition to the refereed papers, the conference featured two FMICS invited talks and two shared (with CONFEST) invited talks. Representing NASA JSC, Dr. Julia Badger delivered a keynote talk on "Application of Formal Methods to Design and Verification of Autonomous Space Systems." Dr. Colin O'Halloran, CTO of D-RiSQ Ltd, UK and Honorary Visiting Professor at the University of York, UK delivered a keynote talk on "Reducing Time to Market through Formal Methods." In conjunction with CONFEST, Professor Ezio Bartocci of TU Wien delivered a keynote talk on "Reasoning About Probabilistic Loops, Moment by Moment" and Professor Ichiro Hasuo of National Institute of Informatics (NII), Tokyo, Japan delivered a keynote talk on "Category Theory for Fast Model Checking Algorithms."

The organizers are grateful to the authors for submitting their work to FMICS 2026 and to the invited speakers for sharing their insights. FMICS 2026 would not have been possible without the collaboration of the Steering Committee, Program Committee, our many external reviewers, and the support of the ERCIM Working Group and the greater Formal Methods Europe community. We are also grateful to the organizers of CONFEST: Daniel Hausmann, David Purser, Patrick Totzke, and Shufang Zhu. The FMICS 2026 website can be found at https://confest-2026.github.io/fmics/.

September 2026

Peter Gorm Larsen
Kristin Yvonne Rozier

# Organization

## Program Committee

| | |
|---|---|
| Jefferson Andrade | Instituto Federal do Espírito Santo |
| Ramesh Bharadwaj | Naval Research Laboratory |
| John Fitzgerald | Newcastle University |
| John Hatcliff | Kansas State University |
| Joseph Kiniry | Galois, Inc. |
| Tsutomu Kobayashi | Japan Aerospace Exploration Agency |
| Peter Gorm Larsen | Aarhus University |
| Tiziana Margaria | University of Limerick |
| Mieke Massink | CNR-ISTI, Pisa, Italy |
| Stephan Merz | Inria Nancy |
| Stefan Mitsch | DePaul University |
| Rosemary Monahan | Maynooth University |
| Tomohiro Oda | Software Research Associates, Inc. |
| Claudio Pinello | Collins Aerospace |
| Anne Remke | WWU Münster |
| Kristin Yvonne Rozier | Iowa State University |
| Cristina Seceleanu | Mälardalen University |
| Martina Seidl | Johannes Kepler University Linz |
| Giulia Sindoni | University of Leeds |
| Bernhard Steffen | TU Dortmund |
| Laura Titolo | Code Metal |
| Christoph Torens | German Aerospace Center, Institute of Flight Systems |
| Jaco van de Pol | Aarhus University |
| Marcel Verhoef | European Space Agency |
| Virginie Wiels | ONERA/DTIS |
| Anton Wijs | Eindhoven University of Technology |
| Naijun Zhan | Institute of Software, Chinese Academy of Sciences |

## Additional Reviewers

Alexis Aurandt
Mikael Bisgaard Dahlsen-Jensen
Markus Frohme
Laura P. Gamboa Guzman
Jan Heemstra
Chris Johannsen
Engel Lefaucheux
Guanhua Lin
Christian Micheletti
Alec Rosentrater
Laurens van der Wal
Shuling Wang
Lisa Willemsen
Hao Wu
Xiong Xu

# Application of Formal Methods to Design and Verification of Autonomous Space Systems

Julia Badger

NASA Johnson Space Center (JSC), USA
julia.m.badger@nasa.gov

**Abstract.** As NASA's Artemis Program accelerates towards the Moon, the consideration of technologies needed for sustained extra-terrestrial presence remains at the forefront. One significant technology gap is the ability to autonomously control complex, safety-critical, integrated habitation and mobility systems across the operational range of the vehicles and missions. The newly formed Moon Base is focused on developing autonomous infrastructure, mobility, and habitation systems that support continuous human presence on the lunar surface. This lofty goal will require international cooperation and significant US commercial production growth areas to achieve. Though Moon Base assets will be developed and operated from all over the world, the Mission Command Center will be central to ensuring that the strategic mission goals to manage the lunar settlement and achieve the relevant science and technology demonstrations are completed. The implementation of this will be highly dependent on strong interoperability agreements and local autonomous control capabilities across the lunar infrastructure. The development of a hierarchical framework for autonomous data management and control is underway to support the distributed, but highly dependent and constrained, control paradigm that results. This talk will discuss the plans for the Moon Base, the development of the autonomous control architecture, and touch on the verification challenges expected.

## Biography

Dr. Julia Badger is the Robotics, Construction, and Automation Lead for Moon Base at NASA-Johnson Space Center. She also serves as the Moon Base Surface Mobility Deputy Lead. She has previously served as the Gateway Autonomy System Manager, Gateway Test and Verification Team lead, and the Robonaut Project Manager. She has been responsible for the research and development of autonomous system capabilities, on the Earth, the International Space Station, the Gateway, and currently, the Moon, that include dexterous manipulation, autonomous spacecraft control and caretaking, and human-robot interfaces. Julia has a BS from Purdue University, and an MS and PhD from the California Institute of Technology, all in Mechanical Engineering. Her work has been honored with several awards, including NASA Software of the Year, Early Career, Director's Commendation, Exceptional Achievement Awards, and the Administrator's Flight Incentive Award.

# Reducing Time to Market through Formal Methods

Colin O'Halloran

D-RiSQ Ltd, UK
coh@drisq.com

**Abstract.** Model Based Software Engineering (MBSE) integrates simulation, automation, and traceability into the development process. By using tools like Simulink and Stateflow developers can simulate system behaviour, automate code generation and maintain traceability from requirements to implementation. The major drawback with MBSE is showing not only that it does what is required, but much more importantly from a certification perspective, that it does not have unwanted functionality, including showing what happens when, not 'if' things go wrong. This challenge is caused by the semantics of the models being unclear, the link between the model and the requirements often being obscure and being able to show that code generated correctly implements the requirements for the model in an efficient and effective manner. The key is to leverage MBSE through evaluating verification artefacts generated by MBSE using Automated Reasoning. A key application of this approach to Robotic and Autonomous Systems is discussed in terms of commercial impact.

## Biography

Colin has over 40 years of experience in high integrity systems, operating as a scientist, consultant and business group manager with RSRE, DERA and QinetiQ. He is an honorary Visiting Professor at the University of York and was previously a full professor of computer science at the University of Oxford. Colin is an internationally recognised expert in the validation and verification of software-based systems using formal methods. At RSRE he developed parts of the MALPAS analysis tool that was used in the assessment of the secondary protection system of the Sizewell B nuclear power station. Within DERA he was the technical authority for the development of the formal semantics of SPARK 83 carried out by PVL Ltd. Within QinetiQ he led the team that developed tools to mathematically verify the flight and engine control software for the Typhoon aircraft as well as the Auto-throttle and Auto-pilot. In 1996 he served on the European Space Agency's Board of Inquiry into the very first launch of Ariane 5 and compiled those parts of the report concerning the software's contribution to the failure. He carried out a survey of certification approaches on behalf of the Director of Helicopter projects following the Chinook crash on the Mull of Kintyre. Since 2012 Colin has been CTO of D-RiSQ Ltd that have developed automated formal methods based mathematical tools covering requirements capture and design verification, backed up by source code and object code verification.

# Contents

# Industrial Adoption of Formal Methods: An Industry Perspective on the Transition to SPARK for Security Critical Firmware Development

Asieh Salehi Fathabadi[1](✉) and Mark Hermeling[2]

[1] University of Southampton, Southampton, UK
a.salehi@soton.ac.uk
[2] AdaCore, New York, USA
mhermeling@adacore.com

**Abstract.** Formal methods offer a compelling but historically under utilized response to the security challenges facing embedded firmware development, now reinforced by CRA and CISA guidance. This paper presents a qualitative case study of two organizations that have made the strategic transition to SPARK, a formally verified, Ada-based language, for security-critical firmware, spanning the semiconductor and automotive safety domains. We characterize the technical, organizational, and economic factors shaping successful adoption, identify key success factors including incremental adoption strategies, structured training, and stakeholder management, and contextualize findings within the evolving regulatory landscape. The study contributes empirical evidence to the discourse on industrial formal methods adoption and provides actionable insights for organizations considering similar transitions.

**Keywords:** Formal Methods · SPARK · Industrial Adoption · Security Critical Systems · Firmware Verification

## 1 Introduction

The security of embedded and firmware software has emerged as one of the defining engineering challenges of the current decade. Attack surfaces that were once considered theoretical have become active vectors: supply chain compromises, boot time vulnerabilities, and root of trust exploits now regularly feature in high profile incidents affecting critical infrastructure, automotive systems, and consumer devices [1,2]. The consequences extend far beyond immediate service disruption: the cost of post deployment security remediation in embedded systems vastly exceeds that of prevention, because firmware and hardware in the field can rarely be updated with the same velocity as conventional software [3].

Regulatory pressure is mounting in parallel with the threat landscape. The European Union's Cyber Resilience Act (CRA) [4], which entered force in 2024


P. Gorm Larsen and K. Y. Rozier (Eds.): FMICS 2026, LNCS 16967, pp. 1–18, 2027.
https://doi.org/10.1007/978-3-032-36849-2_1

and whose principal requirements apply from 2027, imposes enforceable obligations on manufacturers of any product with digital elements sold in the EU market. The CRA explicitly demands that products be designed to be secure by default, that vulnerabilities be addressed promptly throughout a defined support lifecycle, and that manufacturers demonstrate conformity through documented technical evidence. For firmware developers previously relying on informal testing and code review alone, this regime represents a fundamental change in what constitutes an acceptable engineering process.

Against this background, *formal methods*, approaches grounded in mathematical logic to specify and verify software properties, offer a compelling but historically under utilised answer. Formal methods can provide machine checked guarantees of the absence of entire classes of defect: runtime errors, undefined behaviour, memory safety violations, and failures to meet functional specifications. Microsoft reported that 70 percent of all security bugs are memory safety issues [5]. Yet the industrial uptake of formal methods has traditionally been slow, attributed to a combination of the mathematical maturity required, tooling immaturity, and the perceived difficulty of integrating formal techniques into existing industrial workflows [6,7].

This paper examines how a number of organizations have overcome these barriers to transition successfully to SPARK, a formally defined subset of Ada supporting deductive verification, for their most security critical firmware components. Drawing on publicly available case study evidence and practitioner accounts [12,13], we characterize the technical landscape, the adoption strategies employed, the challenges encountered, and the tangible outcomes realised. Although the cases discussed draw on identifiable publicly documented programmes, we deliberately frame the findings at the level of industry patterns and transferable lessons rather than the specifics of individual companies, in the interests of generalisability and sensitivity.

The paper makes the following contributions:

- An empirical characterization of the technical, organizational, and economic factors that drive and constrain industrial adoption of SPARK for security critical firmware;
- A comparative analysis of adoption trajectories across different industry segments, capturing both semiconductor and automotive safety domains;
- A structured set of success factors and anti patterns, grounded in observed practice, for organizations contemplating similar transitions;
- Contextualisation of these findings within the evolving regulatory landscape, specifically the EU Cyber Resilience Act [4].

The remainder of the paper is structured as follows. Section 2 provides background on SPARK. Section 3 characterizes the industry context. Section 4 presents the research design. Section 5 presents the case study evidence. Section 6 analyses the adoption dimensions. Section 7 synthesizes key success factors. Section 8 examines regulatory alignment. Section 9 surveys related work and concludes.

## 2 Background: SPARK and Deductive Verification

**The SPARK Language:** SPARK is a formally defined programming language derived from Ada, specifically designed to enable high integrity software development for systems where correctness, safety, and security are non negotiable requirements [11]. The modern SPARK 2014 release [8], grounded in Ada 2012, substantially extended its expressiveness through contract based specifications and a redesigned verification toolchain, GNATprove [9]. The GNAT compiler and the GNATprove prover are available as open source releases and can be obtained through the Alire package management framework for Ada and SPARK [10].

The key engineering principle underlying SPARK is the elimination of language features that introduce undefined behaviour, ambiguous semantics, or constructs that preclude static analysis. Where Ada already provides strong typing, range checking, and bounded array access, SPARK further restricts pointer use, unrestricted parallelism, and dynamic memory allocation patterns that defeat modular reasoning. In exchange for these constraints, SPARK enables sound, scalable deductive verification.

SPARK adoption guidance, developed jointly by AdaCore and Thales, characterizes five levels of software assurance achievable with increasing analytical effort [14]:

1. **Stone**: Compilation and basic SPARK mode compliance, establishing a valid foundation.
2. **Bronze**: Absence of uninitialized variables and correct information flow across subprograms.
3. **Silver**: Absence of runtime errors (AoRTE), proven through GNATprove.
4. **Gold**: Proof of user defined functional contracts (preconditions, postconditions, invariants), discharged automatically by SMT solvers.
5. **Platinum**: Full functional correctness, where properties beyond SMT automation require manually supplied auxiliary lemmas, a qualitatively different proof engineering effort from Gold.

This graduated framework is strategically important for industrial adoption: it allows organizations to extract immediate, tangible value at lower levels before investing in the expertise required for higher level proofs. In practice, the Silver level, AoRTE, has proven particularly compelling for security critical firmware, because absence of runtime errors directly eliminates entire families of exploitable vulnerability.

**Deductive Verification and GNATprove:** GNATprove [9] is the primary SPARK verification tool. It operates by translating SPARK source code and its contracts into Verification Conditions (VCs), logical formulas that encode the required correctness properties. These VCs are discharged by automated Satisfiability Modulo Theories (SMT) solvers, including CVC5 and Alt Ergo. The analysis is *sound*: if GNATprove raises no unproved checks for a given property, the property is guaranteed to hold for all possible executions.

SPARK analysis is modular: each subprogram is verified in isolation, assuming contracts of called subprograms. This modularity is critical for scalability in large industrial codebases. Teams can focus SPARK on the highest criticality components while interfacing with C via a Foreign Function Interface (FFI), preserving compatibility with existing infrastructure.

Within the broader formal methods landscape, SPARK occupies a distinctive niche: it delivers deductive verification directly on production source code, without requiring a separate modelling step or an abstraction layer. This contrasts with approaches such as model checking [15], where properties are verified on abstract models that may not faithfully capture implementation behaviour, or theorem proving environments such as Coq [16] and Isabelle [17], where the gap between proof artefact and deployed code requires manual bridging. For firmware development, where the code *is* the artefact, SPARK's direct source level approach offers significant practical advantages.

Within the deductive verification landscape for other languages, related approaches include Dafny [32], which targets a dedicated verification language; Frama-C [33] and VerCors [34], which bring deductive verification to C and concurrent Java/C respectively. SPARK's distinguishing characteristic in the firmware context is that it targets a production systems language with a defined operational semantics and direct FFI interoperability with C, without requiring a separate modelling or translation step.

## 3 Industry Context and the Security Challenge

**The Escalating Threat Landscape:** The embedded systems and firmware domain faces a qualitatively different security challenge today compared with a decade ago. Attack campaigns have become more sophisticated, better resourced, and more targeted at supply chain and pre boot attack surfaces. Root of trust components, the firmware elements responsible for establishing the security foundation at system startup, represent particularly high value targets because a compromise at this level undermines all subsequent security guarantees, regardless of the quality of higher level software.

Two structural factors exacerbate this challenge. First, the field update problem: unlike cloud or desktop software, firmware in deployed hardware is costly and sometimes impossible to update. A security flaw discovered post shipment may require expensive hardware recalls, over the air update infrastructure investments, or acceptance of residual risk. Second, the verification gap: conventional development languages for embedded systems, particularly C and C++, provide no compile time or mathematical guarantee against runtime errors, undefined behaviour, or information flow violations. The rich ecosystem of static analysis tools for C and C++ provides valuable assistance but remains incomplete and unsound in the general case.

The regulatory community has responded to this verification gap with increasingly direct guidance. The United States Cybersecurity and Infrastructure Security Agency (CISA) has explicitly identified the development of new product lines for critical infrastructure in memory-unsafe languages such as C or C++ as a dangerous practice that "significantly elevates risk to national security, national economic security, and national public health and safety" [27]. This guidance specifically notes that the continued use of memory-unsafe languages where memory-safe alternatives are readily available constitutes a product security bad practice, particularly for systems serving critical infrastructure.

**The Regulatory Dimension:** The EU Cyber Resilience Act [4] fundamentally alters the compliance calculus for embedded and firmware developers. Prior to the CRA, cybersecurity in most embedded product categories was largely self regulated or governed by sector specific standards. The CRA introduces mandatory, lifecycle wide requirements for any product with digital elements sold in the EU market. Key provisions relevant to formal methods adoption include:

- **Security by design**: Products must be architected to prevent entire classes of vulnerability, not merely to pass penetration tests.
- **Documented conformity**: Manufacturers must maintain technical documentation demonstrating how security properties are achieved.
- **Vulnerability management**: Manufacturers must actively handle vulnerabilities throughout the declared support period, which for most categories is at least five years.
- **Penalties**: Non compliance may result in penalties of up to €15 million or 2.5% of global annual turnover.

SPARK's mathematical proof artefacts are well suited to meeting the documented conformity requirement. A machine checked proof that a firmware component is free from runtime errors and satisfies its security contracts provides a qualitatively stronger assurance argument than test coverage statistics alone, and one that is directly auditable.

**Why Existing Approaches Fall Short:** The limitations of conventional approaches to security assurance in firmware have become increasingly apparent. Code review, while valuable, does not scale linearly with codebase complexity and is subject to reviewer fatigue and gaps in coverage. Dynamic testing, including fuzzing, finds many vulnerability classes effectively but cannot provide completeness guarantees. Penetration testing is necessarily reactive and discovery-bounded. Static analysis for C/C++ spans a wide range of capabilities. Unsound tools such as Infer and CodeQL are widely used in industry and provide valuable signal, but cannot guarantee the absence of reported clean defect classes. Sound, industrially deployed abstract interpretation tools, most notably Astrée [35], which has been used for years on safety-critical avionics code, provide stronger guarantees, but impose restrictions on the code they can analyse. The deductive verification ecosystem for C also exists: Frama-C [33] supports contract based deductive verification of C programs, and CompCert based proof workflows [36] provide formally verified compilation. These are credible approaches for high assurance C development. The organisations in our case studies nonetheless chose SPARK over these alternatives, principally for three reasons: SPARK combines source level verification with a language whose operational semantics fully eliminate undefined behaviour; it provides FFI interoperability with existing C codebases without requiring those codebases to be verified; and the five level assurance framework offers a clear incremental adoption roadmap that the C-based alternatives do not replicate.

## 4 Research Design

**Research Goal:** This study aims to characterize the technical, organizational, and economic factors that shape successful industrial adoption of SPARK for security-critical firmware, addressing the gap identified by Woodcock et al. [7] in the empirical evidence base for formal methods in industry.

**Methodology:** We adopt a qualitative case study approach following Yin's framework [31], suited to "how" and "why" questions about complex organizational and technical phenomena that cannot be captured through controlled experiments or survey instruments.

**Case Selection:** Cases were selected on the basis of two criteria: (1) they represent large scale, completed or substantially progressed SPARK adoptions in security-critical firmware; and (2) they are documented in publicly available, independently verifiable sources. At the time of writing, the two cases presented here, a major semiconductor manufacturer (Case A) and an automotive safety supplier (Case B), are the only adoptions meeting both criteria. The limited number of cases reflects the early stage of industrial SPARK adoption rather than a deliberate sampling choice, and we acknowledge this as a scope limitation.

**Data Sources and Analysis:** Primary data sources are official AdaCore case study publications [12,13] and publicly available practitioner presentations and press releases [23,24]. These sources are not peer-reviewed, and one author's affiliation with AdaCore introduces a potential for confirmatory bias; we declare this explicitly (see Conflict of Interest statement). Analysis proceeded by identifying recurring themes across the two cases using thematic coding against the dimensions of technology adoption established in the literature [7]: technical barriers, organizational enablers, economic factors, and outcome metrics. Findings are reported at the level of observed patterns, with explicit qualification of scope where generalization is not warranted.

**Limitations:** The study does not address why other organizations have not adopted SPARK, nor does it represent sectors beyond semiconductor hardware and automotive safety. Broader generalization requires a larger and more diverse evidence base, which we identify as a priority for future work.

## 5 Case Studies: Industry Transition to SPARK

The following case studies are drawn from publicly available documentation, including official case study publications and practitioner presentations. We present the material at the level of industry practice patterns, characterizing each adoption in terms of motivation, approach, and outcome.

### 5.1 Case Study A: Semiconductor Manufacturer, Root of Trust Firmware

**Organization and Context:** The first case [13] involves a major international semiconductor company whose System on Chip (SoC) products are deployed across millions of devices, including systems requiring the highest standards of automotive safety and data centre integrity. The security critical firmware components of concern include those embedded in the root of trust architecture as well as early boot firmware executing on utility processors. Modern SoCs depend on extensive software to initialize memory buses, communication devices, and application processors before the main operating system can run. This early boot software executes at the lowest privilege levels, before any operating system or application software, and establishes the foundational security properties of the entire platform. The security of the SoC stands or falls with the security of this early boot software, making it a primary target for formal verification.

**Motivation for Change:** The organization had accumulated substantial experience managing security vulnerabilities in C based firmware. It recognized two related problems. First, the technical problem: C's permissive semantics make it very difficult to achieve the completeness of assurance required for root of trust components, even with significant investment in testing and review. Second, the organizational problem: demonstrating to customers and regulators that the firmware meets its security guarantees requires more than test evidence, it requires a form of assurance that can be presented, understood, and audited. SPARK's mathematically grounded proofs, backed by automated tooling, offered a plausible answer to both. Obtaining acceptance required sustained advocacy and a technically credible demonstration that the approach would work in practice.

**Adoption Approach:** The transition was executed incrementally. New SPARK components were written from scratch for the highest criticality firmware elements, rather than attempting a comprehensive migration of existing C code. This greenfield approach allowed the team to avoid the complexity of brownfield migration while establishing a clear proof of concept for stakeholders. The SPARK components were designed to interoperate with the existing C codebase via a carefully defined FFI boundary, allowing gradual expansion of the SPARK footprint over time.

Training was a significant investment. The organisation developed in house SPARK expertise through a combination of external training provided by the language toolchain vendor and internal mentorship. The growth in trained developers over the adoption period was substantial, scaling from a small founding team to over fifty practitioners across multiple product lines within approximately four years. This scaling trajectory reflects a deliberate strategy to build a self sustaining internal capability rather than maintaining permanent external dependency.

**Outcomes:** The formal SPARK components now ship in production hardware. The organisation is able to provide customers and regulators with machine checked proof that the root of trust components are free from runtime errors and that their information flow contracts are satisfied. SPARK's determinism property, the guarantee that the same input always produces the same output, with no hidden state or undefined behaviour, is particularly valued for root of trust applications where predictability is a security requirement in its own right. The approach has demonstrated the ability to combine formal guarantees with production quality, high performance embedded code.

### 5.2 Case Study B: Automotive Safety Systems, ASIL D Component Development

**Organisation and Context:** The second case [12] involves an organisation specialising in autonomous and advanced driver assistance systems (ADAS), where software correctness is foundational to functional safety. The relevant regulatory framework is ISO 26262, the road vehicles functional safety standard, which classifies software components by their Automotive Safety Integrity Level (ASIL), ranging from ASIL A (lowest) to ASIL D (highest). ASIL D components, which can directly affect vehicle safety, require the most rigorous verification.

**Motivation for Change:** The organisation adopted a risk stratified approach to language selection. For components at ASIL C and ASIL D levels, where formal verification is strongly recommended by ISO 26262, SPARK was selected following a systematic evaluation of formal methods technologies. The evaluation criteria included the ability to eliminate undefined behaviour, the tractability of formal verification for the target code, the availability of tool qualification artefacts for the ISO 26262 process, and practical scalability for team based development. SPARK satisfied all four criteria to a degree that alternative technologies did not.

**Adoption Approach:** The adoption strategy was explicitly criticality stratified. Components classified at the highest ASIL levels were implemented in SPARK; lower criticality components were retained in C++, provided the associated risks were managed through other means. This mixed language strategy reduced the organizationaldisruption of transition while focusing formal verification effort where its value is highest.

A key enabler was the existence of SPARK's five level assurance framework, which allowed the team to define a concrete adoption roadmap. The team targeted Silver level (AoRTE) as the baseline for all SPARK components, with Gold level contracts applied to the most critical functionality. This staged approach provided clear milestones and allowed progressive expansion of formal coverage as team expertise matured.

**Outcomes:** SPARK components in ASIL C and D categories are now in active development and verification, with the SPARK proof artefacts contributing directly to the safety case. The ability to produce machine checked proof of functional correctness and absence of runtime errors has strengthened the organisation's certification position and provides a documented basis for ASIL compliance that goes beyond conventional testing approaches. The modular nature of SPARK verification has also proved practically important: the ability to verify components in isolation, making explicit the contract assumptions at each interface, aligns naturally with the component based architecture of modern ADAS systems.

**Summary of Case Evidence:** Table 1 summarises the key dimensions of the two case studies.

**Table 1.** Summary of Industry SPARK Adoption Cases

| Dimension | Case A (Semiconductor) | Case B (Automotive) |
|---|---|---|
| Domain | Root of trust firmware | ADAS/functional safety |
| Previous language | C/C++ | C++ |
| Regulatory driver | Customer/regulator assurance | ISO 26262, ASIL C/D |
| Adoption mode | Greenfield components | Criticality stratified |
| SPARK assurance level | Silver, Gold | Silver, Gold |
| Scale (trained developers) | 5 → 50+ over 4 years | Team scale, growing |
| Production status | Shipping in production hardware | Active development |
| Key benefit | AoRTE, determinism proofs | Formal safety case contribution |

# 6 Analysis of Adoption Dimensions

## 6.1 Technical Dimension

**Language Transition:** The most frequently cited technical challenge is the transition from C or C++ to a language with substantially different idioms and constraints. SPARK's restricted subset, prohibiting arbitrary pointer arithmetic, unchecked type conversions, and forms of concurrency that defeat static analysis, requires engineers to re examine design patterns that are second nature in C. In practice, the restriction is experienced differently depending on context: engineers working at the firmware level, where dynamic memory allocation is already avoided for performance and determinism reasons, find SPARK's constraints less disruptive than might be expected.

The interoperability of SPARK with C via FFI has been a practically important enabler. It allows teams to introduce SPARK components incrementally, at the security critical boundary, without requiring the entire codebase to be rewritten. This compositionality, SPARK code can call C code and be called from C code, with well defined contract boundaries, is essential for industrial adoption at scale.

**Proof Engineering:** A recurring theme in both cases is the importance of investing in contract design rather than treating contracts as post hoc annotations. Contracts, preconditions, postconditions, loop invariants, and type invariants, serve a dual purpose: they are the specification against which the implementation is verified, and they are the machine readable documentation of intent. Getting contracts right requires both software engineering skill and familiarity with the language of formal specification, which is a distinct competency from conventional programming.

Teams found that the effort to write good contracts was not uniformly distributed. Contracts for simple, straightforward functions are trivially written and proved. The effort concentrates at interfaces with complex state, with security critical invariants, and at the boundaries of the SPARK/C interoperation. Both cases emphasised the value of focusing formal verification effort at the highest criticality components rather than attempting uniform coverage.

**Toolchain Integration:** GNATprove integrates with both GNAT Studio and Visual Studio Code, which reduced the toolchain integration burden. Development teams valued the ability to run proofs incrementally during development, receiving feedback analogous to a sophisticated type checker, rather than treating formal verification as a separate, deferred activity. This integration of proof into the development workflow, rather than relegating it to a distinct verification phase, was reported as a significant contributor to developer acceptance.

### 6.2 Organizational Dimension

**Stakeholder Management:** Both cases highlight that the primary barriers to adoption were organizationalrather than technical. Engineering teams with deep C expertise required persuasion that SPARK was practical, learnable, and worth the investment. Management required business cases demonstrating concrete return. Customers and regulators required explanation of what machine checked proofs mean and why they are stronger than test evidence.

The framing adopted in the most successful adoption programmes was important. Rather than presenting SPARK as a *replacement* for existing practice, implying that previous work was inadequate, successful advocates presented it as an *amplifier*: a way of making the existing security and quality discipline more effective by giving it mathematical backing. This framing reduced defensiveness and aligned the case for change with organizationalpride in engineering quality.

**Training and Skill Development:** Both cases invested significantly in structured training. Entry level SPARK training focused on the language syntax, the contract annotation language, and the operation of GNATprove. Advanced training addressed proof engineering, how to write contracts that are verifiable without manual guidance, how to manage cases where automation does not suffice, and how to structure code to facilitate proof. The availability of mentorship support from the toolchain vendor, combining training with project specific guidance, was noted as particularly valuable in the early phases of adoption.

The developer scaling trajectory in Case A, from a founding team of approximately five to over fifty trained developers across multiple product lines within four years, represents a realistic and achievable target for organizations making a serious investment. The trajectory was not linear: significant acceleration occurred once a critical mass of internal expertise was established, creating a self sustaining learning community.

**Process Integration:** Integrating SPARK into existing development processes required adaptation of code review practices, continuous integration pipelines, and documentation standards. Code review needed to encompass both the SPARK source and its contracts; reviewers required enough understanding of formal specifications to evaluate contract quality. Continuous integration was configured to run GNATprove as part of the build pipeline, so that proof obligations were checked continuously rather than only at designated verification milestones.

### 6.3 Economic Dimension

**Costs:** The direct costs of SPARK adoption include toolchain licensing, training, and the additional development time required to write and prove contracts. The training investment is substantial: becoming productive with SPARK proof engineering takes longer than simple language familiarisation. Toolchain costs are comparable with other professional embedded development environments.

An often underestimated cost is the intellectual investment in contract design. Well written contracts require careful thought about the intended behaviour of each component, including invariants that may previously have been implicit. While this investment is real, practitioners in both cases noted that the discipline of making implicit assumptions explicit frequently revealed latent design issues, defects that would eventually have surfaced as bugs or vulnerabilities at far greater cost.

**Benefits:** The economic case for SPARK adoption at the highest criticality tier rests on several converging arguments [4]. First, the cost of post deployment security remediation for firmware vulnerabilities is very high, in some cases, requiring hardware recalls or field update campaigns. Machine checked proof that eliminates entire vulnerability classes provides insurance against this tail risk. Second, the ability to demonstrate provable security properties to customers and regulators has commercial value, differentiating products in markets where security assurance is a purchasing criterion. Third, the CRA's penalties for non compliance, up to €15 million or 2.5% of total worldwide annual turnover, whichever is higher, provide a significant direct financial incentive to invest in technically credible security assurance.

Both cases reported that verification costs for the SPARK components were lower than would have been required to achieve comparable assurance through exhaustive testing. This finding aligns with theoretical arguments about the relative efficiency of deductive proof versus test based approaches for properties of the absence of defect form, and is particularly pronounced for the Silver level (AoRTE), where GNATprove's automation is mature and proof success rates are high.

## 7 Key Success Factors

Synthesising the evidence across both cases, we identify the following key success factors for industrial SPARK adoption:

**Incremental and Risk Stratified Adoption:** The most successful approaches did not attempt to mandate SPARK across entire codebases. Instead, they applied SPARK selectively to the highest criticality components, where the investment in formal verification is most clearly justified and where the value of machine checked guarantees is most directly communicated to stakeholders. Greenfield development of new security critical components in SPARK, interfacing with the existing codebase via well defined FFI boundaries, has proved more tractable than comprehensive legacy migration. This incremental approach limits early phase productivity loss, produces demonstrable results that sustain organisational commitment, and allows expertise to accumulate progressively.

**Investment in Contract Design as Engineering Practice:** The evidence from both cases, consistent with the adoption guidance developed by AdaCore and Thales [14] and the practitioner experience reported in [18], points to contract design as a primary engineering activity rather than a post-hoc annotation task. Contracts, preconditions, postconditions, loop invariants, and type invariants, serve a dual purpose: they are the specification against which the implementation is verified, and they are machine readable documentation of intent. Both cases invested in contract review as a standard part of their code review process and maintained contracts alongside code throughout the development lifecycle. This discipline also produced a secondary benefit: making implicit assumptions explicit frequently revealed latent design issues that would otherwise have surfaced as bugs or vulnerabilities at greater cost.

**Structured Training and Expert Mentorship:** Both cases found that a combination of structured training and ongoing mentorship was essential, particularly in the early phase of adoption. Training that covers both the language and the proof engineering discipline is necessary; tool operation alone is insufficient. Mentorship that provides project specific guidance, helping teams navigate proof failures, contract design choices, and the structure of formal verification evidence, accelerates the transition from theoretical understanding to practical competence.

The identification and development of internal SPARK champions, engineers who combine technical depth in formal verification with credibility among peers, was reported as a high value investment. These champions serve as the primary vector for spreading capability within the organisation and are essential for the self sustaining scaling that both cases achieved.

**Stakeholder Communication and Framing:** The narrative framing of the transition matters. Presenting SPARK adoption as a natural evolution of the organisation's existing commitment to engineering quality, rather than as a rejection of previous approaches, reduces resistance and builds alignment. Translating the language of formal verification, soundness, proof obligations, verification conditions, into terms meaningful to each audience (security engineers, management, customers, regulators) is a distinct skill that successful programmes invested in developing.

For customers and regulators, the message is essentially: "We can now demonstrate, with mathematical certainty, that these specific security properties hold, not just claim it based on test results." This is a qualitatively different assurance claim, and communicating its significance effectively is as important as achieving it technically.

**Toolchain Integration with Development Workflow:** Proof should be integrated into the everyday development workflow, not deferred to a separate verification phase. Both cases configured their CI/CD pipelines to run GNATprove automatically, treating proof failures as build failures. This integration normalises proof as part of development discipline, provides rapid feedback to developers, and prevents the accumulation of unproved obligations that become increasingly costly to address later.

## 8 Regulatory Alignment and Future Outlook

**SPARK and the EU Cyber Resilience Act:** The EU Cyber Resilience Act [4] creates a regulatory environment in which the value proposition of SPARK for security critical firmware is significantly strengthened. The CRA's requirement for documented, auditable evidence of security conformity aligns directly with what SPARK proof artefacts provide. The CRA's demand for security by design, building products that prevent vulnerability classes rather than merely detecting and patching them, maps onto SPARK's ability to provide machine checked absence of runtime errors and information flow violations.

We anticipate that the CRA will act as a significant accelerant for formal methods adoption in the embedded and firmware domain over the 2025–2030 period. organizations that have already established SPARK capability will be well positioned to demonstrate CRA conformity for their highest risk components. organizations beginning adoption now, targeting the 2027 compliance deadline, face a realistic but demanding timeline.

**Extending Adoption, Multi Language and Hybrid Approaches:** An important practical observation from both case studies is that SPARK adoption does not require all or nothing commitment. The ability to interoperate with C and to deploy SPARK selectively on the highest criticality components within a mixed language system makes SPARK adoption compatible with the engineering reality of organizations with large existing codebases. This hybrid approach is not a compromise: it reflects a principled risk stratification strategy in which formal verification effort is concentrated where it delivers most value.

Future toolchain developments, including improvements to the automation of proof at higher assurance levels and extensions of SPARK's formal semantics, are expected to reduce the effort required for Gold level proofs, potentially making full functional correctness verification accessible to a wider range of applications and teams.

**Implications for Standards and Certification:** The growing body of evidence from industrial SPARK deployments is gradually influencing the standards landscape. The DO-178C avionics standard already accommodates formal methods, and the ISO 26262 functional safety standard recommends formal verification at the highest ASIL levels. We anticipate that evidence from the adoption cases described here will contribute to the empirical base informing future standard revisions, potentially making formal methods a more prominent element of the required assurance argument for security critical embedded systems under the CRA framework.

**The Trust-Safety Divide: Beyond Technical Compliance:** A critical challenge for SPARK adoption extends beyond technical verification: the gap between formal safety guarantees and stakeholder trust [28]. Systems can be mathematically proven safe yet fail to gain human trust, while stakeholders may over trust systems with weaker assurance [29]. This *trust-safety divide* represents a fundamental fragmentation between technical and social dimensions of safety, requiring verification processes that are accessible and responsive to diverse stakeholder needs throughout the verification lifecycle [30].

For SPARK deployment, this manifests concretely: verification conditions and proof obligations remain comprehensible primarily to formal methods experts, yet regulatory bodies, customers, and end-users must make trust decisions about formally verified systems. Both case studies in Sect. 5 identified stakeholder communication as a primary organizational challenge.

The CRA's requirement for "documented technical evidence" implicitly recognizes this divide: conformity must be not only achieved but also demonstrable to non-expert assessors. Current practice addresses this through dedicated communication strategies and demonstration systems, but systematic approaches for trust-calibrated verification, where proof systems generate both correctness guarantees and stakeholder appropriate trust evidence, represent an important direction for future SPARK tooling and methodology development.

## 9 Related Work and Conclusion

**Related Work:** The challenge of industrial adoption of formal methods has been studied extensively. Woodcock et al. [7] conducted a comprehensive survey of formal methods in practice, identifying key barriers including the mathematical expertise requirement, the lack of tool support at industrial scale, and the absence of evidence of effectiveness. The present paper contributes to closing the evidence gap identified in that survey, albeit in a specific language and technology context.

The experience of Altran and Thales in adopting SPARK, documented in [14, 18], established the five level assurance framework that has become the standard adoption roadmap. Their reports of progressive adoption, with Bronze and Silver levels providing immediate practical value, are consistent with the patterns observed in our cases. Dross et al. [19] describe SPARK 2014 in industrial context; Barnes [20] provides a comprehensive language reference.

The application of SPARK in the railway safety domain [19] and the Tokeneer security kernel [21] represent earlier case studies of SPARK at scale in demanding domains, predating the current generation of tooling. The present work extends this body of evidence to the firmware and automotive domains, which have not previously been documented at this level of detail in the formal methods literature.

The broader question of formal methods adoption in industry is addressed by Woodcock et al. [7], whose survey remains the primary reference for adoption barriers and enablers. The state of model checking in practice is surveyed by Kroening et al. [15]. In contrast to model checking approaches, SPARK's direct source level verification avoids the abstraction gap between model and implementation, a significant practical advantage for firmware verification.

The regulatory dimension of formal methods has received less academic attention than the technical dimension. Rushby [22] argues that certification of critical systems requires not only correct software but demonstrable correctness, a structured assurance argument comprehensible to regulators, not just mathematically rigorous proof. This tension between formal rigour and regulatory comprehensibility maps directly onto the CRA's documented conformity requirement and the trust-safety divide discussed in Sect. 7. This paper contributes an updated analysis in the context of the EU Cyber Resilience Act [4].

**Conclusion:** This paper has examined the industrial transition to SPARK for security critical firmware development through two case studies spanning the semiconductor and automotive safety domains. The evidence demonstrates that large scale SPARK adoption is achievable, with key challenges as much organisational as technical.

The evidence from these two cases suggests that SPARK's combination of an incrementally adoptable assurance framework, direct source level verification, and mature toolchain automation can be tractable for industrial teams without prior formal methods background, enabling meaningful formal guarantees on security-critical components within realistic timescales. Whether this finding generalizes beyond the semiconductor and automotive safety domains, or to organizations without access to comparable training and mentorship resources, warrants further investigation. The scaling of trained developer communities from small founding teams to organizations of fifty or more practitioners across multiple product lines within four years is a practically significant achievement.

The organizational findings reinforce the importance of incremental risk stratified adoption, investment in contract design as a first class engineering activity, structured training and mentorship, and deliberate stakeholder communication. Their combination and SPARK-specific adaptations add practical value for organisations planning similar transitions.

The EU Cyber Resilience Act [4] substantially strengthens the business case: SPARK's proof artefacts provide exactly the documented, auditable assurance evidence the CRA demands, at a rigour conventional testing cannot match. We expect this to accelerate adoption significantly over the next five years.

Limitations: This study draws on two cases from a single technology supplier's published evidence base. The findings should be interpreted as existence proofs, demonstrating that large scale SPARK adoption is achievable, rather than as a basis for strong generalisations about adoption rates or barriers across industry.

Future work should extend the evidence base to additional sectors and to unsuccessful adoptions, for a more balanced empirical picture.

**Acknowledgements.** Conflict of Interest: One author (M. Hermeling) is employed by AdaCore, the toolchain vendor that supports the open source technology that is the subject of this study. The primary data sources for the case studies are publicly available AdaCore publications. Readers should apply appropriate scrutiny to the findings with this in mind. The academic author (A. Salehi Fathabadi) has no financial relationship with AdaCore. The analysis and interpretation presented here are the authors' own, and findings are framed as patterns observed in these two cases rather than general claims about SPARK adoption.

## References

1. Easterly, J., Fanning, T.: The attack on colonial pipeline: what we've learned & what we've done over the past two years. CISA (2023). https://www.cisa.gov/news-events/news/attack-colonial-pipeline-what-weve-learned-what-weve-done-over-past-two-years (Accessed March 2026)
2. CISA, FBI, NSA: Advanced Persistent Threat Compromise of Government Agencies, Critical Infrastructure, and Private Sector Organizations (SolarWinds Orion). Alert AA20-352A (2021). https://www.cisa.gov/news-events/cybersecurity-advisories/aa20-352a (Accessed March 2026)
3. McConnell, S.: Code Complete: A Practical Handbook of Software Construction, 2nd edn. Microsoft Press, Redmond, WA (2004)
4. European Union: Regulation (EU) 2024/2847 of the European Parliament and of the Council on horizontal cybersecurity requirements for products with digital elements (Cyber Resilience Act), October 2024. https://eur-lex.europa.eu/legal-content/EN/TXT/PDF/?uri=CELEX:32024R2847 (Accessed March 2026)

5. Microsoft: 70 percent of all security bugs are memory safety issues. https://www.zdnet.com/article/microsoft-70-percent-of-all-security-bugs-are-memory-safety-issues/ (Accessed March 2026)
6. Hoare, T., Misra, J.: Verified software: theories, tools, experiments – vision of a grand challenge project. In: Meyer, B., Woodcock, J. (eds.) Verified Software: Theories, Tools, Experiments (VSTTE 2005). Lecture Notes in Computer Science, vol. 4171, pp. 1–18. Springer (2008)
7. Woodcock, J., Larsen, P.G., Bicarregui, J., Fitzgerald, J.S.: Formal methods: practice and experience. ACM Comput. Surv. **41**(4) (2009)
8. Schanda, F.L.F., Matthews, S.R.: A language for safety and security. In: Proceedings of the 9th IET International Conference on System Safety and Cyber Security (SSCS 2014). Institution of Engineering and Technology (IET) (2014)
9. AdaCore, Formal Verification with GNATprove https://docs.adacore.com/spark2014-docs/html/ug/en/gnatprove.html#formal-verification-with-gnatprove (Accessed March 2026)
10. Alire Project: ALIRE: Ada LIbrary REpository. https://alire.ada.dev (Accessed March 2026)
11. AdaCore, The SPARK Programming Language. https://www.adacore.com/languages/spark (Accessed March 2026)
12. AdaCore: Zenseact Chooses SPARK for Automotive Safety. AdaCore Case Study (2026). https://www.adacore.com/case-studies/zenseact-chooses-spark-for-automotive-safety (Accessed March 2026)
13. AdaCore: NVIDIA – Adoption of SPARK Ushers in a New Era in Security-Critical Software Development. AdaCore Case Study (2025). https://www.adacore.com/case-studies/nvidia-adoption-of-spark-new-era-in-security-critical-software-development (Accessed March 2026)
14. AdaCore, Thales: Implementation Guidance for the Adoption of SPARK. AdaCore (2018). https://www.adacore.com/books/implementation-guidance-spark (Accessed March 2026)
15. Kroening, D., et al.: Model Checking, 2nd edition. MIT Press (2018)
16. The Coq Development Team: The Coq Proof Assistant Reference Manual. INRIA (2023). https://coq.inria.fr (Accessed March 2026)
17. Nipkow, T., Wenzel, M., Paulson, L.C.: Isabelle/HOL: A Proof Assistant for Higher Order Logic. Springer LNCS 2283 (2002)
18. Moy, Y., Chapman, R., Dross, C., Guitton, J.: Practical formal verification for reliable software. In: Proceedings of the 14th International Workshop on Automated Verification of Critical Systems (AVoCS)(2018)
19. Dross, C., Efstathopoulos, P., Lesens, D., Méry, D., Moy, Y.: Rail, space, security: three case studies for SPARK 2014. In: Proceedings of the ERTS (2014)
20. Barnes, J.: High Integrity Software: The SPARK Approach to Safety and Security. Addison Wesley (2003)
21. Barnes, J.: Experiences in the industrial use of formal methods. Electron. Commun. EASST (2011)
22. Rushby, J.: Formal methods and the certification of critical systems. Technical Report CSL 93 7, SRI International (1993)
23. AdaCore: AdaCore enhances security critical firmware with NVIDIA. Press Release, February 2019. https://www.adacore.com/press/adacore-enhances-security-critical-firmware-with-nvidia (Accessed March 2026)
24. AdaCore: Formal Methods for an Insecure World. AdaCore Blog (2025). https://www.adacore.com/blog/formal-methods-for-an-insecure-world (Accessed March 2026)

25. ISO 26262 1:2018 Road vehicles - Functional safety, 2nd edition. International Organization for Standardization (2018)
26. RTCA/EUROCAE: DO 178C / ED 12C: Software Considerations in Airborne Systems and Equipment Certification (2011)
27. CISA: Product Security Bad Practices. U.S. Cybersecurity and Infrastructure Security Agency (October 2023). https://www.cisa.gov/resources-tools/resources/product-security-bad-practices (Accessed March 2026)
28. Salehi Fathabadi, A.: The trust-safety divide: a critical gap in human-robot interaction research. In: TRUST 2025: SCRITA and RTSS Workshop at RO-MAN (2025)
29. Akintunde, M., et al.: Actual trust in multiagent systems. In: Proceedings of the 23rd International Conference on Autonomous Agents and Multiagent Systems (AAMAS) (2024)
30. Salehi Fathabadi, A., Stein, S.: Human-centred formal verification: a vision for bridging technical rigour with stakeholder needs in autonomous systems. In: Rigorous State-Based Methods. Lecture Notes in Computer Science. Springer (2026)
31. Yin, R.K.: Case study research and applications: design and methods, 6th edn. In: ISBN 9781506336169, SAGE Publications, Thousand Oaks, CA (2018)
32. Leino, K.R., M.: Dafny: an automatic program verifier for functional correctness. In Logic for Programming, Artificial Intelligence, and Reasoning (2010)
33. Kirchner, F., Kosmatov, N., Prevosto, V., Signoles, J., Yakobowski, B.: Frama-C: A software analysis perspective. Formal Aspects Comput. **27**(3), 573–609 (2015). https://doi.org/10.1007/s00165-014-0326-7
34. Amighi, A., et al.: Verification of concurrent systems with VerCors. In: Formal Methods for Executable Software Models (2014)
35. Delmas, D., Souyris, J.: Astrée: from Research to industry. In: Nielson, H.R., Filé, G. (eds.): Static Analysis. SAS 2007 (2007)
36. Leroy, X.: Formal verification of a realistic compiler. Commun. ACM **52**(7), 107–115 (2009)

# A Formally Verified N-Dimensional Safety Shield for Autonomous Systems

Benjamin Puyobro[1(✉)], Paolo Crisafulli[2], and Burkhart Wolff[3]

[1] LMF, Université Paris-Saclay, IRT SystemX Paris, 91120 Palaiseau, France
bpuyobro@lmf.cnrs.fr
[2] IRT SystemX, 91120 Palaiseau, France
paolo.crisafulli@irt-systemx.fr
[3] LMF, Université Paris-Saclay, Paris, France
wolff@lmf.cnrs.fr

**Abstract.** One of the challenges of autonomous vehicles today is to formally verify safety properties for complex scenarios that include realistic modeling. Initial results have appeared for longitudinal scenarios, but formal treatments of multi-dimensional cases are rare. In this paper, we propose a formally verified Safety Shield model that is generalized to N dimensions. The hybrid-system model is developed in Isabelle/HOL and relies on libraries developed in a cyber-physical system verification project. We believe that our work is of interest to industry as a way to integrate formally verified safety "watch-dogs" for control-systems based on components of mixed reliability such as AI-based algorithms in autonomous vehicles.

**Keywords:** Process-Algebra · Cyber-Physical Systems · Concurrency · Physical Environment · autonomous vehicles · Isabelle/HOL

## 1 Introduction

As Cyber-Physical Systems (CPS) such as robots or Autonomous Vehicles (AV) are a developing industrial field, the need for safety verification is widening. These systems are characterized by a digital controller connected via actuators and sensors to a physical environment; verification techniques therefore involve a combination of discrete computations, communication *and* continuous environment models, which is particularly challenging and problematic for purely test-based techniques due to the astronomic number of possible test cases. Therefore, there is an important opportunity for formal methods, in particular formal proof methods, to address the verification problem of CPS. Several approaches for CPSs have been proposed in the literature [9,13,14,32,47]. The development of certification standards such as [54] confirms the economic and societal relevance of the subject.

In this paper, we discuss a verification technique for a special case of CPS, notably *driving strategies* as introduced in the influential paper *On a Formal*


P. Gorm Larsen and K. Y. Rozier (Eds.): FMICS 2026, LNCS 16967, pp. 19–38, 2027.
https://doi.org/10.1007/978-3-032-36849-2_2

*Model of Safe and Scalable Self-driving Cars* [51], which define Responsibility-Sensitive Safety (RSS). Driving strategies are abstract, non-deterministic algorithms that propose, based on the physical state of surrounding cars, a set of possible accelerations. In more detail, a driving strategy ds is a function:

$$\mathsf{ds} : \mathsf{global\_state} \Rightarrow \mathsf{time\text{-}interval} \Rightarrow \mathsf{acceleration\ set}$$

where the global_state is basically a table with the physical state of all *actors* (cars), comprising position, speed, current acceleration, extension, potential accelerations, etc. For a given time-interval, it is assumed that a chosen current acceleration is considered constant. If each actor chooses a current acceleration from the potential accelerations at some point in time t, then the physical kinematics permits to calculate the future global_state after t + time-interval. A sequence of global_state's is called a *generated scenario*, if it is generated from the driving strategies and kinematics of all actors. A driving strategy is considered safe wrt. a property P, if all states in all possible generated scenarios satisfy P. Safe driving strategies can be used as "watch-dogs" over, for example, untrusted AI-based algorithms suggesting a particular route and driving behavior (cf. [12,48] for this use case).

We developed in [13] a formal theory in which driving strategies can be formulated and proven to be safe in Isabelle/HOL. Over the years, a number of driving strategies have been formally specified and analysed [12,48]; all these models were mostly in a modeling setup for a single-lane. In this paper, we present 2-dimensional scenarios such as intersections and multilane highways, for which we provide formal semi-automated proofs of safety in the sense of no-collision.

Our approach will work for 3-dimensional scenarios as well, for example for collision avoiding strategies for drones or driving strategies involving road slopes. Moreover, once the formalization and the invariants have been established, other researchers have successfully reused these invariants in different proof systems without difficulty[1].

Admittedly, the formal definitions of driving strategies and the necessary invariants for the proofs in Isabelle/HOL are not exactly an easy read. However, producing *randomly* generated scenarios from them and using them in animations is both instructive for engineers and engaging. Therefore, after introducing the technical background and the necessary formal machinery in Sect. 2, we present the driving strategies and their safety proofs in Sect. 3. In Sect. 4, we assess the applicability of our model through simulations and a quantitative comparison of the safety distances associated with the driving strategies. We then discuss related work in Sect. 5 and conclude in Sect. 6, outlining directions for future research.

[1] Idir Aït-Sadoune in Rhodin, personal communication.

## 2 Modeling Cyber-Physical Systems in Isabelle/HOL

Isabelle is a major interactive proof assistant implementing higher-order logic (HOL). As an LCF-style theorem prover, it is based on a small logical core for trustworthiness without requiring—yet supporting—proof objects.

The Isabelle distribution comes with a number of library theories constructed solely from definitional axioms; among them basic data-types for sets, lists, arithmetics, and a substantial part of analysis. In the Isabelle eco-system, there is an archive of formal proofs (the Isabelle/AFP [5]), which runs its content routinely and helps to maintain the quite substantial body of theories provided by about 500 contributors. Among them, there are theories relevant for this paper like extensions to HOL-Analysis [28, 41] or theories on Process-Algebras [4, 5].

### 2.1 The Dynamic Modelisation Using HOL-Analysis

To model a hybrid or cyber-physical system, it is necessary to provide a model of the "physical environment" into which the system is embedded and to which it is connected via sensors and actuators. The scientific challenge of this type of systems is to formally analyse the *interaction* of both, to characterize possible trajectories and establish properties like "safety" of these systems.

In our case, the HOL-Analysis library is most relevant. It provides a collection of more or less basic definitions and results of real and complex analysis. Moreover, it enables the reasoning over complex mathematical objects such as differential equations and transcendental functions arising from modeling physical behavior. We will use this to model continuous dynamics (or: *kinematics*) of our autonomous vehicles.

### 2.2 Modeling Kinematics

HOL-Analysis permits to formalize a wide range of kinematics; however, throughout this paper, we will use only a simple one that we call *standard kinematics*. Standard kinematics assumes that a chosen acceleration is constant throughout a chosen time interval, that the acceleration has immediate effect, and that no external forces occur (slopes, air-resistance, etc.).

We characterize standard kinematics by a second-order *ordinary differential equation* (ODE):

$$\ddot{x}(t) = a$$

which can be rewrited in a first-order ODE:

$$\dot{X}(t) = F(t, X(t)) \quad \text{where } X(t) = \begin{pmatrix} x(t) \\ \dot{x}(t) \end{pmatrix} \text{ and } \forall x_1, x_2. F\left(t, \begin{pmatrix} x_1 \\ x_2 \end{pmatrix}\right) = \begin{pmatrix} x_2 \\ a \end{pmatrix}$$

Starting from $X_0 = \begin{pmatrix} x_0 \\ v_0 \end{pmatrix}$, it boils down to:

$$X(t) = \begin{pmatrix} x_0 + v_0 t + \frac{1}{2} a t^2 \\ v_0 + at \end{pmatrix}$$

Accelerations with a sign opposite to the velocity, i.e. braking, will result in a vehicle that comes to a standstill rather than eventually going backwards. Therefore, we distinguish two cases in our kinematic depending on whether the vehicle reached a stop or not:

$$(p_i, v_i, a_i)(t) = \begin{cases} \left(p_i + t\, v_i + \frac{t^2}{2}\, a,\ v_i + t\, a,\ a\right) & \text{if } v_i\left(v_i + ta\right) \geq 0 \\ \left(p_i - \dfrac{v_i^2}{2a},\ 0,\ a\right) & \text{otherwise} \end{cases}$$

Necessary properties for the analytic solution such as monotonicity with respect to time and acceleration for this kinematic model can be easily proven using the tools provided by the HOL-Analysis library. For the purpose of this paper, we start with a *definition* in Isabelle/HOL of the standard kinematics via its analytic solution:

**Isabelle**

```
definition ‹kinematic δt σ i a ≡
        if speed(σ i) * (speed (σ i) + (δt * a)) ≥ 0
        then σ i ⦇pos:= pos (σ i) + δt * speed (σ i) + δt²/2 * a,
                  speed := speed (σ i) + δt * a, acc := a⦈
        else σ i ⦇pos := pos (σ i) - speed (σ i)² / (2 * a),
                 speed := 0, acc := a⦈›
```

Isabelle/HOL supports a notation for extensible records similar to functional programming languages such as OCaml or SML. Records were written ⦇$\mathsf{field}_1$ := $\mathsf{E}_1$, ..., $\mathsf{field}_n$ := $\mathsf{E}_n$⦈ where the field-names can be used as projections into the record. Note that the ⦇pos := _, speed := _, acc:= _⦈-records here correspond to the "local actor states" mentioned in the introduction, while the function $\sigma$ represents the "global state" yielding for each index i the local state of $\sigma$ i.

### 2.3 Safe Minimal Distances

Assuming the worst-case that the front-$\sigma$ engages in a full-brake, and assuming the standard kinematics, a *minimal safe distance* can be calculated. The original RSS model [51] is based on the idea that a driving strategy that respects this minimal distance is safe in the sense that it will never permit a collision. The calculations according to the above assumptions result in this formula for the safe minimal distance in the RSS model (Fig. 1):

$$d_{\text{min}} = \frac{v_i + v_{i,\rho}}{2}\,\rho_i + \frac{v_{i,\rho}^2}{2a_{\text{minbrake}}i} + \frac{|v_j| + v_{j,\rho}}{2}\,\rho_j + \frac{v_{j,\rho}^2}{2a_{\text{minbrake}}j}. \qquad (1)$$

where $v_{i\ \rho} = |v_i| + \rho_i\, a_{\text{maxaccel}}i$ and $v_{j,\rho} = |v_j| + \rho_j\, a_{\text{maxaccel}}j$.

**Fig. 1.** RSS Safe Distance Formula

In order to stay as close as possible to this idea, we define a *set* of safety distances, resulting for the set of possible accelerations. Our version of this concept formulated Isabelle/HOL reads like this:

Isabelle

```
definition ‹opposite_way v_l v_r i j ≡
            v_l² / (2 * a_minbrake i) + v_r² / (2 * a_minbrake j) ›
definition ‹same_way v i ≡
            v² / (2 * a_minbrake i)›
definition ‹safe_distance σ i j ≡
            (|speed(σ i)| + |speed(σ i)| + ϱ i * a_maxaccel i)/2*ϱ i
          + (|speed (σ j)| + |speed(σ j)| + ϱ j * a_maxaccel j)/2 * ϱ j
            + opposite_way (|speed (σ i)| + σ i * a_maxaccel i)
                    (|speed (σ j)| + σ j * a_maxaccel j) i j›
```

This version takes vehicles traveling in opposite directions into account. The minimal safe distance is defined such that both vehicles have enough time to brake to a full stop without colliding. It is calculated as the sum of the absolute value of the distances the vehicles can travel during their minimal reaction cycle (sense, plan, act), represented here by ϱ i or ϱ j, and the braking distance that each vehicle can cover once it has applied the correct reaction (braking).

## 2.4 The Driving Strategy

Another good example of usefulness of the library provided by Isabelle/HOL is the driving strategy. In our model, the driving strategy is the set of possible accelerations available to a vehicle at a given synchronization instant. HOL-Analysis supports basic reasoning and notation used for sets in mathematics.

Isabelle

```
definition ‹driving_strategy i j σ ≡
      if speed(σ i) > 0 then
         if safe_distance σ i j ≤ vehicles_distance σ i j then
          {-a_maxbrake i .. a_maxaccel i} else {-a_maxbrake i .. -a_minbrake i}
      else if speed(σ i) < 0 then
         if safe_distance σ i j ≤ vehicles_distance σ i j then
          {- a_maxaccel i .. a_maxbrake i} else {a_minbrake i .. a_maxbrake i}
      else if speed(σ i) = 0 then
         if safe_distance σ i j > vehicles_distance σ i j then
          {0} else {- a_maxaccel i .. a_maxaccel i}›
```

This driving strategy is already an extension of [12]. If the vehicle respects the safety distance with the vehicle in front of it, it is free to act as it chooses. However, if this is not the case, it must brake (or remain at zero velocity if it was already zero).

### 2.5 Time-Based Scenarios and Safe Scenarios

We will consider a *scenario* as an infinite sequence of events. Formally, we define events by the disjoint sum of time-intervals (bounded by some model-parameter $\Delta$T) and global states. In Isabelle/HOL, this is represented as follows[2]:

Isabelle
```
datatype ('v) events = time  (of_time : ℝ)              — time step
                     | scene (of_scene:‹('v scene›)     — global state sync
```

Here, the scene's are our global states (so, the $\sigma$-table in the previous definitions.) Global states are parameterized with the polymorphic vector type 'v which is restricted to real normed vector types such as $\mathbb{R}$, $\mathbb{R}^2$, $\mathbb{R}^3$. This way, the speed, pos and acc etc. can actually represent vectors of one or more dimensions.

Thus, a generated scenario is an infinite sequence

⟨time t, scene $\sigma$, time t', scene car', time t'', scene car'', ...⟩

where the global state $\sigma^{(i+1)}$ is constructed via the chosen kinematic from global state $\sigma^{(i)}$ after the time interval time$^{(i)}$.

The set of all generated scenarios of an actor-system A will be denoted by $\mathcal{T}$, the *traces of* A. We will say that an actor system *is safe for a property* P iff:

∀t∈$\mathcal{T}$ A. ∀i∈ℕ\{0}. P(of_scene(t(2*i)))

i.e. all global states in all generated scenarios satisfy P. Note that the global states occur in even positions in a scenario.

The safety property relevant for this paper is formalized as follows in Isabelle/HOL:

Isabelle
```
definition ‹Uni_Dimensional_Invariant σ sid ≡
    ∀i∈sid. ∀j∈sid-{i}. global_minimal_distance σ i j < vehicles_distance σ i j›
```

where sid is the finite set of actor-identities and the construction of global_minimal_distance[3] and vehicles_distance is straight-forward from the definitions of the previous subsections.

## 3 The General N-Dimensional Case

We previously developed theories that addresses vehicle safety with respect to collisions for scenarios involving vehicles driving on a single lane (one-dimensional) and in the same direction [12,13]; the general case of vehicles moving in arbitrary directions was left as future work. The objective of this work is to address this limitation and find techniques for the general N-dimensional case.

It turns out that the N-dimensional case can be sliced into driving strategies using the crucial generalization dimension-by-dimension.

---

[2] Our presentation is actually a slight simplification of the version used in our theories.

[3] This definition is detailed in the next section.

### 3.1 A Generalized Theory for Any Given Dimension

As explained earlier, our model relies on the following principle:

*Any vehicle follows the given driving strategy and respects a minimal distance at all times in the given dimension.*

The proof is based on the fact that the application of the driving strategy in dimension D preserves the minimal distance within in a given time interval $[0..\delta t]$ taking a particular kinematics.

**Isabelle**

```
definition ‹global_minimal_distance σ i j ≡
  if pos(σ i) ≤ pos(σ j) then
     if s(σ i) ≥ 0 ∧ s(σ j) > 0 then same_way σ i j
     else if s(σ i) ≥ 0 ∧ s(σ j) ≤ 0 then opposite_way (s(σ i)) (s(σ j)) i j
        else if s(σ i) ≤ 0 ∧ s(σ j) < 0 then same_way σ j i else 0
  else if s(σ i) ≤ 0 ∧ s(σ j) < 0 then same_way σ i j
     else if s(σ i) ≤ 0 ∧ s(σ j) ≥ 0 then opposite_way (s(σ i)) (s(σ j)) i j
        else if s(σ i) ≥ 0 ∧ s(σ j) > 0 then same_way σ j i else 0›
```

This fairly straightforward case distinction is detailed in Table 1.

**Table 1.** Speed case distinction

| | $v_2 > 0$ | $v_2 = 0$ | $v_2 < 0$ |
|---|---|---|---|
| $v_1 > 0$ | (1) $\frac{v_1^2}{2a_{minbrake}}$ | (2) $\frac{v_1^2}{2a_{minbrake}}$ | (3) $\frac{v_1^2+v_2^2}{2a_{minbrake}}$ |
| $v_1 = 0$ | (4) $\frac{v_2^2}{2a_{minbrake}}$ | (5) 0 | (6) $\frac{v_2^2}{2a_{minbrake}}$ |
| $v_1 < 0$ | (7) 0 | (8) 0 | (9) $\frac{v_2^2}{2a_{minbrake}}$ |

If the vehicles are moving towards each other, they must respect the opposite direction distance. Otherwise, they must satisfy the distance corresponding to vehicles moving in the same direction. If the vehicles are moving away from each other, the required minimal distance is zero.

The distance introduced in [51] defines actually two conceptually different ones: one for the opposite-direction case and one for the same-direction case. However, in this model, it remains unclear on how to combine the two in concrete situations, in particular if two vehicles are initially traveling in the same direction, come to a stop and then start moving toward each other. Since vehicles in our model are allowed to change directions freely, this situation has to be covered by our proof.

The deeper reason that our proof succeeds is: based on our definitions, we ensure that same_way and opposite_way distances are equal when the vehicles' velocities are zero. This permits a smooth transition between the different cases.

Finally, without going into detail for reasons of space restrictions[4], we obtain via a series of lemmas covering the different cases involving two vehicles the necessary proofs that the required minimal distance is preserved when all vehicles follow the driving strategy. Since this minimal distance is strictly positive, a collision is therefore impossible.

[4] the full formal proof is available [27].

### 3.2 The Generalization to N-Dimensions

*Kinematic.* We use the kinematic defined in Sect. 2 applied to each dimension: The notations car·j and a$j are just accessors to the j-th coordinate of each object.

We handle the multi-dimensional setting by a decomposition of the N-dimensional space into N generalized distances and driving strategies. All notions, defined in the generalized single-dimension case, are automatically lifted to each dimension. Technically, we exploit the capacity of Isabelle/HOL to define vectors of arbitrary finite size and to define accessors for each of their coordinates.

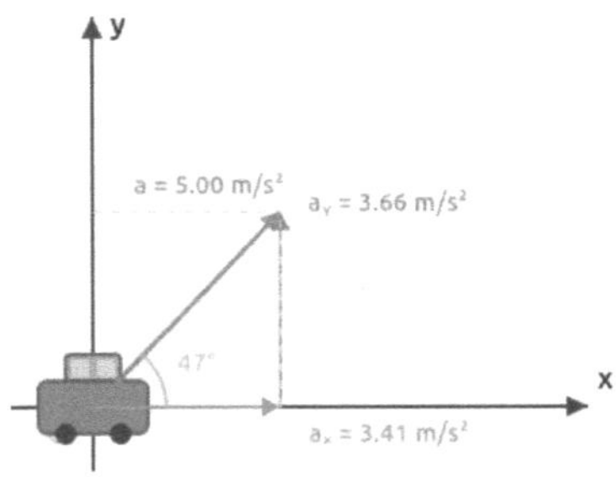


**Fig. 2.** Two Dimensional Case

For the global state car, it will return the position, speed, acceleration etc. on the j-axis. Isabelle's theories also provide a kind of quantification χ j. X j over the components of a product (Fig. 2).

Isabelle

```
definition ‹kinematic_ND δt σ i a ≡
  σ i (|pos   := χ j. pos (kinematic δt (σ·j) i (a$j)),
       speed := χ j. speed (kinematic δt (σ·j) i (a$j)),
       acc   := χ j. acc (kinematic δt (σ·j) i (a$j)) |)›
```

*Driving Strategy.* Our driving strategy, based on the single-dimensional one, is defined as follows: It selects, for each pair of vehicles, a dimension along which they must follow the driving strategy with respect to one another:

Isabelle

```
SOME s. global_minimal_distance (σ·s) i j < vehicles_distance (σ·s) i j
```

Note that the SOME s. P(s) is denoting the Hilbert-Choice operator of HOL. This has the effect that a driving strategy can "randomly select" a dimension and respect its minimal distances, i.e. it is completely free in the other dimensions. Therefore, the N-Dimensional acceleration-ranges are the following:

$$acc = \begin{pmatrix} a_0 \in \text{acceleration range} \\ \vdots \\ a_s \in \text{driving strategy} \\ \vdots \\ a_m \in \text{acceleration range} \end{pmatrix}$$

Note that if we consider two different pairs of vehicles, they do not necessarily have to respect the same minimal distances along the same dimension, even if the two pairs share a common vehicle.

Our goal, as mentioned in Sect. 2 is to prove the following property:
$\forall t \in \mathcal{T}\ A.\ \forall i \in \mathbb{N} \setminus \{0\}.\ P(of\_scene(t(2*i)))$

In our case, P is a no-collision property, but we prove a stronger invariant, from which we want to derive the desired no collision property:

```
Isabelle
definition ‹inv_ND σ idS ≡
        ∀i∈idS. ∀j∈⋂n. dangerous_vehicles (σ·n) i.
            ∃n. global_minimal_distance (σ·n) i j < vehicles_distance (σ·n) i j›
```

In other words, we restrict the invariant to a sub-set of vehicles that are "dangerous" in order to make our model more realistic (Fig. 3).

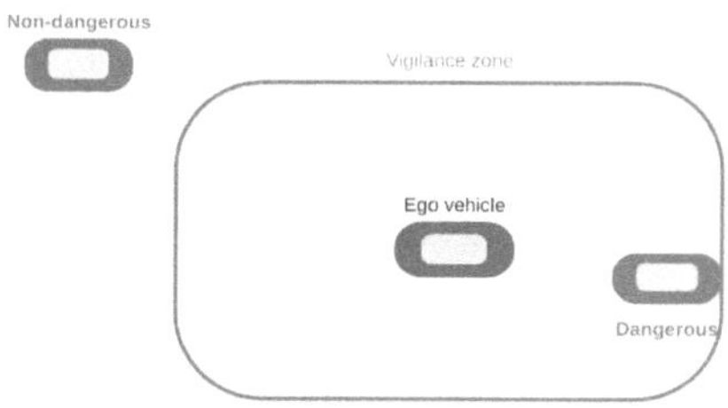


**Fig. 3.** Two Dimensional Case

Dangerous vehicles are those that lie within the region defined by the safe distance in all dimensions. A vehicle is considered dangerous if its actual distance to the ego vehicle is smaller than the safe distance in every dimension. If this is not the case, our model proves that vehicle cannot become dangerous within $\delta t$ before the next global state, i.e. it can be safely ignored.

This invariant finally expresses the following:

*For any vehicle in the scene, if you take any of the dangerous vehicles surrounding him, then there exist a dimension in which the minimal distance is respected.*

We would like to emphasize a particular aspect of our model: Our generalization to N dimensions does not depend on a specific definition of the kinematics, the driving strategy, or the minimal distances. As soon as a proof is established in the single dimension, it can be generalized to arbitrary dimensions.

In our formal theory in Isabelle/HOL, we present this part in a so-called *locale*, i.e. a parameterized theory depending of properties of the actors (kinematic, driving strategy etc.). When instantiated, it gives you the proof obligations for the assumptions of the parameter. Once discharged, it generates the safety theorems for a safety shield in a N-dimensional scenario regarding collisions.

## 4 Assessment of Model Applicability

This section presents the assessment of the applicability of the proposed safety-shield. We first motivate its use by situating its inspiration, Responsibility-Sensitive Safety, within the autonomous driving domain. We then instantiate the parameters of our model as required for simulation and quantitative analysis. Building on these elements, we evaluate the proposed driving strategies through simulation and assess the resulting safety distances.

### 4.1 Industrial Context

As explained in Sect. 1, our approach is derived from RSS, one of the few safety models that define a formal notion of safety and have been integrated into industrial autonomous driving stacks [40,51]. In parallel, safety assurance for autonomous systems is increasingly structured around standards such as ISO 21448 (SOTIF) [54] and ISO 34502 [55], which promote scenario-based validation and safety case construction. While these standards do not prescribe specific safety models, a formal approach such as RSS provides a robust basis for supporting their requirements. More broadly, RSS is becoming part of a wider ecosystem of safety approaches, with applications spanning learning-based systems [1], motion planning [33], motion control [62], runtime safety shields [2], and risk assessment [36]. RSS can therefore be viewed as a key component of autonomous vehicle safety engineering: it provides requirements, design principles, and implementation guidance during development, while also serving as a reference model for assessment and validation. In this context, our approach builds on an industrially influential safety model and extends its formal verification to many-dimensional settings.

## 5 Numerical Parameters for Road-Based Hybrid Systems

In order to perform simulations and distances applicability assessments, we need to choose numerical values for the parameters:

- $\rho$, response time of the vehicle;
- $a_{maxaccel}$, maximum acceleration of the vehicle during the response interval;
- $a_{minbrake}$, minimum braking deceleration ensuring collision avoidance.

*Response Time.* The response time of a human is generally estimated at 1 s [57]. For an onboard computing system, a reaction time of 0.1 s is targeted by engineers for autonomous vehicles; however, it may not currently be realistic to use such a value for simulations, as explained in [38,50]. Numerical evaluations will therefore be carried out in a range of 0.5 s to 1 s, with automated vehicles' reaction time set to 0.5 s.

*Maximum Acceleration.* The maximum acceleration is evaluated based on the time required for a vehicle starting from rest to reach 100 km/h. Typical passenger vehicles in the 130–150 hp range exhibit acceleration times from 0 to 100 km/h on the order of 8–10 s, as observed across representative models' specifications (Toyota Corolla [46,59], Volkswagen Golf [60], Ford Focus [45,58]). We therefore retain the maximum corresponding acceleration, namely 8 s to reach $27.8\,\mathrm{m\,s^{-1}}$, which yields an average acceleration of: $27.8/\ 8 = 3.47\,\mathrm{m\,s^{-1}}$.

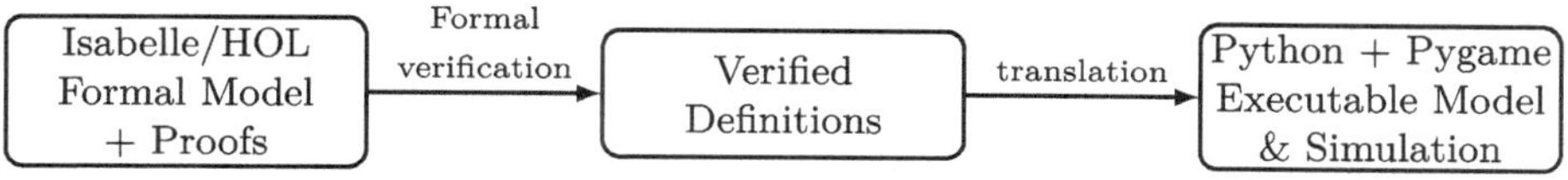


**Fig. 4.** Tool chain from formal verification to simulation.

*Minimum Deceleration* $a_{minbrake}$. We adopt the value 5.8 m s$^{-1}$, which corresponds to the legal minimum for a passenger vehicle ( [56], Annex 3, §2.1.1(B)).

*Maximum Deceleration* $a_{maxbrake}$. We adopt the value 11 m s$^{-2}$ as a strong dry-road braking upper bound [29, 49].

### 5.1 Evaluation via Simulation

In this section, we present simulations of our safety shield in operation across a range of scenarios. Simulations complement formal verification by enabling the detection of undesirable behaviors arising from unrealistic modeling assumptions, thereby revealing when the model or its parameter choices are not adequate. The simulation is deliberately not physically realistic: vehicle motion is modeled using simple axis-wise kinematics, and accelerations are selected randomly within bounds permitted by our safety shield. Rather than aiming at accurate driving behavior or parking strategies, the goal is to stress-test the safety constraints themselves, showing that—even under non-deterministic and potentially erratic motion— collisions are avoided in representative two-dimensional scenarios. Since the driving strategy is sufficiently simple, it can be implemented in virtually any modern programming language. For our experiments, we chose Python as the implementation language.[5]

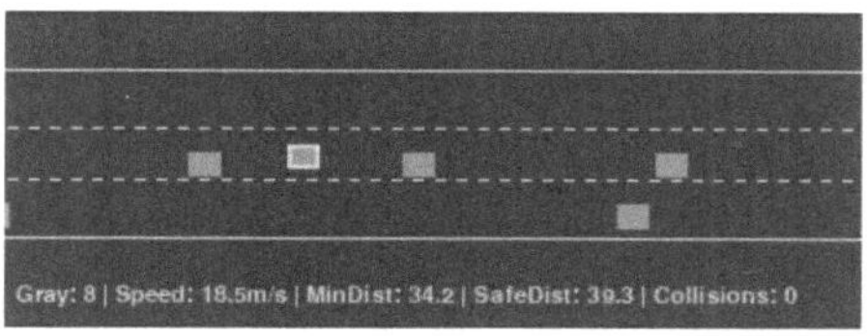


**Fig. 5.** Highway Scenario

[5] Part of the simulation code (specifically the visualization component), was generated with the assistance of artificial intelligence tools. The code is fully available on Github [27] and the repository homepage provides animated versions of the figures shown below (Figs. 4 and 5).

**Highway Scenario.** A three-lane highway scenario is considered in which the ego vehicle, controlled by a driving strategy constrained by our safety shield, must navigate from left to right through traffic. The maximum speed of the gray vehicles is constrained to a lower value (relative to the scale chosen in the simulation) so that the ego vehicle can perform overtaking maneuvers.

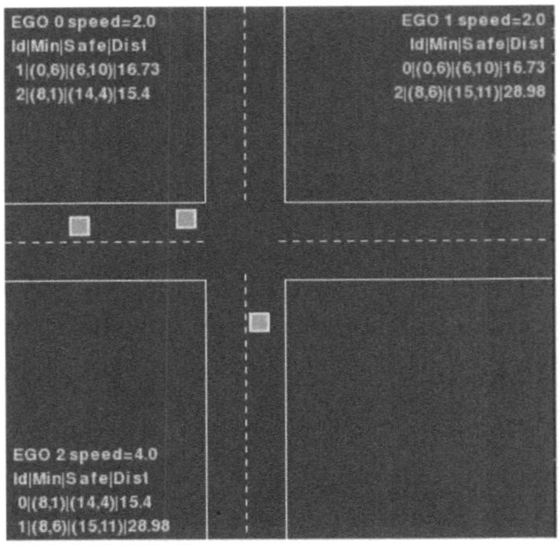


**Fig. 6.** Intersection Scenario

**Crossing Roads Scenario.** Another particularly interesting scenario is that of an intersection between two roads: Vehicles appear randomly at 0 velocity at the four corners of the intersection and must cross it, as turning back is not allowed. In our simulation, the crossing proceeds without issue. Vehicles may use any lane. A more constrained scenario, in which vehicles are required to remain within their lane, would be more realistic; however, since our simulation is fully unconstrained, it also encompasses those cases (Figs. 6 and 7).

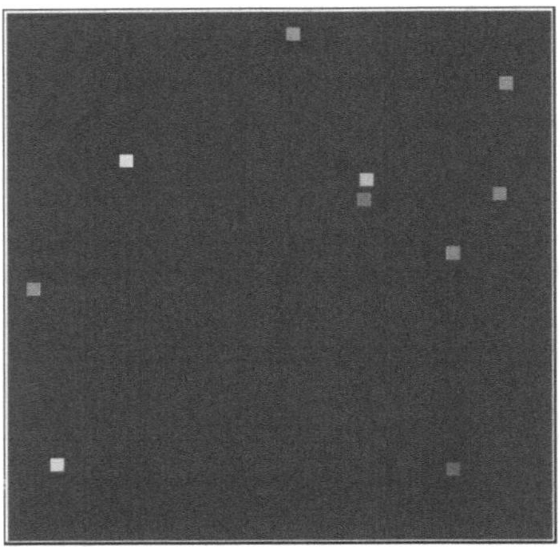

**Fig. 7.** Parking Lot Scenario

**Parking Lot Scenario.** The original RSS article [51] identifies unstructured roads as among the most complex settings. A typical example is a parking lot, which we over-approximate by allowing vehicles to move freely within a bounded area. Vehicles are generated randomly at zero velocity and evolve without predefined trajectories, provided that they adhere to the prescribed driving strategy. In our simulations, collisions may occasionally occur depending on the chosen parameter values, in particular the reaction time. These can be traced back to situations where vehicles are expected to be at rest but, due to numerical approximations, exhibit residual motion and make contact.

## 5.2 Assessment of the Safety Distances

There has been a substantial body of work criticizing the longitudinal safety distance defined in RSS for the longitudinal same-direction scenario as overly conservative in real-world driving conditions, as well as refining and optimizing this distance to improve its practical applicability [10,21,61]. These studies indicate that only the distance travelled while accelerating during the response time is subject to criticism and optimization, i.e., the minimal distance $d_{min}$, which depends solely on braking distances, is not challenged.

Therefore, to evaluate the distances induced by our safety shield, we rely on $d_{min}$ as the basis for comparison. For simplicity, we assume identical values for $a_{minbrake}$ for the two vehicles under consideration. Collecting data from the Crossing Roads scenario we can illustrate Sect. 3 and Table 1.

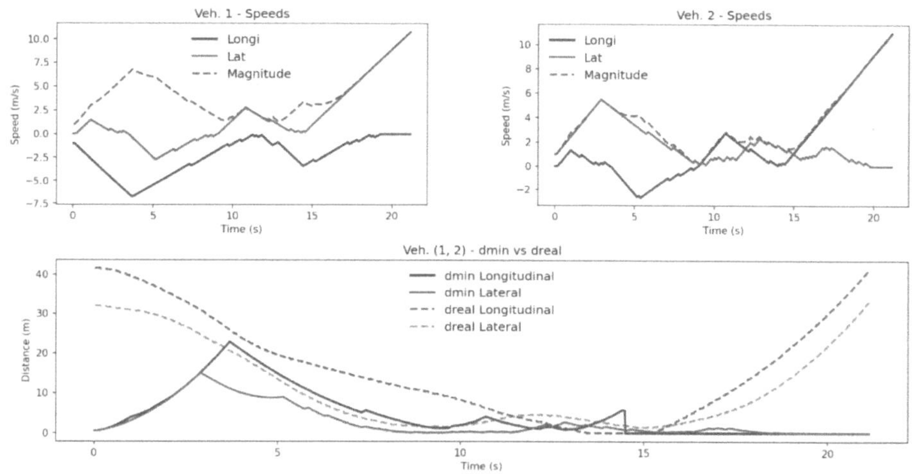


**Fig. 8.** Speed and Minimal Distance Data from Crossing Roads Scenario

We can clearly see in Fig. 8 that the vehicles move toward each other (situation (9) of Table 1), thus enforcing braking along the last axis that became unsafe. Both speeds (lateral and longitudinal) for both vehicles decrease towards 0. While the vehicles are close to each other and a collision remains possible in at least one direction (all cases except (5) and (7)), the speeds remain low. Finally, they pass each other, and at least one direction becomes completely safe (situations (5) and (7)), allowing them to continue towards their destination.

*Minimal Distance Comparison.* In our previous work [12,13], we defined a minimum distance for longitudinal same-direction scenarios as $d_{min\_opti} = \max\left(0, \frac{v_1^2}{2a_{minbrake}} - \frac{v_2^2}{2a_{maxbrake}}\right)$.

Figure 9 compares $d_{min\_opti}$ with $d_{min\_same\_way}$ and $d_{min\_opposite\_way}$. At first glance, the minimal distances in our model appear more conservative, in particular $d_{min\_same\_way}$ compared to $d_{min\_opti}$. We do

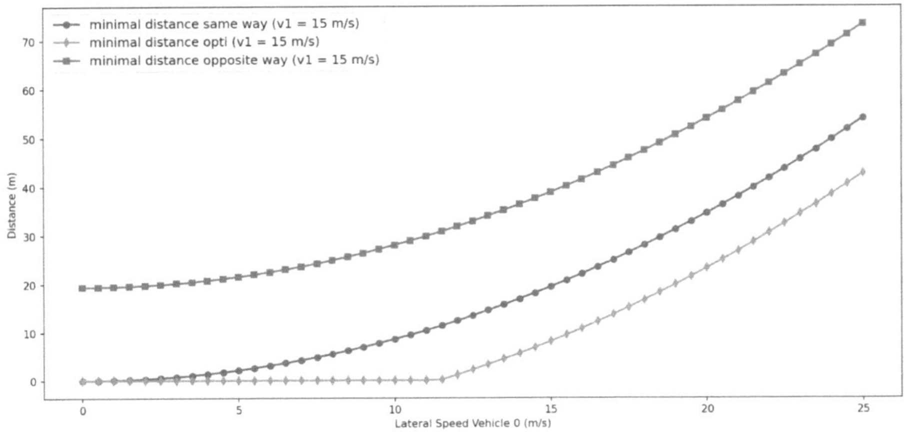


**Fig. 9.** Minimal Distance Comparison for two vehicles v0 (ego) and v1(other)

not optimize $d_{min}s$ for this case in the present work, in order to retain a simpler model, given that this formula has already been proven safe in the aforementioned work. The remaining minimal distances are nevertheless justified for the corresponding situations: for lateral approach, the approaching vehicle must cover its braking distance; for head-on motion, both vehicles must cover their braking distances to reach a complete stop without collision. Finally, for these two situations (lateral or head-on), violations of the corresponding safety distances are inherently transient. This contrasts with the longitudinal same-direction case, where unsafe configurations may persist over time.

To sum up, while our model prioritizes simplicity over optimality in same-direction situations, it yields physically justified bounds for lateral and head-on cases, making it all the more suited to crossing-road and free-evolution scenarios.

### 5.3 Implementation Effort

The adoption of formal methods in industrial settings is often accompanied by concerns regarding development effort and cost. In this section, we provide indicative orders of magnitude for the effort required by the proposed approach. Obtaining the present formal proof required approximately *three person-months*. This estimate does not include the one-dimensional proofs established in our previous work [12,13], on which the present work builds. The development of the simulation prototype required approximately *one week*. Most of this effort was devoted to constructing the environment, while the translation of the safety shield into Python proved to be straightforward, as the underlying definitions remain relatively simple, especially using nowadays llms.

Such costs must be weighed against the high level of reliability and formal safety guarantees achieved through formal verification.

## 6 Related Work

There are numerous approaches to model and analyse CPSs, from simulation-based approaches, which are common in the emerging autonomous vehicle industry, to model-checking approaches, for which tools include [3,18,19,26], or more recently [11,17,31] (see [20] for a survey). While simulations raise the question of the coverage of the problem space, model-checking approaches typically suffer from too coarse abstractions from the continuous physical environment.

Model-checking approaches are concerned, existing approaches include discrete time point based temporal logics and discrete time automata [6,25,37]; they address car control and collision avoidance specifically.

Numerical approaches to compute the reachable sets in ODE's have been used in the work [30,39] for a number of scenarios, among them also two-dimensional ones. In practice, they require particular hypothesis on step-sizes and numerical stability and will be limited by strong assumptions on the structure of ODE's when considering more complex kinematics. This also holds for approaches such as [24] and [35], which tackled the non-collision problem from a testing perspective.

Proof-based approaches, similar to ours, include Differential Hoare Logics [16,42], also using Isabelle/HOL. Event-B and the Rodin platform have also been proposed to formalize CPSs as abstract machines [8,15,53]. They have in common to model continuous time and the physics via the usual Newtonian differential equations. This also holds for the work done in KeyMaera and KeyMaera X systems [7,47], Strauss and Mitsch [52] which use use first-order dynamic logic. Along this line, Prebet, Teuber, and Platzer [48] use differential dynamic logic (dL) to prove absence of collision on an infinite time horizon for longitudinal driving. However, our model is universally *time-triggered* (any sampling smaller than $\Delta \mathsf{T}$ is considered) which makes a transition to simulations and implementations easier.

Regarding multi-dimensional models, examples can be found in the literature that focus on specific cases [23,34,37], particularly addressing intersection-related problems. There is also a strong similarity—atleast concerning the results—with DAIDALUS [43,44], a PVS-based library of formally verified detect and avoid algorithms for Unmanned Aircraft Systems developed by the NASA.

We extend the previously cited work by providing a general formal proof within a multi-dimensional setting that could be considered wider than what previously existed. Our model—albeit starting from a very abstract characterization—is nevertheless fairly easy to convert to simulations and concrete implementations.

## 7 Conclusion

We have presented a formally verified driving strategy for autonomous vehicles based on the Responsibility-Sensitive Safety (RSS [51]) framework, extended to the general N-dimensional case. Our approach demonstrates that collision avoidance can be rigorously established for multi-dimensional scenarios using Isabelle/HOL, significantly extending prior work limited to one-dimensional settings.

A key contribution of this work lies in the dimension-by-dimension generalization, which enables the lifting of single-dimensional invariants to arbitrary dimensions. This provides a scalable foundation for reasoning about complex driving environments while maintaining strong formal guarantees.

In addition to the theoretical development, we validated the approach through simulations and quantitative analysis. The results indicate that the proposed safety distances, although conservative, remain compatible with practical driving constraints, and highlight the impact of key parameters such as reaction time and acceleration.

Overall, this work supports the integration of formally verified safety shields as runtime assurance mechanisms in autonomous systems, complementing less reliable components such as AI-based controllers.

As future work, we would like to explore the following directions:

- extensions of the underlying proof architecture towards truly cyber-physical models involving synchronous communication, non-determinism *and* differential equations (as [13]),
- model more complex kinematics and road topologies,
- goal-aware driving strategies [22,30,39],
- towards models involving computer security aspects, and
- automatically generate from our specifications executable code or simulation environments.

**Acknowledgement.** This work has been supported by the French government under the *France 2030* program, as part of the SystemX Technological Research Institute.

## References

1. Abouelazm, A., Michel, J., Gremmelmaier, H., Joseph, T., Schörner, P., Zöllner, J.M.: Balancing progress and safety: a novel risk-aware objective for RL in autonomous driving. arXiv preprint arXiv:2505.06737 (2025). https://arxiv.org/abs/2505.06737
2. ABZ Conference: ABZ 2025 case study (2025). https://abz-conf.org/site/2025/casestudy/. Accessed 11 Apr 2026
3. Asarin, E., Dang, T., Maler, O.: The d/dt tool for verification of hybrid systems. In: Brinksma, E., Larsen, K.G. (eds.) CAV 2002. LNCS, vol. 2404, pp. 365–370. Springer, Heidelberg (2002). https://doi.org/10.1007/3-540-45657-0_30
4. Ballenghien, B., Taha, S., Wolff, B.: HOL-CSPM - architectural operators for HOL-CSP. Arch. Formal Proofs **2023** (2023). https://www.isa-afp.org/entries/HOL-CSPM.html
5. Ballenghien, B., Taha, S., Wolff, B., Ye, L.: HOL-CSP version 2.0. Arch. Formal Proofs (2019). Formal proof development. https://isa-afp.org/entries/HOL-CSP.html

6. Bannour, B., Niol, J., Crisafulli, P.: Symbolic model-based design and generation of logical scenarios for autonomous vehicles validation. In: IEEE Intelligent Vehicles Symposium, IV 2021, Nagoya, Japan, 11–17 July 2021, pp. 215–222. IEEE (2021). https://doi.org/10.1109/IV48863.2021.9575528
7. Beckert, B., Platzer, A.: Dynamic logic with non-rigid functions. In: Furbach, U., Shankar, N. (eds.) IJCAR 2006. LNCS (LNAI), vol. 4130, pp. 266–280. Springer, Heidelberg (2006). https://doi.org/10.1007/11814771_23
8. Butler, M.J., Abrial, J., Banach, R.: Modelling and refining hybrid systems in Event-B and Rodin. In: Petre, L., Sekerinski, E. (eds.) From Action Systems to Distributed Systems - The Refinement Approach, pp. 29–42. Chapman and Hall/CRC (2016). https://doi.org/10.1201/b20053-5
9. Vintr, T., Vintrova, V., Stefanec, M., Rozsypalek, Z., Rekabi-Bana, F., Arvin, F.: Frequency map enhancement revisited and extended for biohybrid robotics. In: Cavalcanti, A., Foster, S., Richardson, R. (eds.) Towards Autonomous Robotic Systems, TAROS 2025. LNCS, vol. 16045. Springer, Cham (2026). https://doi.org/10.1007/978-3-032-01486-3_8
10. Chai, C., Zeng, X., Wu, X., Wang, X.: Evaluation and optimization of responsibility-sensitive safety models on autonomous car-following maneuvers. Transp. Res. Rec. **2674**(11), 662–673 (2020). https://doi.org/10.1177/0361198120948507
11. Chen, X., Ábrahám, E., Sankaranarayanan, S.: Flow*: an analyzer for non-linear hybrid systems. In: Sharygina, N., Veith, H. (eds.) CAV 2013. LNCS, vol. 8044, pp. 258–263. Springer, Heidelberg (2013). https://doi.org/10.1007/978-3-642-39799-8_18
12. Crisafulli, P., Durier, A., Puyobro, B., Wolff, B.: Polychronous rss in a process-algebraic framework - a case study. In: Leuschel, M., Ishikawa, F. (eds.) Rigorous State-Based Methods, vol. 15728, pp. 249–268. Springer, Cham (2026). https://doi.org/10.1007/978-3-031-94533-5_15
13. Crisafulli, P., Taha, S., Wolff, B.: Modeling and analysing cyber-physical systems in HOL-CSP. Robot. Auton. Syst. **170**, 104549 (2023). https://doi.org/10.1016/J.ROBOT.2023.104549
14. Derler, P., Lee, E.A., Sangiovanni-Vincentelli, A.: Modeling cyber-physical systems. Proc. IEEE (Special Issue on CPS) **100**(1), 13–28 (2012). http://chess.eecs.berkeley.edu/pubs/843.html
15. Dupont, G., Ameur, Y.A., Singh, N.K., Pantel, M.: Formally verified architectural patterns of hybrid systems using proof and refinement with Event-B. Sci. Comput. Program. **216**, 102765 (2022). https://doi.org/10.1016/j.scico.2021.102765
16. Foster, S., Huerta y Munive, J.J., Struth, G.: Differential Hoare logics and refinement calculi for hybrid systems with Isabelle/HOL. In: Fahrenberg, U., Jipsen, P., Winter, M. (eds.) RAMiCS 2020. LNCS, vol. 12062, pp. 169–186. Springer, Cham (2020). https://doi.org/10.1007/978-3-030-43520-2_11
17. Fränzle, M., Herde, C., Teige, T., Ratschan, S., Schubert, T.: Efficient solving of large non-linear arithmetic constraint systems with complex Boolean structure. J. Satisf. Boolean Model. Comput. **1**(3-4), 209–236 (2007). https://doi.org/10.3233/sat190012
18. Frehse, G.: PHAVer: algorithmic verification of hybrid systems past HyTech. Int. J. Softw. Tools Technol. Transf. **10**(3), 263–279 (2008). https://doi.org/10.1007/s10009-007-0062-x
19. Frehse, G., et al.: SpaceEx: scalable verification of hybrid systems. In: Gopalakrishnan, G., Qadeer, S. (eds.) CAV 2011. LNCS, vol. 6806, pp. 379–395. Springer, Heidelberg (2011). https://doi.org/10.1007/978-3-642-22110-1_30

20. Geretti, L., et al.: ARCH-COMP22 category report: continuous and hybrid systems with nonlinear dynamics. In: Frehse, G., Althoff, M., Schoitsch, E., Guiochet, J. (eds.) Proceedings of 9th International Workshop on Applied Verification of Continuous and Hybrid Systems (ARCH22). EPiC Series in Computing, vol. 90, pp. 86–112. EasyChair (2022). https://doi.org/10.29007/fnzc, https://easychair.org/publications/paper/JrQ4
21. Hassanin, O., Wang, X., Wu, X., Xu, X.: Efficiency performance and safety evaluation of the responsibility-sensitive safety in freeway car-following scenarios using automated longitudinal controls. Accid. Anal. Prev. **177**, 106799 (2022). https://doi.org/10.1016/j.aap.2022.106799, https://www.sciencedirect.com/science/article/pii/S0001457522002342
22. Hasuo, I., et al.: Goal-aware RSS for complex scenarios via program logic. IEEE Trans. Intell. Veh. **8**(4), 3040–3072 (2023). https://doi.org/10.1109/tiv.2022.3169762
23. Haydon, J., Bondu, M., Eberhart, C., Dubut, J., Hasuo, I.: Formal verification of intersection safety for automated driving (2023). https://arxiv.org/abs/2308.06785
24. Hekmatnejad, M., Hoxha, B., Fainekos, G.: Search-based test-case generation by monitoring responsibility safety rules (2020). https://doi.org/10.48550/ARXIV.2005.00326, https://arxiv.org/abs/2005.00326
25. Hekmatnejad, M., et al.: Encoding and monitoring responsibility sensitive safety rules for automated vehicles in signal temporal logic. In: Proceedings of the 17th ACM-IEEE International Conference on Formal Methods and Models for System Design, MEMOCODE '19. Association for Computing Machinery, New York, NY, USA (2019). https://doi.org/10.1145/3359986.3361203, https://doi-org.ezproxy.universite-paris-saclay.fr/10.1145/3359986.3361203
26. Henzinger, T.A., Ho, P.-H., Wong-Toi, H.: HyTech: a model checker for hybrid systems. In: Grumberg, O. (ed.) CAV 1997. LNCS, vol. 1254, pp. 460–463. Springer, Heidelberg (1997). https://doi.org/10.1007/3-540-63166-6_48
27. HOL-CyberPhi Project: Autonomous_Simulations (2026). https://github.com/holcyberphi-code/Autonomous_Simulations. GitHub repository. Accessed 07 Apr 2026
28. Immler, F., Hölzl, J.: Ordinary differential equations. Archive of Formal Proofs, April 2012. Formal proof development. https://isa-afp.org/entries/Ordinary_Differential_Equations.html
29. Jeppsson, H., Lubbe, N., Isaksson-Hellman, I.: Real life safety benefits of increasing brake deceleration in car-to-pedestrian accidents: simulation of vacuum emergency braking. Accid. Anal. Prev. **111**, 311–320 (2018). https://doi.org/10.1016/j.aap.2017.12.001
30. Kochdumper, N., Gassert, P., Althoff, M.: Verification of collision avoidance for commonroad traffic scenarios. In: Frehse, G., Althoff, M. (eds.) 8th International Workshop on Applied Verification of Continuous and Hybrid Systems (ARCH21). EPiC Series in Computing, Brussels, Belgium, 9 July 2021, vol. 80, pp. 184–194. EasyChair (2021). https://doi.org/10.29007/1973
31. Kong, S., Gao, S., Chen, W., Clarke, E.: dReach: $\Sigma$-reachability analysis for hybrid systems. In: Baier, C., Tinelli, C. (eds.) TACAS 2015. LNCS, vol. 9035, pp. 200–205. Springer, Heidelberg (2015). https://doi.org/10.1007/978-3-662-46681-0_15
32. Li, W., et al.: Formal design, verification and implementation of robotic controller software via RoboChart and RoboTool. Auton. Robots **48**(6-7), 14 (2024). https://doi.org/10.1007/S10514-024-10163-7

33. Lin, P., Javanmardi, E., Jiang, Y., Hu, D., Zhang, S., Tsukada, M.: eRSS-RAMP: a rule-adherence motion planner based on extended responsibility-sensitive safety for autonomous driving (2024). https://arxiv.org/abs/2409.02503
34. Loos, S.M., Platzer, A.: Safe intersections: at the crossing of hybrid systems and verification. In: Yi, K. (ed.) ITSC, pp. 1181–1186 (2011). https://doi.org/10.1109/ITSC.2011.6083138
35. Loos, S.M., Platzer, A., Nistor, L.: Adaptive cruise control: hybrid, distributed, and now formally verified. In: Butler, M., Schulte, W. (eds.) FM 2011. LNCS, vol. 6664, pp. 42–56. Springer, Heidelberg (2011). https://doi.org/10.1007/978-3-642-21437-0_6
36. Lu, D., Du, H., Wu, Z., Yang, S.: Risk assessment in autonomous driving: a comprehensive survey of risk sources, methodologies, and system architectures. Auton. Intell. Syst. **5**(1), 24 (2025). https://doi.org/10.1007/s43684-025-00112-1
37. Maierhofer, S., Moosbrugger, P., Althoff, M.: Formalization of intersection traffic rules in temporal logic. In: 2022 IEEE Intelligent Vehicles Symposium (IV), pp. 1135–1144 (2022). https://doi.org/10.1109/IV51971.2022.9827153
38. Makridis, M., Mattas, K., Borio, D., Giuliani, R., Ciuffo, B.: Estimating reaction time in adaptive cruise control system. In: 2018 IEEE Intelligent Vehicles Symposium (IV), pp. 1312–1317 (2018). https://doi.org/10.1109/IVS.2018.8500490
39. Manzinger, S., Pek, C., Althoff, M.: Using reachable sets for trajectory planning of automated vehicles. IEEE Trans. Intell. Veh. **6**(2), 232–248 (2021). https://doi.org/10.1109/TIV.2020.3017342
40. Mobileye: Responsibility-Sensitive Safety (RSS). https://www.mobileye.com/technology/responsibility-sensitive-safety/. Accessed 09 Apr 2026
41. y Munive, J.J.H.: Matrices for odes. Arch. Formal Proofs (2020). Formal proof development. https://isa-afp.org/entries/Matrices_for_ODEs.html
42. y Munive, J.J.H., Foster, S., Gleirscher, M., Struth, G., Laursen, C.P., Hickman, T.: IsaVODEs: interactive verification of cyber-physical systems at scale. J. Autom. Reason. **68**, 21 (2024). https://api.semanticscholar.org/CorpusID:273492134
43. Muñoz, C.A.: DAIDALUS: Detect and AvoID alerting logic for unmanned systems (2023), version 2.0.4, LAR-19282-1, NASA Langley Research Center. https://github.com/nasa/daidalus
44. Muñoz, C., et al.: DAIDALUS: detect and avoid alerting logic for unmanned systems. In: 2015 IEEE/AIAA 34th Digital Avionics Systems Conference (DASC), pp. 5A1-1–5A1-12 (2015). https://doi.org/10.1109/DASC.2015.7311421
45. Parkers: Ford Focus Hatchback (2018) ST-Line 1.5 EcoBoost 150PS Auto 5d – Specifications (2026). https://www.parkers.co.uk/ford/focus/hatchback-2018/st-line-(sync3-dab-naviagtion-system)-15-ford-ecoboost-150ps-auto-5d/specs/. Accessed 28 Apr 2026
46. Parkers: Toyota Corolla Hatchback (2019) 1.8 Hybrid Design 5dr CVT – Specifications (2026). https://www.parkers.co.uk/toyota/corolla/hatchback-2019/18-hybrid-design-5dr-cvt/specs/. Accessed 28 Apr 2026
47. Platzer, A.: Logical Foundations of Cyber-Physical Systems. Springer, Cham (2018). https://doi.org/10.1007/978-3-319-63588-0
48. Prebet, E., Teuber, S., Platzer, A.: Verification of autonomous neural car control with KeYmaera X. In: Leuschel, M., Ishikawa, F. (eds.) Rigorous State-Based Methods, ABZ 2025. LNCS, vol. 15728, pp. 288–307. Springer, Cham (2025). https://doi.org/10.1007/978-3-031-94533-5_17
49. Radu, A.I.: Comparison of passenger vehicle braking distance when travelling on snow and asphalt at different velocities. IOP Conf. Ser. Mater. Sci. Eng. **898**(1), 012002 (2020). https://doi.org/10.1088/1757-899X/898/1/012002

50. Rydzewski, A., Czarnul, P.: Human awareness versus autonomous vehicles view: comparison of reaction times during emergencies. In: 2021 IEEE Intelligent Vehicles Symposium (IV), pp. 732–739 (2021). https://doi.org/10.1109/IV48863.2021.9575602
51. Shalev-Shwartz, S., Shammah, S., Shashua, A.: On a Formal Model of Safe and Scalable Self-driving Cars. arXiv e-prints arXiv:1708.06374 (2017)
52. Strauss, M., Mitsch, S.: Slow down, move over: a case study in formal verification, refinement, and testing of the responsibility-sensitive safety model for self-driving cars. In: Prevosto, V., Seceleanu, C. (eds.) Tests and Proofs, TAP 2023. LNCS, vol. 14066, pp. 149–169. Springer, Cham (2023). https://doi.org/10.1007/978-3-031-38828-6_9
53. Su, W., Abrial, J., Zhu, H.: Formalizing hybrid systems with Event-B and the Rodin platform. Sci. Comput. Program. **94**, 164–202 (2014). https://doi.org/10.1016/j.scico.2014.04.015
54. Technical Committee ISO/TC 22, Subcommittee SC 32: Road vehicles—Safety of the intended functionality. techreport ISO 21448:2022. International Organization for Standardization. https://www.iso.org/standard/77490.html
55. Technical Committee ISO/TC 22, Subcommittee SC 33: Road vehicles — Test scenarios for automated driving systems — Scenario-based safety evaluation framework, November 2022. https://www.iso.org/standard/78951.html, edition 1, published November 2022
56. United Nations Economic Commission for Europe: UN Regulation No 13-H – Uniform provisions concerning the approval of passenger cars with regard to braking [2023/401] (2023). https://op.europa.eu/publication-detail/-/publication/c432329d-b3e5-11ed-8912-01aa75ed71a1. official Journal of the European Union, L 60, 24 February 2023, pp. 1–60. Accessed 28 Apr 2026
57. Wikipedia contributors: Assured clear distance ahead — table of perception-reaction times (2024). Revision ID: 1344132024. https://en.wikipedia.org/w/index.php?title=Assured_clear_distance_ahead&oldid=1344132024#Table_of_perception-reaction_times
58. Wikipedia contributors: Ford focus (fourth generation) — Wikipedia, the free encyclopedia (2026). https://en.wikipedia.org/w/index.php?title=Ford_Focus_(fourth_generation)&oldid=1350523669. Accessed 28 Apr 2026
59. Wikipedia contributors: Toyota corolla — Wikipedia, the free encyclopedia (2026). https://en.wikipedia.org/w/index.php?title=Toyota_Corolla&oldid=1347056469. Accessed 28 Apr 2026
60. Wikipedia contributors: Volkswagen Golf Mk8 — Wikipedia, the free encyclopedia (2026). https://en.wikipedia.org/w/index.php?title=Volkswagen_Golf_Mk8&oldid=1348847435. Accessed 28 Apr 2026
61. Xu, X., Wang, X., Wu, X., Hassanin, O., Chai, C.: Calibration and evaluation of the responsibility-sensitive safety model of autonomous car-following maneuvers using naturalistic driving study data. Transp. Res. Part C Emerg. Tech. **123**, 102988 (2021). https://doi.org/10.1016/j.trc.2021.102988, https://www.sciencedirect.com/science/article/pii/S0968090X21000231
62. Yu, T., Tang, Y., Chen, R., Zhao, S.: Optimization of adaptive cruise control strategies based on the responsibility-sensitive safety model. Vehicles **7**(2), 28 (2025). https://doi.org/10.3390/vehicles7020028, https://www.mdpi.com/2624-8921/7/2/28

# Deductive Verification of a Patricia Trie with Creusot

Téo Bernier[1,2(✉)], Frédéric Loulergue[2], and Nikolai Kosmatov[1]

[1] Thales Research and Technology, cortAIx Labs, Palaiseau, France
{teo.bernier,nikolai.kosmatov}@thalesgroup.com,
teo.bernier@univ-orleans.fr

[2] Université d'Orléans, INSA Centre Val de Loire, LIFO UR 4022, Orléans, France
frederic.loulergue@univ-orleans.fr

**Abstract.** Beyond their practical value, space-efficient mutable containers provide instructive use cases for deductive verification, in particular for Rust implementations, where ownership and borrowing simplify some aliasing concerns without eliminating the need for functional proofs. This paper reports on a verification case study of a Patricia trie implemented in safe Rust, specified and verified with Creusot. The code targets a concrete setting: keys are fixed-length arrays of Boolean values, and leaf contents are generic. The verified API is a finite-map interface comprising empty trie construction, mutation-based insertion and deletion, as well as lookup. The case study exposes the main proof challenges of compressed prefix trees: destructive updates, splitting at the first differing bit, and maintaining a global correspondence between explicit node prefixes and the extensional key–value relation represented by the trie. We prove functional correctness of lookup and updates, extensional properties such as the uniqueness of the value associated with a key, and client scenarios that validate the contracts on both symbolic and concrete executions.

## 1 Introduction

Beyond their practical value, mutable data structures provide an important source of case studies for formal methods. In particular, they expose the interaction between complex memory behaviors, logical abstractions, and the limits of proof automation [8,9,19,22,25,31,36,38,39,42]. They are used as building blocks in numerous service modules and applications, and therefore the correctness of their implementations is essential.

Compared to unsafe memory languages like C/C++, Rust brings a strong ownership discipline and eliminates large classes of memory errors. Yet, deductive verification is still needed to establish correct functional behavior of low-level containers. Recent work on Rust verification has explored a variety of approaches, ranging from semantic foundations to automated and auto-active verification tools [1,24,26,27,33]. In this landscape, Creusot [2,18,21] appears particularly attractive because it covers a large subset of Rust features [17] and relies on


P. Gorm Larsen and K. Y. Rozier (Eds.): FMICS 2026, LNCS 16967, pp. 39–59, 2027.
https://doi.org/10.1007/978-3-032-36849-2_3

Why3 [11] to generate proof obligations (or verification conditions), which enables them to be proved by multiple solvers including Alt-Ergo [14], Z3 [16] and cvc5 [4].

Among various mutable data structures, Patricia tries [23,35] provide an interesting target for formal verification. They offer fast prefix lookup and a compact representation of bitstring keys. From a practical point of view, they are used, for example, in Linux kernel routing, in the Haskell maps library, which is extensively used in GHC, the Glasgow Haskell Compiler, in Ethereum (Merkle Patricia Tries), and for runtime support for dynamic verification in the E-ACSL plugin [28] of the Frama-C industrial analysis platform. The latter is implemented in C and initially motivated our choice for this specific structure since the correctness of the analysis depends on the correctness of the Patricia trie implementation.

These examples illustrate their importance for industrial applications. From a verification perspective, Patricia tries combine several specification and proof difficulties: the specification has to encode the *common prefix logic* and the *key-based structural invariants*, and the proof must show that internal nodes always store *compressed prefix* information, updates perform *structural rewiring* correctly, and the intended semantics is that of a *finite map* from keys to values.

This paper reports on a deductive verification case study of a Patricia trie written in *safe* Rust and annotated for Creusot. The companion artifact [6] provides the considered implementation of a Patricia trie, where keys are represented by arrays (of fixed size) of Booleans and values can be of any type. The verified interface is a small map-like API with constructors, lookup, insertion, and removal. We estimate the overall effort required to perform this case study as approximately 6 person-months, which included learning the Creusot tool and proving several simpler versions first. The full verification can be replayed using the artifact Dockerfile, which relies on Creusot version 0.11.0, Why3, Alt-Ergo, Z3 and cvc5.

*Contributions.* The contributions of this case study include:

- formal verification using Creusot of a Patricia trie implementation in Rust with a finite-map-style API;
- a specification based on an abstract key–value relation and an explicit prefix-classification data type that bridges compressed branching and extensional map reasoning;
- a presentation of the verification methodology combining logical/executable pairings, bit-level lemmas, snapshots, and localized assertions to prove destructive updates in Creusot;
- a discussion of the current scope and limitations.

*Outline.* The remainder of the paper is structured as follows. Section 2 recalls the Rust and Creusot notions needed in the following sections. Section 3 presents the target data structure, Patricia tries. Section 4 describes the verified API and its specification. Section 5 explains the verification approach and the main proof results. Section 6 discusses related work, and Sect. 7 concludes and gives future research directions.

## 2 Background: Rust and Creusot

Since its introduction, the Rust programming language has attracted significant attention. It is designed as a low-level systems language, offering an alternative to traditional languages such as C and C++, while providing stronger safety guarantees and richer abstractions without incurring performance penalties. In particular, Rust offers a variety of high-level features, including ownership and borrowing, algebraic data types and pattern matching, generic programming, traits and dynamic dispatch, as well as support for iterators, combinators, and higher-order functions.

These features, together with the goal of ensuring memory safety without relying on a garbage collector, are enabled by integrating underlying concepts such as linearity [3,34], ownership [12] and borrowing [37] directly into the type system. By encoding resource management within types, Rust enables static tracking of variable usage and memory access patterns. This approach allows the compiler to automatically free memory at appropriate points in the program, thereby achieving safe and efficient memory management without garbage-collection overhead.

Creusot [18] is a deductive verifier for Rust that targets ordinary source code annotated with contracts, logical functions, and proof-oriented assertions. From a practical perspective, its main advantage is that verification remains close to the implementation: the verification engineer works directly in Rust, without translating the code into a separate proof language in a proof assistant.

Creusot translates annotated Rust programs to the intermediate verification framework Why3 [11], where verification conditions are discharged by SMT solvers. Its specification language, Pearlite, supports first-order reasoning over contracts, algebraic data types, and ghost code, while snapshots and proof assertions provide explicit control at mutation points. Creusot follows an auto-active methodology: most proof obligations are generated automatically, but the user can still guide the provers with auxiliary lemmas and local assertions.

Our target implementation of a Patricia trie stays within a tame fragment of the Rust language: it uses mutable references and heap allocation through Box, but no *unsafe* code. Yet, its correctness depends on nontrivial semantic properties: prefix-based routing, extensional map behavior, and preservation of invariants under destructive updates. Creusot is expressive enough to state these properties at the source-code level, yet lightweight enough to keep the proof architecture tied to the actual code.

## 3 Verification Target: Patricia Tries

A binary trie stores keys as root-to-leaf paths whose edges are labeled by bits. If many keys share a long prefix, an ordinary trie contains a chain of unary internal nodes before the first genuine branch. A *Patricia trie* (also known as a *radix tree* or *compressed trie*) is a variant of the trie data structure in which chains of

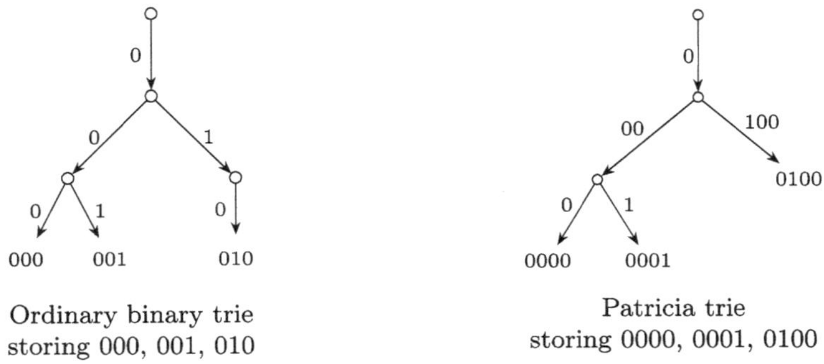


**Fig. 1.** Compression in a Patricia trie. The target implementation stores at each internal node the corresponding prefix: the longest common prefix of the keys in its subtree.

unary nodes are compressed into single edges, yielding a more space-efficient representation [23,35]. Thus, each internal node corresponds to the longest common prefix shared by the keys in its subtree. Figure 1 illustrates this compression.

The verified implementation uses an explicit-prefix view, where each internal node stores the longest prefix shared by all keys in the corresponding subtree. The main exported structure is `PTrie<K,V>`, implemented as a wrapper around an optional root node, `Option<PNode<K,V>>`. The recursive data type `PNode<K,V>`, which remains internal to the implementation, has three constructors: a branching node `Node{prefix,left,right}`, a leaf `Leaf{key,value}`, and a transient constructor `Tmp`, which is used during updates. Keys are abstracted by the trait `Key`; the artifact provides, in particular, an array implementation `AKey([bool; KEY_SIZE])` with `KEY_SIZE = 32` and a machine-word implementation `UKey(usize)`. A prefix is represented as a full key together with a length indicating how many leading bits are significant. The remaining bits are ignored. The values stored in the PTrie have type parameter `V`.

*Lookup* starts at the root and repeatedly compares the given key with the prefix stored in the current internal node. If the key extends it, the next bit determines whether the search continues on the left or on the right. If the key diverges before the end of the prefix, the search stops immediately.

*Insertion* follows prefixes until the first mismatch with the given key, and then rewrites the tree so that the mismatch becomes a new branching point. Insertion modifies the PTrie and returns an optional value. At the top level, if the PTrie is empty, insertion creates a single leaf root and returns `None`. Otherwise, it delegates to recursive node insertion. In a leaf, if the inserted key is equal to the stored key, the value is updated in place and the old value is returned. If the keys differ, insertion computes their longest common prefix, replaces the current leaf by a branching node, and places the old and new leaves on the left or right according to the first differing bit. In an internal node, insertion compares the new key against the stored prefix. If the key still belongs below the node, insertion recurses into the designated child; if it diverges before the end of the current prefix, insertion creates a fresh parent node above the current subtree.

*Deletion* of a given key works by following the compressed prefixes until the algorithm can decide one of three cases: the key is absent in the current subtree, the key is deeper in one subtree, or the key is stored in an immediate leaf. At each internal node, the algorithm compares the query key with the prefix stored in that node. If the query disagrees with that prefix before the prefix ends, then the key cannot occur anywhere in that subtree, so deletion stops immediately and returns failure. If the query key agrees with the stored prefix, then the next relevant bit determines whether the algorithm continues in the left subtree or in the right subtree. Once the algorithm has chosen a side, two cases may occur. If the selected child is itself an internal node, deletion continues recursively there. If the selected child is a leaf, the algorithm compares the full key stored in that leaf with the query key. In case they differ, the key is not present and deletion fails; otherwise, the leaf is removed.

The Patricia-trie-specific step occurs after a successful removal of such a leaf. Since the current internal node then has only one remaining child, the algorithm immediately compresses the Patricia trie by removing that internal node as well and replacing it with the surviving sibling. In other words, deletion not only removes the key, but also restores the compressed Patricia shape instead of leaving a useless unary branch.

At the top level, the same principle applies to the root: if the PTrie is empty, deletion fails. If the PTrie consists of a single leaf, deletion either removes that leaf or leaves the PTrie unchanged. Otherwise, deletion proceeds with the recursive process described above.

*A Representative Scenario from the Artifact.* To validate the expected results, we exercise the verified API on various sequences of operations on a PTrie. In function `main_akey` of the companion artifact [6], this is done concretely on a fresh PTrie using four distinct 32-bit keys:

$$a = 0^{32}, \quad b = 0000\,1100\,1\,0^{23}, \quad c = 0000\,1000\,1\,0^{23}, \quad d = 1^{32},$$

where $0^k$ and $1^k$ denote runs of $k$ identical bits. These keys induce the compact Patricia trie shown in Fig. 2. This example is useful throughout the case study because it exhibits two characteristic update patterns of the implementation: a local split between $b$ and $c$ below the prefix 00001, and a top-level split separating the mostly-zero family $\{a, b, c\}$ from the all-one key $d$.

The generic symbolic client function `generic_symbolic_client` checks the same sequence of insertions, updates, lookups, and removals using four arbitrary distinct keys on an arbitrary PTrie. The function `main_ukey` instantiates the same client for machine-word keys.

## 4 API Specification

The contracts shown in this section are written in Pearlite, the logical specification language of Creusot. API preconditions and postconditions are given

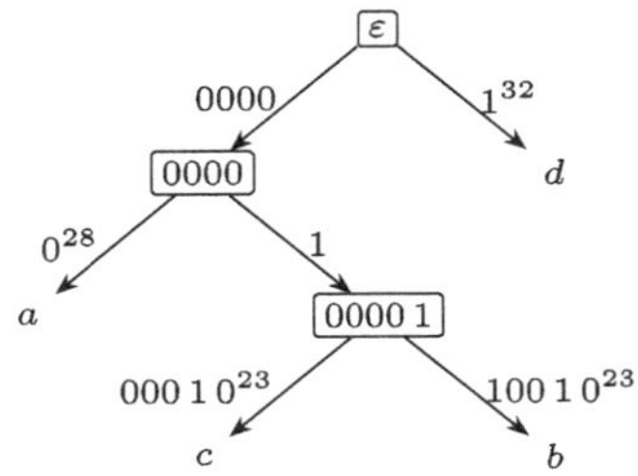


**Fig. 2.** Patricia trie storing keys $a = 0^{32}$, $b = 0000\,1100\,1\,0^{23}$, $c = 0000\,1000\,1\,0^{23}$, $d = 1^{32}$. This trie is used in the concrete client scenario implemented by `main_akey` in the companion artifact [6]. Internal nodes are labeled by the corresponding prefixes.

by `#[requires(...)]` and `#[ensures(...)]` attributes, respectively. Functions annotated with `#[logic]` are logical functions: they are used in specifications and proofs, but are not part of the executable API. In the code, we systematically use the suffix `_log` for logical functions, pretty-printed as a lower subscript "$_l$" in the paper. The attribute `#[check(terminates)]` asks Creusot to prove termination of the corresponding executable function.

Pearlite formulas reuse a Rust-like expression syntax, extended with logical constructs such as universal and existential quantification, written for instance `forall<var: Type>` and `exists<var: Type>`. They also introduce new logic operators used in the contracts below. For an expression `e`, `e@` denotes its logical view, as provided by the `View` trait, for example, the view of the `usize` type is the logical `Int` type. For an expression denoting a mutable borrow, `^e` denotes its final, or prophesied, value, that is, the value it will have when the borrow is released. Finally, `==>` denotes logical implication. These notations are used only in specifications and proofs, and do not affect the executable behavior of the verified API.

With this notation in place, we now describe the public specification of the Patricia trie. The API has two main components: the key abstraction `Key` and the Patricia-trie structure `PTrie<K: Key, V>`.

`Key` extends both `Copy` and `View`. In the case of keys, the corresponding logic model is a sequence of bits (i.e. `Seq<bool>`) . The `Key` trait requires both logical and executable functions for: the length of a key (`len`), getting the $i^{th}$ bit of a key (`bit(i)`), and getting the index of the first different bit of two keys (`diff(key)`). The trait also requires two lemmas that establish the equivalence of model equality and extensional bitwise equality of two keys.

We provide two implementations of this trait: one for fixed-size Boolean arrays and one for unsigned integers.

The central abstraction of the specification is the predicate:

`ptrie.contains`$_l$`(k, v)`

which states that the PTrie stores the association of key $k$ with value $v$.

```
1118    #[logic(open)]
1119    pub fn is_empty_l(&self) -> bool {
1120              {
1121          forall<key: &K, value: V> !self.contains_l(key, value)
1122      }
1123    }
1124
1125    #[requires(self.inv_l())]
1126    #[ensures(result == self.is_empty_l())]
1127    pub fn is_empty(&self) -> bool
1134
1135    #[ensures(result.inv_l())]
1136    #[ensures(result.is_empty_l())]
1137    pub fn new() -> Self
```

**Fig. 3.** Verified PTrie API: vacuity test and creation.

```
1223    #[requires(self.inv_l())]
1224    #[ensures(forall<value: &V> result == Some(value) ==>
1225                                self.get_l(key) == Some(*value))]
1226    #[ensures(result == None ==> self.get_l(key) == None)]
1227    #[ensures(forall<value: &V>
1228      self.contains_l(key, *value) == (result == Some(value)))]
1229    #[ensures(!(exists<other_value: V>
1230      self.contains_l(key, other_value)) == (result == None))]
1231    pub fn get(&self, key: &K) -> Option<&V>
```

**Fig. 4.** Verified PTrie API: lookup.

The logical function $\texttt{get}_l$ is specified as the functional view of $\texttt{contains}_l$: it returns `Some(v)` exactly when the predicate holds for `v`, and `None` otherwise. At this level, the PTrie is understood extensionally as a partial map.

Figure 3 presents the first two verified functions of the API. Lines 1118–1123 define $\texttt{is\_empty}_l$: `#[logic]` indicates it is a logic function whose purpose is to be called in contracts or logical annotations. It is used on Lines 1126 and 1136 in the contracts of the executable function `is_empty` and the constructor of empty PTrie, `new`.

Note that both operations refer to $\texttt{inv}_l$. This predicate expresses formally conditions on the `PTrie` structure so that it has the properties of a Patricia trie, in particular that the routing using bits is correct. This invariant is detailed in the next section because it is a key element of the verification.

Figure 4 shows the contract for the lookup function. Either the PTrie contains a value associated with the given key and a reference to this value is returned (Lines 1224–1225), or there is no value associated with this key and `None` is returned (Line 1226). It is also expressed using $\texttt{contains}_l$. This can only be ensured for well-formed tries respecting the invariant (Line 1223).

There is a variant when one is interested in a mutable reference to the searched value: `get_mut`, shown in Fig. 5. The Patricia trie itself is borrowed mutably. Creusot models a mutable borrow as carrying two logical views of the borrowed place: its current value, written `*r`, and its final prophesied value, written `^r`. For `get_mut`, the returned `value: &mut V` escapes to the caller, so `^value` is not fixed at the moment `get_mut` returns. It denotes the value that

```
1239    #[requires(self.inv_l())]
1240    #[ensures((^self).inv_l())]
1241    #[ensures(forall<value: &mut V> result == Some(value) ==>
1242        self.get_l(key) == Some(*value) &&
1243        (^self).get_l(key) == Some(^value))]
1244    #[ensures(result == None ==>
1245          self.get_l(key) == None &&
1246          (^self).get_l(key) == None)]
1247    #[ensures(forall<other_key: &K, other_value: V>
1248        key@ != other_key@ ==>
1249        ((^self).contains_l(other_key, other_value) ==
1250        self.contains_l(other_key, other_value)))]
1251    pub fn get_mut(&mut self, key: &K) -> Option<&mut V>
```

**Fig. 5.** Verified PTrie API: lookup for mutable reference.

```
1276    #[requires(self.inv_l())]
1277    #[ensures((^self).inv_l())]
1278    #[ensures((^self).contains_l(&key, value))]
1279    #[ensures(forall<other_key: K, other_value: V>
1280      key@ != other_key@ ==>
1281        ((^self).contains_l(&other_key, other_value) ==
1282          self.contains_l(&other_key, other_value)))]
1283    #[ensures(forall<other_value: V>
1284      self.contains_l(&key, other_value) ==
1285      (result == Some(other_value)))]
1286    #[ensures(!(exists<other_value: V>
1287      self.contains_l(&key, other_value)) == (result == None))]
1288    #[check(terminates)]
1289    pub fn insert(&mut self, key: K, value: V) -> Option<V>
```

**Fig. 6.** Verified PTrie API: insertion.

the mutable reference will have when the caller eventually stops using it, once it has reached its final value. This is why `*value == ^value` is not a valid post-condition: it would claim that no future write through the returned reference can change the value of the reference. The situation for `^self` is related: because `value` is a mutable borrow into `self`, the final view `^self` must account for the future final value of that borrowed subpart. So `^self` is not merely "the trie at the instant of return" either. It is the trie after the outstanding mutable borrow has been resolved, with the borrowed entry updated according to `^value`. The invariant is preserved (Line 1240). If the function returns a reference then its value is related to the key in the pre-state and its prophesied value is also related to the same key (Lines 1241–1243), otherwise it is absent from both (Lines 1244–1246). For all the other keys, the pre-state and prophesied state for the Patricia trie are equivalent in the sense for a given key, either they contain the same value or they both do not associate a value to this key (Lines 1247–1250).

Insertion (Fig. 6) preserves the invariant (Line 1277), adds the new binding, i.e. it is contained in the trie at the end of the call (Line 1278), preserves all associations for all keys logically different from the given key (Lines 1279–1282), and returns the previous value if one existed (Lines 1283–1285) or returns `None` otherwise (Lines 1286–1287).

Removal is specified symmetrically: it preserves the invariant (see Fig. 7, Line 1304), removes the queried binding if present (Line 1306), leaves all values of other keys untouched (Lines 1307–1310), and returns the deleted value if the key was previously stored, or `None` if it was not (Lines 1311–1314).

## 5 Verification Approach and Results

The verification follows the implementation layers, where each layer introduces the logical facts needed by the next one. The key layer provides the bit-level view of keys, the prefix layer specifies the relation between keys and prefixes, the node layer specifies and proves the recursive algorithms, and the wrapper layer exposes the public finite-map API.

The first layer is the key abstraction described previously.

The second layer is the prefix layer, centred on the `APrefix<K>` type. A value `APrefix(k,n)` represents the prefix of length `n` of the key `k`. Bits of `k` at positions greater than or equal to `n` are ignored. Thus, several values of type `APrefix<K>` can represent the same prefix, as long as their keys match on their first `n` bits. The invariant of `APrefix<K>` requires `n` to be strictly smaller than the key length, which ensures that there is always a next bit after the prefix.

The comparison operation on prefixes is central to the implementation. Comparing a key with a prefix returns a value of type `KPCmp<K>`. In a tuple `KPCmp (is_right,opt_prefix)`, `opt_prefix` indicates whether the key matches the

```
1304 #[requires(self.inv_l())]
1305 #[ensures((^self).inv_l())]
1306 #[ensures(forall<value: V> !(^self).contains_l(key, value))]
1307 #[ensures(forall<other_key: K, other_value: V>
1308   key@ != other_key@ ==>
1309     ((^self).contains_l(&other_key, other_value) ==
1310     self.contains_l(&other_key, other_value)))]
1311 #[ensures(forall<value: V>
1312   self.contains_l(key, value) == (result == Some(value)))]
1313 #[ensures(!(exists<value: V>
1314   self.contains_l(key, value)) == (result == None))]
1315 pub fn remove(&mut self, key: &K) -> Option<V>
```

**Fig. 7.** Verified PTrie API: removal.

| Layer | Main proof facts | Role |
|---|---|---|
| Keys | lemma_eq_bits, lemma_bits_eq | Relate equality of logical key views to equality of all bits. |
| Prefixes | lemma_kp_eq_cmp_none$_l$, same_view_cmp_none$_l$, lemma_same_view_cmp_none$_l$ | Recover the branch-classification facts needed when a key matches a prefix. |
| Nodes | lemma_leaf_contains_exact, lemma_node_always_contains_at_least_one, lemma_only_one_value_per_key, lemma_contains_key_eq | Establish subtree-level properties of contains$_l$: exact leaf membership, non-emptiness, determinism, and key-view extensionality. |
| Wrapper | lemma_empty_is_none, lemma_only_one_value_per_key, lemma_contains_key_eq | Lift node-level properties to the public PTrie interface. |

**Fig. 8.** Overview of lemmas

prefix or diverges from it. If the key matches the prefix up to its length, then `opt_prefix` is `None` and `is_right` is the first bit of the key after the prefix, and determines the child to follow. If instead the key diverges before the end of the compared prefix, then `opt_prefix` is `Some(prefix)` where `prefix` is the longest common prefix of the key and the compared prefix. In this case, `is_right` is the bit of the key at the divergence position, and is used when insertion creates a new branching node. In both cases, `is_right` indicates whether the key should be routed to the left or to the right branch, with `false` for the left branch and `true` for the right branch.

The third layer is the internal tree `PNode<K,V>`. This is where the recursive algorithms for lookup, mutable lookup, insertion, and deletion are verified. Its constructors are described in Sect. 3. The public wrapper `PTrie<K,V>` forms the fourth layer: it handles the empty-root case and exposes the verified API described in Sect. 4.

*Invariant.* The main invariant is defined first on internal nodes and then lifted to the wrapper. For nodes, $\texttt{inv}_l$ is the conjunction of two predicates. Predicate $\texttt{only\_nodes\_and\_leaves}_l$ excludes the transient constructor `Tmp` from stable states. This constructor is introduced only by destructive updates. Predicate $\texttt{prefix\_includes}_l$ states the routing principle of Patricia tries. For every binding contained in a node, the stored prefix must classify the key consistently: a key routed left can occur only in the left subtree, a key routed right can occur only in the right subtree, and a key that does not match the stored prefix cannot occur below the node at all. The wrapper invariant $\texttt{PTrie:,!:inv}_l$ applies the same node invariant to the optional root, with the empty trie represented by `None`.

*Proof-Guiding Constructs.* Besides contracts, the proof can be guided using two constructs provided by Creusot. Macro `snapshot!(e)` records the logical value of expression `e` at a given program point. This is particularly useful before destructive updates, it allows to reason about previous states, but it can also be used to add specific lemmas into the proof context. Macro `proof_assert!(P)` introduces an intermediate assertion: Creusot generates a verification condition for proposition `P`, and once it is proved, the proposition is available to prove the following obligations. These constructs do not affect the executable Patricia-trie operations.

*Auxiliary Lemmas.* The verification relies on a few lemmas, summarized in Fig. 8. These lemmas are defined and proved using lemma functions. As already mentioned, the key lemmas connect equality of logical views with pointwise equality of bits. Prefix lemmas explain the case where a key has the same logical view as the key used to build a prefix, which is needed when the prover must recover that the prefix comparison returns the `None` case. Node lemmas establish elementary facts about the represented relation, in particular exact membership for a leaf, non-emptiness of well-formed nodes, functionality of the map relation, and extensionality with respect to key views. Wrapper lemmas lift these facts from nodes to `PTrie`.

```
807 #[logic]
808 #[requires(self.invₗ())]
809 #[ensures(exists<key: &K, value: V> self.containsₗ(key, value))]
810 pub fn lemma_node_always_contains_at_least_one_element(&self) {
811   match self {
812     Node { left, .. } => left.lemma_node_always_contains_at_least_one_element(),
813     Leaf { key, value } => {
814       proof_assert!(self.containsₗ(key, *value));
815     }
816     _ => (),
817   }
818 }
```

**Fig. 9.** Definition and proof of `lemma_node_always_contains_at_least_one_element`.

Figure 9 shows one example of a lemma function. The precondition on Line 808 requires the node to be well formed. The postcondition on Line 809 states that such a node contains at least one key-value pair. The proof on Lines 811–817 follows the recursive structure of the `PNode` type: for an internal node, it is enough to recurse on one child (Line 812), for a leaf, the stored key-value pair is a direct witness of the existential quantifier. However, a `proof_assert!` (Line 814) is still needed to make this fact explicit to the SMT solvers. This proof illustrates a common proof pattern used in the node layer, several other lemmas follow the same style: they perform case analysis, proceed by recursive calls when needed, and expose intermediate facts through local assertions.

One role of lemma functions is to state facts that SMT solvers do not derive directly from recursive definitions. This is particularly visible in the update operations, where the proof must relate the pre-state of a mutable node to the rebuilt post-state.

Another role is to isolate complex facts in smaller proof contexts with carefully chosen hypotheses, which can make the resulting verification conditions easier for SMT solvers to discharge than in more saturated contexts.

*A Representative Proof.* Deletion is the most characteristic update proof because it combines prefix routing, ownership-preserving mutation, and compression of the tree shape. Figure 10 shows the core recursive operation on `PNode`.

The proof follows the algorithmic structure. The current prefix first classifies the queried key (Fig. 10, Line 1021). If the key belongs to the left branch, the proof inspects the left child (Line 1022). If this child is a leaf with the same key view, the leaf is removed and the current node is replaced by the right sibling (Lines 1023–1032). This is the Patricia-specific compression step: deletion does not leave a unary internal node behind. The right branch is symmetric.

The proof annotations in this code are concentrated at the points where the shape changes. The call to `take` moves a child or the current node out of place while leaving `Tmp` (Lines 1028 and 1032). The post-state invariant excludes this temporary value once reconstruction is complete. The snapshot of `lemma_leaf_contains_exact` records that the selected leaf denotes exactly one binding before it is moved (Line 1026). The local `proof_assert!` steps make

```
1003 impl<K: Key, V> PNode<K, V> {
1008   #[requires(self.inv_l())]
1009   #[requires(match self {Node {..} => true, _ => false})]
1010   #[ensures((^self).inv_l())]
1011   #[ensures(forall<value: V> !(^self).contains_l(key, value))]
1012   #[ensures(forall<other_key: K, other_value: V> key@ != other_key@ ==>
1013     ((^self).contains_l(&other_key, other_value) == self.contains_l(&other_key, other_value)))]
1014   #[ensures(forall<value: V> self.contains_l(key, value) == (result == Some(value)))]
1015   #[ensures(!(exists<value: V> self.contains_l(key, value)) == (result == None))]
1016   #[check(terminates)]
1017   #[variant(self.height())]
1018   pub fn remove(&mut self, key: &K) -> Option<V> {
1019     if let Node { prefix, left, right } = self {
1020               { key.lemma_eq_bits(key) };
1021       match prefix.kp_cmp(key) {
1022         KPCmp(false, None) => match &mut **left {
1023           Leaf { key: leaf_k, value: leaf_v } => {
1024             let diff = leaf_k.diff(key);
1025             if diff == K::len() {
1026                      {left.lemma_leaf_contains_exact(key, *leaf_v)};
1027                          (left.contains_l(key, *leaf_v));
1028               let removed_leaf = left.take();
1029               let Leaf { value: leaf_v, .. } = removed_leaf else {
1030                 unreachable!()
1031               };
1032               *self = right.take();
1033               Some(leaf_v)
1034             } else {
1035               None
1036             }
1037           }
1038           _ => left.remove(key),
1039         },
1040         //
```

**Fig. 10.** Deletion on internal Patricia-trie nodes.

explicit the membership and absence facts needed by the post-condition after the sibling has been promoted (Line 1027).

At the wrapper level, `PTrie::remove` deals with the cases that do not belong to the recursive node algorithm (see Fig. 11, Line 1315). If the root is absent, removal returns `None` (Line 1341). If the root is a single leaf, it either removes that leaf or restores it unchanged (Lines 1320–1332). Otherwise, it delegates to `PNode::remove` and wraps the resulting root again (Lines 1335–1338).

*Clients.* Verifying the different algorithms is necessary, but the proven contracts also need to be usable in practice. To ensure that the specification is sufficiently complete and usable, we define several scenarios manipulating Patricia tries.

First, to check that the public contracts expose the expected map-like behavior, the proof-oriented wrappers `map_new`, `map_insert`, and `map_remove` restate the API in a functional style. They show that the imperative operations can be composed as map updates over the logical function $\texttt{get}_l$.

Then, the generic client executes a longer scenario with four pairwise distinct symbolic keys. It checks insertion into an arbitrary initial trie, deletion of a freshly inserted binding, repeated insertion of existing keys, lookup after updates, and removal of the four distinguished keys. The concrete clients instantiate the same scenario for Boolean-array keys and unsigned-integer keys.

```
pub fn remove(&mut self, key: &K) -> Option<V>
{
  let root = self.root.take();
  match root {
    Some(node) => match node {
      Leaf {
        key: leaf_key,
        value: leaf_value,
      } => {
        let diff = leaf_key.diff(key);
        if diff == K::len() {
          Some(leaf_value)
        } else {
          self.root = Some(Leaf {
            key: leaf_key,
            value: leaf_value,
          });
          None
        }
      }
      mut node => {
        let res = node.remove(key);
        self.root = Some(node);
        res
      }
    },
    None => None,
  }
}
```

**Fig. 11.** Deletion on a Patricia trie.

Finally, the integer-key client uses `#[bitwise_proof]` and six trusted assertions to record the concrete bit inequalities that make its four test keys distinct. The core PTrie API itself does not rely on these trusted assertions. This scenario shows that the public API remains usable with a machine-word key representation.

*Verification Results.* Figure 12 gives a breakdown of the nonblank, noncomment lines of the verified Rust artifact. The count separates the executable body from the lines introduced for specification and proof, and reports this decomposition for each implementation layer. The columns are defined as follows: Ex. Body represents the executable functions' implementation, i.e. the executable source code. Ex. Spec. denotes the contracts and tool-specific annotations attached to executable functions. This is the part most relevant to users who instantiate new key types or rely on the public API. Ex. Proof refers to the local proof-guiding constructs used inside executable functions. It reflects the additional proof effort needed to help SMT solvers discharge the verification conditions. Log. Def. captures the logical functions' specifications and bodies. These functions define the logical model used by the proof and reflect part of the complexity of each layer. This category also includes the proof-guiding lines that are zero for all layers except the prefix layer, where it takes two lines. Lemmas counts the lemma functions' definitions, and proof artifacts. It gives an indication of the amount and complexity of the auxiliary facts needed to prove each layer. Total gives the total number of nonblank, noncomment lines for the layer. Verif. contains all lines that are not executable-body lines, i.e. the lines added to specify the program, define its logical model, and guide the proof. Ratio measures the number of verification lines per executable-body line. It gives an indication of the verification overhead for each layer.

| Layer | Ex. Body | Ex. Spec | Ex. Proof | Log. Def. | Lemmas | Total | Verif. | Ratio |
|---|---|---|---|---|---|---|---|---|
| Keys | 74 | 40 | 1 | 118 | 32 | 265 | 191 | 2.58 |
| Prefixes | 37 | 35 | 0 | 121 | 44 | 237 | 200 | 5.41 |
| Nodes | 154 | 36 | 12 | 83 | 60 | 345 | 191 | 1.24 |
| Wrapper | 82 | 53 | 6 | 41 | 27 | 209 | 127 | 1.55 |
| Clients | 81 | 15 | 72 | 0 | 0 | 168 | 87 | 1.07 |
| Total | 428 | 179 | 91 | 363 | 163 | 1224 | 796 | 1.86 |

**Fig. 12.** Detailed statistics of the specification and the implementation (lines of code).

Overall, the artifact contains 428 lines of executable body and 796 verification-related lines, giving a ratio of 1.86 verification lines per executable-body line. However, the distribution is not uniform across layers. The prefix layer has the highest ratio, because it defines prefixes, their relation with the keys, and the routing logic. It has the largest number of verification lines, even though it is the smallest layer in terms of executable code.

In contrast, the node layer has the largest executable body, but a limited verification overhead. It is the first layer that substantially uses lemmas and local assertions, since the recursive algorithms require some proof guidance. Compared to the amount of executable code analyzed, however, the proof effort remains relatively low, and many lemmas simply follow basic case analysis and recursive calls.

The wrapper layer mostly reuses the node-layer specifications and instantiates wrapper versions of the node lemmas.

Finally, the client layer contains most of the executable proof-guiding lines, as it checks that the verified contracts work as expected. This also suggests that the current public API could be more optimized for SMT solvers, as most of the difficulty comes from the executable code proof effort.

| Prover | Calls | Min | Avg | Max |
|---|---|---|---|---|
| `alt-ergo@2.6.2` | 394 | 5 ms | 30 ms | 1100 ms |
| `z3@4.15.8` | 27 | 7 ms | 29 ms | 240 ms |
| `cvc5@1.3.3` | 13 | 22 ms | 339 ms | 1100 ms |
| **Overall** | 434 | 5 ms | 39 ms | 1100 ms |

**Fig. 13.** Proof timing statistics reported by `why3find`.

Experiments were run on a MacBook Pro (Apple M4 Max chip, 16 cores and 128 GB of memory), running macOS version 26.3.1 on `arm64`, with Creusot version 0.11.0, Why3 version 1.8.2 and WHY3FIND version 1.2.0, and the following SMT provers: Alt-Ergo version 2.6.2, Z3 version 4.15.8, cvc5 version 1.3.3. The wall clock for proving the 434 goals the first time (i.e. first instance of `cargo creusot prove`), using only one job, is around 4 m30 s. Table 13 shows, for each prover, how many verification conditions were proved and the minimum, average and maximum time spent to prove these conditions. The provers are listed in the order they were tried. The timeout was set to 6 s.

*Lessons Learned.* Prior to this verification case study on a Rust implementation of Patricia tries, we conducted an attempt to verify a similar implementation in C using the Frama-C verification platform [29]. As in the present work, we did not strictly focus on an existing real-life code, but took the liberty to create a simplified version inspired by real-life implementations. We allocated a similar level of effort to the verification of the C version. Although we already had experience with Frama-C, we were unable to complete the verification within the allocated time. Only the insertion function was partially verified without addressing complete functional properties of Patricia tries. The inability of solvers to automatically discharge the generated proof obligations prevented us from going further: even for our partial specification, there were around 70 interactive proofs to create and maintain (mostly via proof scripts in the interactive proof assistant of Frama-C) out of around 700 proof obligations. This was due in particular to a significant number of separation annotations and the need to maintain a companion ghost structure, similar to the one used for linked list [8,9] but adapted to match the tree topology. Similar difficulties were also encountered in the TPM2-TSS verification case study [44] involving linked lists. Targeting a Patricia trie, more complex structural invariants further increased the difficulty.

The Rust verification avoids these problems thanks to the Rust type system. As the internal node only uses a simple recursive definition, the type system invariants ensure the separation between a node and its children. These experiments suggest that Rust implementations of complex memory structures are easier to verify than comparable C implementations. Furthermore, instead of lemmas proven in the Rocq proof assistant [7] which can be necessary when using Frama-C [44], the Rust case study only required lemma functions which we found more convenient and easier to write and prove, since only the inductive step must be explicit, and the solvers complete the proof.

The Rust implementation considered here is not entirely idiomatic. While it constitutes a credible safe realization, some parts have been simplified and are not fully representative of a real-world implementation. For example, some functions on the keys are implemented recursively instead of using iterators. These choices were made to ease the specification development and the proof effort, but with additional effort, it would be possible to reach more realistic versions. Overall, we encountered very few limitations of Creusot in this case study, and we found the familiarization with the tool reasonably easy and fast.

# 6 Related Work

*Verified Data Structures.* Data structures and their manipulations are a common target of verification efforts, such as linked lists [8,9], trees [19], linked data structures including lists and trees [22,25], sets [20], hash tables [39] and generic containers [38] to name a few. Beyond the programming language and specification language, two important aspects vary across these verification efforts. First, how are the specifications written? In particular, is the data structure related to a *model* in the logic specification language to express the data structure API contracts? Second, to what extent is the verification automated: fully automated, partially automated, or mostly interactive?

Blanchard et al. verified a linked list API written in C using as a model either a ghost C array [8] or logic lists in the ACSL specification language [9]. In both cases, the verification is carried out with Frama-C [5,29], which is largely automated but may rely on interactive theorem proving, in particular for lemmas proved by induction. This approach was later made significantly more automated through an auto-active verification [32] methodology for Frama-C [10]. Dross et al. [19] verified red-black trees in SPARK (a subset of Ada), using arrays as the implementation structure. Their proof relies on ghost code and auto-active verification. For JML, Gladisch and Tyszberowicz [25] specify methods on a linked list structure using a pure observer rather than a model. This observer takes a list object and an index and returns the element at the position. They also study a tree structure, where the observer is `boolean reach(Tree a, int depth, Tree b)`, meaning that `b` is a subtree of `a` at depth exactly `depth`.

Filliâtre et al. [22] use an integer-indexed ghost data structure to represent both linked lists and trees implemented in WhyML and proved with Why3. In terms of list representation, their approach is close to the ghost arrays of Blanchard et al. [8], with one significant difference: the predicate relating the data structure to its model is not inductive but universally quantified over integers. This makes the proofs easier, avoiding the need to assist SMT provers with lemmas proved by induction, whether interactively or automatically. Dubois uses a logic set [20] and auto-active verification in Why3. Pottier verifies an imperative hash table data structure implemented in OCaml and verified with CFML, a translator to Rocq (formerly Coq). This approach is mostly interactive.

For object-oriented languages such as Java and Eiffel, a common verification technique consists in attaching abstract models to classes under verification, as in the work of Polikarpova et al. [38]. These models are immutable and introduced solely for specification purposes. Nevertheless, they are expressed as regular classes of the source language, which makes them suitable for runtime assertion checking. In deductive verification, such classes can be translated into logical entities of the underlying provers. The faithfulness of this translation can itself be subject to verification [15].

In our work, we adopt an auto-active verification approach, relying on a few helper lemmas; only three require simple proofs by induction. For keys, we use the Creusot-provided `View` trait to relate a key to its model `Seq<bool>`. In this respect, our approach is close to works that rely on explicit models. For the trie, however, we do not use an explicit model, but instead rely on the $\texttt{contains}_l$ predicate. This is closer to the work of Gladisch and Tyszberowicz, in that the predicate observes the leaves of the trie. The approach of Creusot, unlike that of Polikarpova et al. [38], does not provide `Seq` as a regular pure functional implementation. Nevertheless, in both approaches, the model is translated into logical entities for the underlying provers (in the case of Creusot, through Why3).

*Deductive Verification of* Rust *Programs.* There are two main categories of deductive verifiers for Rust, depending on whether they trust the Rust type system and borrow checker. In the first case, the verifier uses the typing and borrowing information produced by the Rust compiler, together with user annotations, to generate proof obligations. Tools such as Prusti [1] and RefinedRust [24] use permission- or separation-logic-inspired reasoning to track ownership and aliasing properties. They differ substantially in their target fragments: Prusti focuses primarily on safe Rust, whereas RefinedRust is designed for high-assurance reasoning about Rust programs including unsafe components. This style can express low-level aliasing properties, but typically requires more explicit proof structure than SMT-oriented verification of safe Rust fragments. In the second case, the verifier relies on the guarantees enforced by the Rust type system and borrow checker: a large fragment of safe Rust can then be viewed through a functional lens. This makes proof obligations easier to generate and discharge. In practice, this leads to obligations solved either by SMT solvers, as in Creusot [18] and Verus [31], or by proof assistants, as in Aeneas [26].

Recent case studies using Verus also show that Rust verification is scaling toward larger systems [30], including OS and kernel components [13], cluster-management controllers [41], and security-oriented components [43]. Recent work also explores automated specification and proof generation for several data structures [40]. These works are complementary to ours. They demonstrate scale and systems-level verification in Rust, whereas our case study focuses on a compact but proof-intensive mutable data structure, where the central difficulty is the interaction between compressed-prefix reasoning, finite-map specifications, and destructive tree updates in Creusot. Porting our case study to Verus would offer a useful comparison point for evaluating the maturity and scalability of the two tools.

Mutable borrows remain one of the main challenges. To the best of our knowledge, Aeneas and Creusot are currently the only mature representatives of this line of work that handle mutable borrows without severe usability restrictions, such as disallowing them in return positions. This is necessary to deal with functions such as `get_mut`. Moreover, we favor a more automated approach, which motivates our choice of Creusot over Aeneas in this work.

## 7 Conclusion and Future Work

This paper presents a deductive verification case study of a Patricia trie implemented in safe Rust and verified with Creusot. The verified code establishes the functional correctness of a small but meaningful API. Its specification is organized around an abstract key–value relation, while the implementation features some idiomatic imperative Rust, with boxed nodes and destructive updates. The central proof idea is to make prefix classification explicit, both operationally and logically, and to combine this abstraction with a global invariant that partitions the represented keys between subtrees. Automation works well once the right lemmas are in place, but update proofs still require a focused prefix-lemma layer, snapshots of prior states, and a few local assertions. We consider this a positive result for auto-active verification in Rust: even for a compressed mutable tree, the proof remains structured, modular, and close to the code.

A Rust crate implementing Patricia tries exists, namely `patricia_tree` (https://github.com/sile/patricia_tree). While its API is significantly richer, its implementation heavily relies on `unsafe`. This suggests several natural directions for future work. A first direction is to retain the safe implementation of a Patricia trie while extending the API with iterators and prefix-related operations such as splitting a Patricia trie at a given prefix and returning the entry whose key shares the longest common prefix with a query key. A second direction is to study a more low-level implementation of Patricia tries. Full direct verification of arbitrary unsafe Rust is not currently within Creusot's scope. Instead, Creusot supports reasoning about selected unsafe idioms, especially raw pointers and interior-mutable state, through ghost permissions complemented by pointer-liveness information. These features could be explored to verify low-level code. Exploring the combination of Creusot and Gilian is another promising direction for reasoning about code that uses `unsafe` [2].

**Acknowledgment.** Part of this work was supported by ANR (grants ANR-22-CE39-0014, ANR-22-CE25-0018, ANR-24-ASM2-0001). We thank the anonymous referees for helpful comments.

## References

1. Astrauskas, V., et al.: The Prusti project: formal verification for Rust. In: NASA Formal Methods (NFM). LNCS, vol. 13260, pp. 88–108. Springer, Cham (2022). https://doi.org/10.1007/978-3-031-06773-0_5
2. Ayoun, S., Denis, X., Maksimovic, P., Gardner, P.: A hybrid approach to semi-automated Rust verification. Proc. ACM Program. Lang. **9**(PLDI), 970–992 (2025). https://doi.org/10.1145/3729289
3. Baker, H.G.: Use-Once variables and linear objects: storage management, reflection and multi-threading. ACM SIGPLAN Not. **30**(1), 45–52 (1995). https://doi.org/10.1145/199818.199860

4. Barbosa, H., et al.: cvc5: a versatile and industrial-strength SMT solver. In: TACAS 2022. LNCS, vol. 13243, pp. 415–442. Springer, Cham (2022). https://doi.org/10.1007/978-3-030-99524-9_24
5. Baudin, P., et al.: The dogged pursuit of bug-free C programs: the Frama-C software analysis platform. Commun. ACM **64**(8), 56–68 (2021). https://doi.org/10.1145/3470569
6. Bernier, T., Loulergue, F., Kosmatov, N.: VPTrie: deductive verification of a Patricia Trie with Creusot. Companion Artifact. (2026). https://doi.org/10.5281/zenodo.19932306
7. Bertot, Y., Castéran, P.: Interactive Theorem Proving and Program Development. Coq'Art: The Calculus of Inductive Constructions. Springer, Heidelberg (2004). https://doi.org/10.1007/978-3-662-07964-5
8. Blanchard, A., Kosmatov, N., Loulergue, F.: Ghosts for lists: a critical module of Contiki verified in Frama-C. In: Dutle, A., Muñoz, C., Narkawicz, A. (eds.) NFM 2018. LNCS, vol. 10811, pp. 37–53. Springer, Cham (2018). https://doi.org/10.1007/978-3-319-77935-5_3
9. Blanchard, A., Kosmatov, N., Loulergue, F.: Logic against ghosts: Comparison of two proof approaches for a list module. In: ACM Symposium on Applied Computing (SAC), pp. 2186–2195. ACM (2019). https://doi.org/10.1145/3297280.3297495
10. Blanchard, A., Loulergue, F., Kosmatov, N.: Towards full proof automation in Frama-C using auto-active verification. In: Badger, J.M., Rozier, K.Y. (eds.) NFM 2019. LNCS, vol. 11460, pp. 88–105. Springer, Cham (2019). https://doi.org/10.1007/978-3-030-20652-9_6
11. Bobot, F., Filliâtre, J.-C., Marché, C., Paskevich, A.: Let's verify this with Why3. Int. J. Softw. Tools Technol. Transfer **17**(6), 709–727 (2014). https://doi.org/10.1007/s10009-014-0314-5
12. Boyapati, C., Salcianu, A., Beebee, W., Rinard, M.: Ownership types for safe region-based memory management in real-time Java. In: Programming Language Design and Implementation (PLDI), pp. 324–337. ACM (2003). https://doi.org/10.1145/781131.781168
13. Chen, X., Li, Z., Zhang, J., Narayanan, V., Burtsev, A.: Atmosphere: practical verified kernels with Rust and Verus. In: Symposium on Operating Systems Principles, SOSP '25. Association for Computing Machinery, New York, NY, USA (2025). https://doi.org/10.1145/3731569.3764821
14. Conchon, S., Iguernelala, M., Mebsout, A.: A collaborative framework for non-linear integer arithmetic reasoning in Alt-Ergo. In: Symposium on Symbolic and Numeric Algorithms for Scientific Computing (SYNASC), pp. 161–168. IEEE Computer Society (2013). https://doi.org/10.1109/SYNASC.2013.29
15. Darvas, Á., Müller, P.: Proving consistency and completeness of model classes using theory interpretation. In: Fundamental Approaches to Software Engineering (FASE). LNCS, vol. 6013, pp. 218–232. Springer, Heidelberg (2010). https://doi.org/10.1007/978-3-642-12029-9_16
16. de Moura, L., Bjørner, N.: Z3: an efficient SMT solver. In: Ramakrishnan, C.R., Rehof, J. (eds.) TACAS 2008. LNCS, vol. 4963, pp. 337–340. Springer, Heidelberg (2008). https://doi.org/10.1007/978-3-540-78800-3_24
17. Denis, X., Jourdan, J.H.: Specifying and verifying higher-order Rust iterators. In: Sankaranarayanan, S., Sharygina, N. (eds.) Tools and Algorithms for the Construction and Analysis of Systems (TACAS). LNCS, vol. 13994, pp. 93–110. Springer, Cham (2023). https://doi.org/10.1007/978-3-031-30820-8_9

18. Denis, X., Jourdan, J.H., Marché, C.: Creusot: a foundry for the deductive verification of Rust programs. In: Riesco, A., Zhang, M. (eds.) Formal Methods and Software Engineering, ICFEM 2022. LNCS, vol. 13478, pp. 90–105. Springer, Cham (2022). https://doi.org/10.1007/978-3-031-17244-1_6
19. Dross, C., Moy, Y.: Auto-active proof of red-black trees in SPARK. In: NASA Formal Methods (NFM), pp. 68–83 (2017). https://doi.org/10.1007/978-3-319-57288-8_5
20. Dubois, C.: Deductive verification of sparse sets in Why3. In: Protzenko, J., Raad, A. (eds.) Verified Software. Theories, Tools and Experiments (VSTTE). LNCS, pp. 28–46. Springer, Cham (2024). https://doi.org/10.1007/978-3-031-86695-1_3
21. Filliâtre, J.-C., Paskevich, A.: Why3 — where programs meet provers. In: Felleisen, M., Gardner, P. (eds.) ESOP 2013. LNCS, vol. 7792, pp. 125–128. Springer, Heidelberg (2013). https://doi.org/10.1007/978-3-642-37036-6_8
22. Filliâtre, J., Paskevich, A., Danvy, O.: When separation arithmetic is enough. In: Damiani, F., Farrell, M. (eds.) Integrated Formal Methods, IFM 2025. LNCS, vol. 16194, pp. 23–37. Springer, Cham (2026). https://doi.org/10.1007/978-3-032-10794-7_2
23. Fredkin, E.: Trie memory. Commun. ACM **3**(9), 490–499 (1960). https://doi.org/10.1145/367390.367400 Commun. ACM **3**(9), 490–499 (1960). https://doi.org/10.1145/367390.367400
24. Gäher, L., Sammler, M., Jung, R., Krebbers, R., Dreyer, D.: RefinedRust: a type system for high-assurance verification of Rust programs. Proc. ACM Program. Lang. **8**(PLDI), 1115–1139 (2024). https://doi.org/10.1145/3656422
25. Gladisch, C., Tyszberowicz, S.: Specifying linked data structures in JML for combining formal verification and testing. Sci. Comput. Program. **107–108**, 19–40 (2015). https://doi.org/10.1016/j.scico.2015.02.005
26. Ho, S., Protzenko, J.: Aeneas: Rust verification by functional translation. Proc. ACM Program. Lang. **6**(ICFP), 711–741 (2022). https://doi.org/10.1145/3547647
27. Jung, R., Jourdan, J.H., Krebbers, R., Dreyer, D.: RustBelt: securing the foundations of the rust programming language. Proc. ACM Program. Lang. **2**(POPL), 66:1–66:34 (2018). https://doi.org/10.1145/3158154
28. Kosmatov, N., Petiot, G., Signoles, J.: An optimized memory monitoring for runtime assertion checking of C programs. In: Legay, A., Bensalem, S. (eds.) RV 2013. LNCS, vol. 8174, pp. 167–182. Springer, Heidelberg (2013). https://doi.org/10.1007/978-3-642-40787-1_10
29. Kosmatov, N., Prevosto, V., Signoles, J. (eds.): Guide to Software Verification with Frama-C. Core Components, Usages, and Applications. Computer Science Foundations and Applied Logic Book Series, Springer (2024). https://doi.org/10.1007/978-3-031-55608-1
30. Lattuada, A., et al.: Verus: a practical foundation for systems verification. In: 2024 Symposium on Operating Systems Principles (2024). https://doi.org/10.1145/3694715.3695952
31. Lattuada, A., et al.: Verus: verifying rust programs using linear ghost types. Proc. ACM Program. Lang. **7**(OOPSLA), 286–315 (2023). https://doi.org/10.1145/3586037
32. Leino, K.R.M., Moskal, M.: Usable auto-active verification (2010). http://fm.csl.sri.com/UV10/
33. Matsushita, Y., Denis, X., Jourdan, J.H., Dreyer, D.: RustHornBelt: a semantic foundation for functional verification of Rust programs with unsafe code. In: Programming Language Design and Implementation (PLDI), pp. 841–856. ACM (2022). https://doi.org/10.1145/3519939.3523704

34. Minsky, N.H.: Towards alias-free pointers. In: Cointe, P. (ed.) ECOOP 1996. LNCS, vol. 1098, pp. 189–209. Springer, Heidelberg (1996). https://doi.org/10.1007/BFb0053062
35. Morrison, D.R.: PATRICIA - practical algorithm to retrieve information coded in alphanumeric. J. ACM **15**(4), 514–534 (1968). https://doi.org/10.1145/321479.321481
36. Mühlberg, J.T., White, D.H., Dodds, M., Lüttgen, G., Piessens, F.: Learning assertions to verify linked-list programs. In: Calinescu, R., Rumpe, B. (eds.) SEFM 2015. LNCS, vol. 9276, pp. 37–52. Springer, Cham (2015). https://doi.org/10.1007/978-3-319-22969-0_3
37. Noble, J., Vitek, J., Potter, J.: Flexible alias protection. In: Jul, E. (ed.) ECOOP 1998. LNCS, vol. 1445, pp. 158–185. Springer, Heidelberg (1998). https://doi.org/10.1007/BFb0054091
38. Polikarpova, N., Tschannen, J., Furia, C.A.: A fully verified container library. Formal Aspects Comput. **30**(5), 495–523 (2018). https://doi.org/10.1007/s00165-017-0435-1
39. Pottier, F.: Verifying a Hash table and its iterators in higher-order separation logic. In: Certified Programs and Proofs (CPP), pp. 3–16. ACM (2017). https://doi.org/10.1145/3018610.3018624
40. Sun, C., et al.: VeriStruct: AI-assisted automated verification of data-structure modules in Verus. In: Junges, S., Katz, G. (eds.) Tools and Algorithms for the Construction and Analysis of Systems, TACAS 2026. LNCS, vol. 16506. Springer, Cham (2026). https://doi.org/10.1007/978-3-032-22749-2_6
41. Sun, X., et al.: Anvil: verifying liveness of cluster management controllers. In: Conference on Operating Systems Design and Implementation, OSDI'24. USENIX Association, USA (2024)
42. Tafat, A., Marché, C.: Binary Heaps Formally Verified in Why3. Research Report RR-7780, INRIA (2011). https://hal.inria.fr/inria-00636083
43. Zhou, Z., Anjali, Chen, W., Gong, S., Hawblitzel, C., Cui, W.: VeriSMo: a verified security module for confidential VMs. In: Conference on Operating Systems Design and Implementation, OSDI'24. USENIX Association., USA (2024)
44. Ziani, Y., Bernier, T., Kosmatov, N., Loulergue, F., Gracia Pérez, D.: Towards formal verification of a TPM software stack: achievements and opportunities. Formal Asp. Comput. **37**(4) (2025).https://doi.org/10.1145/3743153

# Reasoning About Concurrent Loops and Recursion with Rely-Guarantee Rules

Ian J. Hayes[1(✉)], Larissa A. Meinicke[1], and Cliff B. Jones[2]

[1] School of Electrical Engineering and Computer Science, The University of Queensland, Brisbane, QLD 4072, Australia
ian.hayes@uq.edu.au

[2] School of Computing, Newcastle University, Newcastle upon Tyne, UK

**Abstract.** The objective of this paper is to present general, mechanically verified, refinement rules for reasoning about recursive programs and while loops in the context of concurrency. We make use of the rely-guarantee approach to concurrency that facilitates reasoning about interference from concurrent threads in a compositional manner. Recursive programs can be defined as fixed points over a lattice of commands and hence we develop laws for reasoning about fixed points. Loops can be defined in terms of fixed points and hence the laws for recursion can be applied to develop laws for loops. Unlike many approaches to concurrency, we do not assume that expression evaluation is atomic.

## 1 Introduction

For sequential programs, the Hoare-style verification rule for a while loop [21,31],

$$\boxed{\text{while}}\ \frac{\{p \wedge b \wedge z = z_0\}\ c\ \{p \wedge z \ll z_0\}}{\{p\}\ \textbf{while}\ b\ \textbf{do}\ c\ \textbf{od}\ \ \{p \wedge \neg b\}} \tag{1}$$

makes use of a loop invariant, $p$, that is assumed to hold initially and is maintained by the body of the loop if the loop guard $b$ holds. To show termination, a variant expression $z$ is required to strictly decrease on each iteration according to a well-founded relation $\ll$. Rule (1) is not valid if there are concurrent threads modifying shared variables because interference can (i) invalidate the invariant $p$ or (ii) increase the variant expression $z$ or (iii) interfere with the evaluation of $b$ in such a way that $b$ may not hold at the start of the execution of the loop body or (iv) prevent $\neg b$ holding on exit from the loop.

Finding compositional rules that cope with interference proved challenging (see [15]); Rely/Guarantee (RG) conditions offer a compositional way to develop shared-variable concurrent programs [32–34]; initially the inference rules were presented in the keyword style of VDM [35]; a series of contributions [19,22,23,25,27,30] succeeded in recasting the RG approach in an algebraic style.

When designing a thread $T$, it is assumed that all atomic state-to-state transitions made by its environment (i.e. concurrently running threads) satisfy a rely condition $r$, a relation between program states. To complement this, the implementation of thread $T$


P. Gorm Larsen and K. Y. Rozier (Eds.): FMICS 2026, LNCS 16967, pp. 60–79, 2027.
https://doi.org/10.1007/978-3-032-36849-2_4

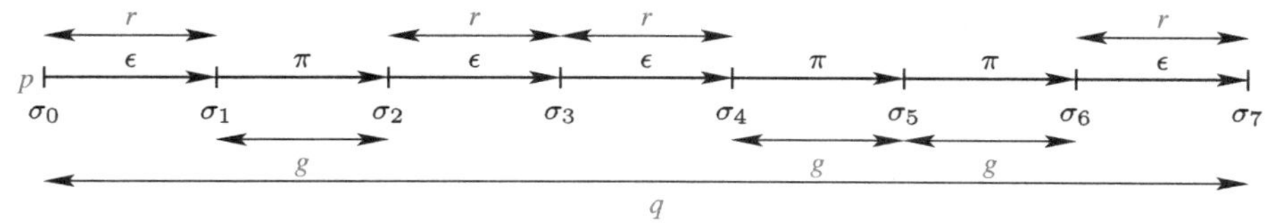


**Fig. 1.** An Aczel trace satisfying a specification with precondition $p$, postcondition $q$, rely condition $r$ and guarantee condition $g$. If the initial state, $\sigma_0$, is in $p$ and all environment transitions ($\epsilon$) satisfy $r$, then all program transitions ($\pi$) must satisfy $g$ and the initial state $\sigma_0$ must be related to the final state $\sigma_7$ by the postcondition $q$, also a relation between states.

must ensure that all program transitions it makes satisfy a guarantee relation $g$, where $g$ must imply the rely condition of every thread running in parallel with $T$. Figure 1 gives an example of an Aczel trace of program and environment transitions [1, 14, 15]. The intricate question of which transitions are to be viewed as atomic is addressed in §2.

This paper develops laws for reasoning about recursion (§3) and while loops (§4) in a rely-guarantee style. The proof of termination of a recursion makes use of well-founded induction with a variant function and a well-founded relation; however, the standard approach of requiring the variant to be reduced by the function body before any recursive calls are made does not deal with interference from other threads reducing the variant in a manner that precludes the function body reducing it. Hence we present an early termination version of the law that allows the function body to either reduce the variant before recursive calls or establish a condition such that a call on the function will not itself make any recursive calls (i.e. it will only use the base case(s) of the function). Because a while loop is defined as a recursive function, our law for while loops is proven in terms of the law for recursion; it too is an early termination version. An example of developing a recursive program that allows concurrent threads to share variables is given in §3.1; the use of a while loop that can terminate prematurely is illustrated in §4.1.

*Related Work.* It is interesting to compare Concurrent Separation Logic (CSL) with the Rely-Guarantee (RG) ideas behind this paper. The aim of Reynolds' Separation Logic is to offer a way to reason about ownership of heap addresses [45]; O'Hearn showed its applicability to concurrent heap programs in [43]. In contrast, the early RG publications were applied to stack variables although there is no reason to avoid programs that employ heaps. Subsequently a variety of CSLs have been applied to reasoning about ownership of other resources including locks. (A useful historical account of the origins and developments of CSLs is [10].) One attempt to classify the application areas of the two approaches is stated by O'Hearn in [43] to be that CSL supports reasoning about race freedom whereas RG allows proofs about "racy" programs. Whilst this is superficially true, it ignores development by reifying abstractions and it is important to remember the initial emphasis of RG research was precisely to provide a compositional development method for shared-variable concurrent programs. For example [36] addresses Asynchronous Communication Mechanisms and presents a development of Hugo Simpson's "four-slot implementation" whose essence is to avoid races on the slots; the RG development identifies the conditions for race freedom at an abstract level. There are two important combinations of CSL and RG rules: RGSep [51] and SAGL [20]; an alternative approach to viewing separation as an abstraction is offered in [37]. Bornat also looked at employing combinations of the approaches on proofs about Simpson's algorithm in [8,9] but [9] does not really use CSL.

Most RG approaches [18, 32–34, 44, 46–49, 53–55], employ laws that only apply if expression evaluation is atomic, which does not reflect the reality of expression evaluation in programming language implementations. Such laws can only be used with expressions that have a single critical reference [7, Definition 2.7, p.27], [2, Definition 2.4]; but the validity of their application in this case cannot be verified within their theories precisely because of the atomicity assumption in their semantics; hence they break the formal chain of reasoning. An exception is the work of Coleman and Jones [11, 12] who develop a fine-grained operational semantics that does not assume expression evaluation is atomic, however, the rules they develop are restricted to simple special cases of our rules. We assume neither expression evaluations nor assignment commands are executed atomically (see [26]). □

## 2 Wide-Spectrum Language

This section introduces our wide-spectrum language that incorporates both specification and programming language commands [6]. Our approach follows that used for the sequential refinement calculus [3,41] but extends it with concurrency, which requires a richer semantics based on Aczel traces [1, 14, 15]. The underlying theory is based on our earlier research [19, 22, 23, 25, 27, 30] and all lemmas and theorems have been proven in our corresponding Isabelle/HOL theories.

*Naming and Syntactic Precedence Conventions.* We use $\Sigma$ for the set of program states; $\sigma$ for program states (i.e. $\sigma \in \Sigma$); $c$ and $d$ for commands; $p$ for sets of program states; $g$, $q$ and $r$ for binary relations between program states; $u$, $v$ and $w$ for program variables; $e$ for expressions; $b$ for boolean expressions, where $\mathbb{B}$ is the set of booleans; and $k$ and $\kappa$ for values. Subscripted versions of the above names follow the same convention. Unary operations and function application have higher syntactic precedence than binary operations. For binary operations, non-deterministic choice ($\vee$) has the lowest precedence, and sequential composition (;) has the highest precedence, except framing ($V : c$) is higher. We use parentheses to resolve all other syntactic ambiguities.

**Values, Left Values and States.** Our theory treats values, left values (variables and indexed array elements) and program states abstractly. For values ($\in$ *Value*) the only constraint is that *Value* contains the distinct boolean values `true` and `false` (so that we can handle boolean guards in conditionals and loops) and the undefined value $\lightning$ (so we can handle divide-by-zero, out of bounds array indexing, etc.). Left values (l-values for short) consist of base variable names ($v \in$ *Identifier*) and indexed array elements (*Indexed A i*), where $A$ is an l-value and $i$ is an index value, similar to the approach used by Dingel [18]. Importantly, evaluation of an l-value for an indexed array element is done before dereferencing its value, so that atomicity is only required for accessing individual array elements, not the whole array.

$$LValue \mathrel{\widehat{=}} Base\ Identifier \mid Indexed\ LValue\ Value. \tag{2}$$

We abbreviate "*Base v*" to "*v*", and "*Indexed A i*" to "*A* [*i*]". L-values could be extended to handle a heap but we do not consider that in this paper.[1] The set of possible program states, $\Sigma$, is a mapping from l-values to values: $\Sigma \mathrel{\widehat{=}} LValue \to Value$.

**Command Lattice.** Our language consists of a complete distributive lattice of commands, $\mathcal{C}$, with partial order, $c \succeq d$, meaning command $c$ is refined (or implemented) by command $d$, so that non-deterministic choice ($c \vee d$) is the lattice join and strong conjunction ($c \wedge d$) is the lattice meet. The lattice is complete so that, for a set of commands $C$, non-deterministic choice, $\bigvee C$, and strong conjunction, $\bigwedge C$, are defined as the least upper bound and greatest lower bound, respectively, and the bottom and top elements of the lattice are $\bot$ and $\top$, respectively. The lattice operators are considered part of our wide spectrum language. Given a complete lattice we can define least ($\mu$) and greatest ($\nu$) fixed points of monotone functions.[2] Programming language functions are defined via *parametrised commands*, that is, they are of type, $Value \to \mathcal{C}$.

**Aczel Trace Semantics and Primitive Operations.** The semantic model for the lattice of commands consists of sets of Aczel traces [1, 14, 15]. An Aczel trace consists of a possibly infinite sequence of state-to-state transitions each of which is labeled as either a program ($\pi$) or environment ($\epsilon$) transition, as in Fig. 1. A trace may be either terminating, aborting or incomplete. Sets of traces corresponding to commands are prefix closed (i.e. they contain all incomplete prefix traces of a trace) and abort closed (i.e. they contain all possible extensions of an aborting trace). The language includes the following three binary operators:

$c \mathbin{;} d$, sequential composition, that is associative, has the null command, $\boldsymbol{\tau}$, as its neutral element, and distributes arbitrary non-deterministic choices in its left argument (3) and non-empty non-deterministic choices in its right argument (4). A trace of $c \mathbin{;} d$ consists of the gluing concatenation of a terminating trace of $c$ and a trace of $d$, or an incomplete (including infinite) or aborting trace of $c$. A *gluing concatenation* of a terminating trace $tr_1$ with a trace $tr_2$ requires that the final state of $tr_1$ equals the initial state of $tr_2$ and these two states become a single state in the concatenation.

$c \parallel d$, parallel composition, that is associative, commutative, and distributes non-empty non-deterministic choices in both its arguments (5) because $\parallel$ is commutative. Because each trace records *both* the behaviour of the program *and* its environment, parallel composition is synchronous [23, 30, 40], and a trace of $c \parallel d$ consists of a matching of a trace of $c$ and a trace of $d$, where a program transition $\sigma \xrightarrow{\pi} \sigma'$ of $c$

[1] Because a heap corresponds to an anonymous array with indices being pointer values, the theory for handling arrays could be used to handle a heap.

[2] In other works on the refinement calculus [3, 4], the dual lattice is used (i.e. with the reverse ordering), so greatest fixed points in our theory correspond to least fixed points in theirs.

matches an environment transition $\sigma \xrightarrow{\epsilon} \sigma'$ of $d$ to give $\sigma \xrightarrow{\pi} \sigma'$ for $c \parallel d$ (or vice versa) and an environment transition $\sigma \xrightarrow{\epsilon} \sigma'$ for both $c$ and $d$ matches to give the same environment transition for $c \parallel d$. Note that a program transition of $c$ cannot match a program transition of $d$, leading to the interleaving of their program transitions. If either $c$ or $d$ aborts, so does $c \parallel d$. A terminating trace of $c \parallel d$ corresponds to matching terminating traces of $c$ and $d$.

$c \Cap d$, weak conjunction, that is associative, commutative, idempotent, and distributes non-empty non-deterministic choices in both its arguments (6) because $\Cap$ is commutative. A trace of $c \Cap d$ is either a trace of both $c$ and $d$, or it is an aborting trace of $c$ that equals an incomplete trace of $d$ up to the point of abort of $c$ (or vice versa). Weak conjunction ($c \Cap d$) behaves as both $c$ and $d$ unless either $c$ or $d$ aborts, in which case the weak conjunction aborts. Termination of $c \Cap d$ corresponds to termination of both $c$ and $d$, that is, both $c$ and $d$ execute the same terminating trace.

$$\textstyle\bigvee_{c \in C} (c \mathbin{;} d) = (\bigvee_{c \in C} c) \mathbin{;} d \tag{3}$$
$$\textstyle\bigvee_{c \in C} (d \mathbin{;} c) = d \mathbin{;} (\bigvee_{c \in C} c) \qquad \text{if } C \neq \emptyset \tag{4}$$
$$\textstyle\bigvee_{c \in C} (c \parallel d) = (\bigvee_{c \in C} c) \parallel d \qquad \text{if } C \neq \emptyset \tag{5}$$
$$\textstyle\bigvee_{c \in C} (c \Cap d) = (\bigvee_{c \in C} c) \Cap d \qquad \text{if } C \neq \emptyset \tag{6}$$

**Primitive Commands.** A command is *infeasible* in a state, $\sigma$, if it cannot make any transition from $\sigma$ and it can neither terminate nor abort in state $\sigma$. The language includes five primitive commands:

$\bot$ is the command that is everywhere infeasible. It is the least command in our lattice; it satisfies $\bot \mathbin{;} c = \bot$, for any command $c$.

$\tau\, p$ is an instantaneous test that the current state $\sigma$ is in the set of states $p$: if $\sigma \in p$, $\tau\, p$ terminates, otherwise it is infeasible – note that there is no transition taken by an instantaneous test (in the trace semantics, its trace is tagged as terminated);

$\pi\, r$ is an atomic program command that may perform a program transition $\sigma \xrightarrow{\pi} \sigma'$ if $(\sigma, \sigma') \in r$ and then terminate, otherwise it is infeasible if $\sigma \notin \mathbf{dom}\, r$;

$\epsilon\, r$ is an atomic environment command that may perform an environment transition $\sigma \xrightarrow{\epsilon} \sigma'$ if $(\sigma, \sigma') \in r$ and then terminate, otherwise it is infeasible, and

$\top$ is Dijkstra's abort command [16, 17] that can do any behaviour whatsoever. It is the greatest command. Aborting behaviour is irrecoverable, (i.e. $\top \mathbin{;} c = \top$ for any $c$).

For tests, $\tau\, p_1 \succeq \tau\, p_2$ if $p_1 \supseteq p_2$, and both $\pi\, r_1 \succeq \pi\, r_2$ and $\epsilon\, r_1 \succeq \epsilon\, r_2$ hold if $r_1 \supseteq r_2$. Tests/atomic commands are everywhere infeasible for the empty set/relation: $\tau\, \emptyset = \pi\, \emptyset = \epsilon\, \emptyset = \bot$. A command is considered *atomic* if it is of the form, $\pi\, g \vee \epsilon\, r$, for some relations $g$ and $r$, that is, it can only make a single transition, which may be either a program ($\pi$) transition in $g$ or an environment ($\epsilon$) transition in $r$.

The command $\boldsymbol{\tau}$ is the test that always succeeds (7). The assert command, $\{\!|p|\!\}$, aborts if the current state is not in $p$, otherwise it terminates immediately (8), where $\overline{p} = \Sigma - p$. Property (9) gives an alternative form for an assert command. Note that $\{\!|\emptyset|\!\} = \top$ and $\{\!|\Sigma|\!\} = \boldsymbol{\tau}$. The command $\alpha\, r$ allows either a program or an environment transition, provided it satisfies $r$ (10). The abbreviations $\boldsymbol{\pi}$ and $\boldsymbol{\epsilon}$ allow any program

(12) or environment (13) transition, respectively, and $\boldsymbol{\alpha}$ allows any transition, program or environment (14), where univ is the universal relation between program states (11). Note the bold fonts for $\boldsymbol{\tau}$, $\boldsymbol{\pi}$, $\boldsymbol{\epsilon}$ and $\boldsymbol{\alpha}$.

$$\boldsymbol{\tau} \mathrel{\widehat{=}} \tau\, \Sigma \quad (7) \qquad \mathsf{univ} \mathrel{\widehat{=}} \Sigma \times \Sigma \quad (11)$$
$$\{\!\!\{p\}\!\!\} \mathrel{\widehat{=}} \boldsymbol{\tau} \vee \tau\, \overline{p}\, ;\top \quad (8) \qquad \boldsymbol{\pi} \mathrel{\widehat{=}} \pi\, \mathsf{univ} \quad (12)$$
$$\{\!\!\{p\}\!\!\} = \tau\, p \vee \tau\, \overline{p}\, ;\top \quad (9) \qquad \boldsymbol{\epsilon} \mathrel{\widehat{=}} \epsilon\, \mathsf{univ} \quad (13)$$
$$\alpha\, r \mathrel{\widehat{=}} \pi\, r \vee \epsilon\, r \quad (10) \qquad \boldsymbol{\alpha} \mathrel{\widehat{=}} \alpha\, \mathsf{univ} \quad (14)$$

Given a set of states $p$ and a relation $r$, $r \rhd p$ is the relation $r$ restricted so that its range elements are within $p$.

$$r \rhd p \mathrel{\widehat{=}} \{(\sigma, \sigma') \in r.\ \sigma' \in p\} \tag{15}$$

Two assertions can be merged (16). A test after an assertion with the same set of states is redundant (17). If $c$ is refined by $d$ from states in $p_1$ and from states in $p_2$, then $c$ is refined by $d$ from states in their union (18), and that property can be generalised to a set of sets of states $P$, rather than just two sets of states (19).

$$\{\!\!\{p_1\}\!\!\}\, ;\{\!\!\{p_2\}\!\!\} = \{\!\!\{p_1 \cap p_2\}\!\!\} \tag{16}$$
$$\{\!\!\{p\}\!\!\}\, ;\tau\, p = \{\!\!\{p\}\!\!\} \tag{17}$$
$$\{\!\!\{p_1 \cup p_2\}\!\!\}\, ;c \succeq d \qquad \text{if } \{\!\!\{p_1\}\!\!\}\, ;c \succeq d \text{ and } \{\!\!\{p_2\}\!\!\}\, ;c \succeq d \tag{18}$$
$$\{\!\!\{\textstyle\bigcup P\}\!\!\}\, ;c \succeq d \qquad \text{if } \forall p \in P.\ \{\!\!\{p\}\!\!\}\, ;c \succeq d \tag{19}$$

The inclusion of assertions makes it possible to reason about Hoare triples.

**Definition 1 (Hoare-triple).** *A command* $c$ establishes *postcondition* $p_1$ *from initial states satisfying* $p$*, written using the Hoare triple,* $\{p\}\ c\ \{p_1\}$*, if and only if,*[3]

$$\{\!\!\{p\}\!\!\}\, ;c \succeq c\, ;\{\!\!\{p_1\}\!\!\}. \tag{20}$$

Note the different braces used in the assertion commands and for the pre and post conditions in the Hoare triple.

**Derived Commands.** Finite ($c^\star$) and possibly infinite ($c^\omega$) iteration of a command $c$ zero or more times can be defined as the least (21) and greatest (22) fixed points, respectively, of the monotone function $(\lambda x.\ \boldsymbol{\tau} \vee c\ ;\ x)$.

$$c^\star \mathrel{\widehat{=}} \mu x.\ \boldsymbol{\tau} \vee c\, ;x \quad (21) \qquad c^\omega \mathrel{\widehat{=}} \nu x.\ \boldsymbol{\tau} \vee c\, ;x \quad (22)$$

A program guarantee command, $\mathbf{guar}_\pi\ g$, ensures that every program transition satisfies the relation $g$ but places no constraints on environment transitions (23). A rely

[3] Note if $c$ does not terminate or aborts, (20) holds because the assertion $\{\!\!\{p_1\}\!\!\}$ is not reached, so this is a weak correctness interpretation of Hoare logic [52]. For our usages here, $c$ is an expression evaluation, which can neither abort nor fail to terminate.

command, **rely** $r$, assumes environment transitions satisfy $r$; if any environment transition does not, it aborts (24), in the same way that an assertion $\{\!|p|\!\}$ aborts if the initial state is not in $p$. The notation $\overline{r}$ stands for the complement of the relation $r$. An evolution command [13], **evolve** $r$, combines a rely of $r$ with a guarantee of $r$ (25). An invariant command, **inv** $p$, assumes $p$ holds initially and then relies on environment transitions maintaining $p$, and guarantees that program transitions maintain $p$, i.e. it satisfies **evolve** $\overrightarrow{p}$, where $\overrightarrow{p}$ is the universal relation restricted so that final states are in $p$ (26). The command **term** only performs a finite number of program transitions but does not constrain its environment (28). The command **idle** can perform only a finite number of stuttering (no change) program transitions but does not constrain its environment (29). The relation $\mathsf{id}$ is the identity relation and $\mathsf{id}_V$ is the identity relation on a set of l-values $V$ (30). The command $V : c$, restricts $c$ so that its program transitions can only modify l-values in the set $V$, called its *frame* (31). Within identity relations and frames an l-value $u$ stands for the singleton set $\{u\}$. The command **opt** $r$ either performs a single program transition satisfying $r$ or it can terminate immediately from states $\sigma$ such that $(\sigma,\sigma) \in r$ (32), that is, $r$ is satisfied by not changing the state. The atomic specification command, $\langle r\rangle$, achieves $r$ via an atomic program transition and allows finite stuttering program transitions (that do not change the state) and arbitrary environment transitions before and after the atomic transition (33); like **opt** $r$, the atomic transition satisfying $r$ may be elided for states $\sigma$ for which $(\sigma,\sigma) \in r$.

$$\mathbf{guar}_\pi\ r \mathrel{\widehat=} (\pi\, r \vee \epsilon)^\omega \quad (23)$$
$$\mathbf{rely}\ r \mathrel{\widehat=} (\boldsymbol{\alpha} \vee \epsilon\, \overline{r}\ ;\ \top)^\omega \quad (24)$$
$$\mathbf{evolve}\ r \mathrel{\widehat=} \mathbf{rely}\ r \Cap \mathbf{guar}_\pi\ r \quad (25)$$
$$\overrightarrow{p} \mathrel{\widehat=} \{(\sigma,\sigma').\ \sigma' \in p\} \quad (26)$$
$$\mathbf{inv}\ p \mathrel{\widehat=} \{\!|p|\!\}\ ;\ \mathbf{evolve}\ \overrightarrow{p} \quad (27)$$
$$\mathbf{term} \mathrel{\widehat=} \boldsymbol{\alpha}^\star\ ;\ \boldsymbol{\epsilon}^\omega \quad (28)$$
$$\mathbf{idle} \mathrel{\widehat=} \mathbf{guar}_\pi\ \mathsf{id} \Cap \mathbf{term} \quad (29)$$
$$\mathsf{id}_V \mathrel{\widehat=} \{(\sigma,\sigma).\ \forall v \in V.\ \sigma'\, v = \sigma\, v\} \quad (30)$$
$$V : c \mathrel{\widehat=} \mathbf{guar}_\pi\ \mathsf{id}_{\overline{V}} \Cap c \quad (31)$$
$$\mathbf{opt}\ r \mathrel{\widehat=} \pi\, r \vee \tau\{\sigma.\ (\sigma,\sigma) \in r\} \quad (32)$$
$$\langle r\rangle \mathrel{\widehat=} \mathbf{idle}\ ;\ \mathbf{opt}\ r\ ;\ \mathbf{idle} \quad (33)$$

The postcondition specification command, $(\!|q|\!)$, for $q$ a relation between states, guarantees to terminate in a final state $\sigma'$ that is related to the initial state $\sigma$ by $q$ (34). The initial test, $\tau\{\sigma\}$, selects those behaviours that start in state $\sigma$ and the final test, $\tau\{\sigma'.\ (\sigma,\sigma') \in q\}$, restricts the behaviours to those satisfying $q$ end-to-end. The nondeterministic choice accumulates those behaviours for all possible starting states $\sigma$.

$$(\!|q|\!) \mathrel{\widehat=} \bigvee \sigma.\ \tau\{\sigma\}\ ;\ \mathbf{term}\ ;\ \tau\{\sigma'.\ (\sigma,\sigma') \in q\} \quad (34)$$

If a specification command is restricted to achieve a final state satisfying $p$, that restriction may be pulled out as a test (35). The composition of binary relations is written, $r_1 \mathbin{⨾} r_2$, where, $(\sigma,\sigma') \in (r_1 \mathbin{⨾} r_2)$ if and only if $(\exists \sigma_1.\ (\sigma,\sigma_1) \in r_1 \wedge (\sigma_1,\sigma') \in r_2)$. A specification command $(\!|r_1 \mathbin{⨾} r_2|\!)$ can be split into two specifications, where the first establishes the precondition $p$ of the second (36). Guarantees (37) and relies (38) distribute over sequential composition, see [39].

$$(\!| q \rhd p |\!) = (\!| q |\!) \; ; \tau \, p \tag{35}$$

$$(\!| r_1 \fatsemi r_2 |\!) \succeq (\!| r_1 \rhd p |\!) \; ; \{\!| p |\!\} \; ; (\!| r_2 |\!) \tag{36}$$

$$\mathbf{guar}_\pi \, g \Cap c_1 \; ; c_2 = (\mathbf{guar}_\pi \, g \Cap c_1) \; ; (\mathbf{guar}_\pi \, g \Cap c_2) \tag{37}$$

$$\mathbf{rely} \, r \Cap c_1 \; ; c_2 = (\mathbf{rely} \, r \Cap c_1) \; ; (\mathbf{rely} \, r \Cap c_2) \tag{38}$$

**Expressions.** Our treatment of expressions is based on that in [26] and the reader is referred there for more details. We distinguish between l-values expressions (*lve*) and expressions (*e*). The syntax of expressions includes constants ($\kappa$), dereferencing of l-value expressions ($*lve$), unary operators ($\ominus \, e$), and binary operators ($e_1 \oplus e_2$). L-value expressions consist of either a variable $v$ or an indexed array reference $lve[e]$, in which *lve* is an l-value expression (thus allowing multi-dimensional arrays) and $e$ is an index expression. The notation $[\![e]\!]_\sigma$ stands for the value of expression $e$ in state $\sigma$; it has the standard inductive definition over the structure of expressions [26].

In a sequential program the value of an expression is uniquely determined by the state in which it is evaluated, whereas in a concurrent context its value depends on the sequence of states that occur during its evaluation. Hence for a given initial state, an expression may evaluate to different values depending on any interleaving environment transitions between its accesses to variable values. To allow for such non-determinism, we represent the evaluation of an expression $e$ to a value $k$ by the command $\langle\!| e |\!\rangle_k$, e.g. evaluating a pair of expressions $(e_1, e_2)$ to a pair of values $(k_1, k_2)$, evaluates them in parallel: $\langle\!| (e_1, e_2) |\!\rangle_{(k_1,k_2)} = \langle\!| e_1 |\!\rangle_{k_1} \parallel \langle\!| e_2 |\!\rangle_{k_2}$. If $e$ does not evaluate to $k$, $\langle\!| e |\!\rangle_k$ is infeasible. Because expression evaluation is side-effect free, successful evaluation corresponds to the command **idle**, which allows finite stuttering transitions during the evaluation.

Expressions typically occur in a non-deterministic choice over $k$, for example, the only choice that succeeds for $\langle\!| \kappa |\!\rangle_k$ is for $k = \kappa$ and all other choices for $k$ are infeasible. The effect when followed by a command, $c\,k$, that is dependent on $k$, is to select $c\,\kappa$:

$$\bigvee k. \; \langle\!| \kappa |\!\rangle_k ; c\,k = \mathbf{idle} \; ; c\,\kappa.$$

**Programming Language Commands.** A conditional command either evaluates the boolean expression $b$ to `true` and executes $c$, or to `false` and executes $d$ (39). Because our language is not statically typed, the semantics needs to deal with guards that evaluate to a non-boolean, in which case conditionals are defined to abort. Theorem 2 (rely-conditional) below includes an assumption (47) that avoids the case when $b$ evaluates to a non-boolean. A while loop executes $c$ while $b$ evaluates to `true` and then terminates if $b$ evaluates to `false` or aborts if $b$ evaluates to a non-boolean (40). A greatest fixed point is used because that allows both a finite and an infinite number of iterations, and hence allows one to address termination of loops. For a parameterised command, $f$, that is, $f$ is of type $Value \rightarrow \mathcal{C}$, the command, **call** $f\,e$, evaluates its argument $e$ to $k$ and then executes $f\,k$; the **idle** at the end allows for stuttering transitions to effect the return (41). The parameter passing mechanism is call-by-constant, that is, the actual parameter $e$ is evaluated to give the value of the formal parameter but the formal parameter acts as a constant within the procedure body (and hence cannot be modified within the procedure body). If $e$ is a constant $\kappa$, then $\mathbf{call}\, f\, \kappa$ reduces to $\mathbf{idle}\, ; f\, \kappa\, ; \mathbf{idle}$.

$$\mathbf{if}\; b\; \mathbf{then}\; c\; \mathbf{else}\; d\; \mathbf{fi} \mathrel{\widehat{=}} \llparenthesis b \rrparenthesis_{\mathsf{true}} \,;\, c \vee \llparenthesis b \rrparenthesis_{\mathsf{false}} \,;\, d \vee \bigvee\{\llparenthesis b \rrparenthesis_k \,;\, \top \,.\, k \notin \mathbb{B}\} \tag{39}$$

$$\mathbf{while}\; b\; \mathbf{do}\; c\; \mathbf{od} \mathrel{\widehat{=}} \nu x.\ \mathbf{if}\; b\; \mathbf{then}\; c \,;\, x\; \mathbf{else}\; \boldsymbol{\tau}\; \mathbf{fi} \tag{40}$$

$$\mathbf{call}\; f\, e \mathrel{\widehat{=}} \bigvee k.\ \llparenthesis e \rrparenthesis_k \,;\, f\, k \,;\, \mathbf{idle} \tag{41}$$

**Expression Evaluation Under Interference.** Consider the following command,

$$\{\!\!\{p\}\!\!\} \,;\, \mathbf{if}\; b\; \mathbf{then}\; \{\!\!\{p_T\}\!\!\} \,;\, c\; \mathbf{else}\; \{\!\!\{p_F\}\!\!\} \,;\, d\; \mathbf{fi}\,. \tag{42}$$

In the sequential case [31], assuming the initial state satisfies the precondition $p$, the assertions $p_T$ and $p_F$ in (42) hold if $p_T$ is taken to be $p \cap b$ and $p_F$ is taken to be $p \cap \neg b$. However, under interference from concurrent threads, the following issues arise:

1. the precondition $p$ may be invalidated by interference;
2. if $b$ evaluates to $\mathsf{true}$, it does not follow that $b$ holds at the start of the **then** branch; and
3. if $b$ evaluates to $\mathsf{false}$, it does not follow that $\neg b$ holds at the start of the **else** branch.

To handle the invalidation of the precondition $p$ by interference, we require that $p$ is stable under the rely condition $r$ [50]. If for a particular example, the precondition $p$ is not stable under $r$, it can be replaced by a weaker precondition that is stable under $r$.

**Definition 2 (stable).** *A set of states, $p$, is* stable *under a relation $r$ if, whenever $\sigma \in p$ and $(\sigma, \sigma') \in r$, then $\sigma' \in p$.*

For reasoning about guard evaluation under interference we make use of a Hoare triple (Definition 1) of the form, $\{p\}\ \ \mathbf{rely}\, r \Cap \llparenthesis b \rrparenthesis_k\ \ \{p_1\}$, which can be read as "$\llparenthesis b \rrparenthesis_k$ establishes $p_1$ from initial states satisfying $p$ under interference satisfying $r$". For the conditional command in (42) executing in a context in which its environment satisfies a rely condition $r$, the assertions $p_T$ and $p_F$ in (42) are valid if the following Hoare triples hold because these triples correspond to evaluating the guard to $\mathsf{true}$/$\mathsf{false}$ under interference satisfying $r$.

$$\{p\}\ \mathbf{rely}\, r \Cap \llparenthesis b \rrparenthesis_{\mathsf{true}}\ \{p_T\} \tag{43}$$

$$\{p\}\ \mathbf{rely}\, r \Cap \llparenthesis b \rrparenthesis_{\mathsf{false}}\ \{p_F\} \tag{44}$$

These address issues (2) and (3) above. To reason about arbitrary expressions, possibly with multiple references to shared variables, we make use of a compositional approach in which we establish a postcondition for a complex expression by first establishing postconditions for each of its component sub-expressions. Our approach does not need the syntactic single critical reference restriction [2, 7] of approaches in which expression evaluation is assumed to be atomic (see [26] for details).

Because expressions are free from side effects, they refine **idle**, and hence we have the following lemma for introducing an expression evaluation. See [26] for a proof.

**Lemma 1** (idle-to-expr-with-post). *For $p$ a set of states, $r$ a relation, $k$ a constant, $e$ an expression, and $P\,k$ a set of states, if $\{p\}$ $\mathbf{rely}\, r \Cap \llparenthesis e \rrparenthesis_k$ $\{P\,k\}$,*

$$\mathbf{rely}\, r \Cap \{\!\!\{p\}\!\!\} \,;\, \mathbf{idle} \succeq \mathbf{rely}\, r \Cap \llparenthesis e \rrparenthesis_k \,;\, \{\!\!\{P\,k\}\!\!\}.$$

**Introducing a Conditional Command.** To introduce a conditional command, separate assumptions are required for the case of the guard $b$ evaluating to $\mathsf{true}$ (45) and to $\mathsf{false}$ (46). A third assumption (47) ensures $b$ evaluates to a boolean value, which rules out the third aborting alternative in the definition of a conditional (39). A fourth assumption (48) requires that $c$ tolerates inference before it starts execution. See [26] for a proof.

**Theorem 2 (rely-conditional).** *If $b$ is a boolean expression, $q$ and $r$ are relations, $c$ is a command, $p$, $p_T$ and $p_F$ are sets of states, and,*

$$\{p\}\ \mathbf{rely}\ r \Cap \langle\!\langle b \rangle\!\rangle_{\mathsf{true}}\ \{p_T\} \quad (45) \qquad \forall k.\ \{p\}\ \mathbf{rely}\ r \Cap \langle\!\langle b \rangle\!\rangle_k\ \{\llcorner k \in \mathbb{B} \lrcorner\} \quad (47)$$

$$\{p\}\ \mathbf{rely}\ r \Cap \langle\!\langle b \rangle\!\rangle_{\mathsf{false}}\ \{p_F\} \quad (46) \qquad \mathbf{rely}\ r \Cap \{\!\!\{p\}\!\!\}\ ;\ c \succeq \mathbf{rely}\ r \Cap \{\!\!\{p\}\!\!\}\ ;\ \mathbf{idle}\ ;\ c \quad (48)$$

*then* $\mathbf{rely}\ r \Cap \{\!\!\{p\}\!\!\}\ ;\ c \succeq \mathbf{if}\ b\ \mathbf{then}\ \mathbf{rely}\ r \Cap \{\!\!\{p_T\}\!\!\}\ ;\ c\ \mathbf{else}\ \mathbf{rely}\ r \Cap \{\!\!\{p_F\}\!\!\}\ ;\ c\ \mathbf{fi}$.

A specification command, $(\!|q|\!)$, being refined to a conditional command (39) must tolerate interference satisfying $r$ in order to allow for the evaluation of the guard and interference before and after the execution of the conditional [11].

**Definition 3 (tolerates).** *A relation $q$* tolerates *interference $r$ from precondition $p$ if $p$ is stable under $r$ and both, $p \lhd (r \fatsemi q) \subseteq q$ and $p \lhd (q \fatsemi r) \subseteq q$.*

If $q$ tolerates $r$ from $p$, then $p \lhd (r^* \fatsemi q \fatsemi r^*) \subseteq q$, where $r^*$ is the reflexive, transitive closure of $r$. That is, $q$ tolerates zero or more $r$ transitions both before and after it, and thus one can introduce **idle** commands before and after a specification command with postcondition $q$ (see [29] for a proof of these properties).

$$\mathbf{rely}\ r \Cap \{\!\!\{p\}\!\!\}\ ;\ (\!|q|\!) = \mathbf{rely}\ r \Cap \{\!\!\{p\}\!\!\}\ ;\ \mathbf{idle}\ ;\ (\!|q|\!)\ ;\ \mathbf{idle} \quad \text{if } q \text{ tolerates } r \text{ from } p \quad (49)$$

**Introducing a Function Call.** A call command first evaluates its actual parameter expression, which may be subject to interference from parallel threads, and hence we make use of assumption (50), which establishes the precondition $P\,k$ for the execution of the body of the function (i.e. $f\,k$). To allow for interference both before and after executing the body of the function, the postcondition relation $q$ must tolerate such interference.

**Theorem 3 (introduce-call).** *If $e$ is an expression, $p$ and $P\,k$ are set of states, $g$, $q$ and $r$ are relations, where $g$ is reflexive and $q$ tolerates $r$ from $p$, and for all $k$,*

$$\{p\}\ \mathbf{rely}\ r \Cap \langle\!\langle e \rangle\!\rangle_k\ \{P\,k\} \quad (50) \qquad \mathbf{guar}_\pi\ g \Cap \mathbf{rely}\ r \Cap \{\!\!\{P\,k\}\!\!\}\ ;\ (\!|q|\!) \succeq f\,k \quad (51)$$

*then,* $\mathbf{guar}_\pi\ g \Cap \mathbf{rely}\ r \Cap \{\!\!\{p\}\!\!\}\ ;\ (\!|q|\!) \succeq \mathbf{call}\,f\,e$ *. See [28] for a proof.*

If $p$ is stable under $r$ and the expression $e$ is invariant under interference satisfying $r$, then $P\,k$ can be taken to be, $p \cap \llcorner e = k \lrcorner$, where the notation, $\llcorner Pr \lrcorner$, stands for the set of states in which the predicate $Pr$ holds, where references to program variables within $Pr$ correspond to their value in the state.

## 3 Recursion

This section develops Theorem 5 (recursion-early) that covers introducing recursion. It uses a variant expression and a well-founded relation $\ll$ to show termination. The well-founded induction principle states that, for a well-founded relation $\ll$ and property $P\,k$ defined on values that are type compatible with $\ll$,

$$(\forall k.\ (\forall j.\ j \ll k \Rightarrow P\,j) \Rightarrow P\,k) \quad \Rightarrow \quad (\forall k.\ P\,k). \tag{52}$$

The notation $\llcorner e_1 \ll e_2 \lrcorner$ abbreviates $\{\sigma\ .\ [\![e_1]\!]_\sigma \ll [\![e_2]\!]_\sigma\}$, where $[\![e]\!]_\sigma$ is the value of $e$ is state $\sigma$. The following lemma lifts well-founded induction to reasoning about refinement of commands using a parametrised variant expression $z$ that is type compatible with a well-founded relation $\ll$. In the following lemma, $s$ and $c$ are parameterised commands, that is, of the form $\lambda y.\ body$, for some $body$. A parameterised command $s$ is refined by another $c$, that is $s \succeq c$, if $\forall y.\ s\,y \succeq c\,y$.

**Lemma 4** (well-founded-variant). *If s and c are parameterised commands, $\ll$ is a well-founded relation, z is a parametrised variant expression (type compatible with $\ll$), and,*

$$\forall k.\ (\forall y.\ \{\!\!\{\llcorner z\,y \ll k \lrcorner\}\!\!\}\ ;\ s\,y \succeq c\,y) \Rightarrow (\forall y.\ \{\!\!\{\llcorner z\,y = k \lrcorner\}\!\!\}\ ;\ s\,y \succeq c\,y) \tag{53}$$

*then $s \succeq c$. See [28] for a proof.*

Theorem 5 applies Lemma 4 for $c$ in the form of the greatest fixed point, $\nu f$, of a monotone function $f$ from parameterised commands to parametrised commands, that is, the type of $f$ is $(Value \rightarrow \mathcal{C}) \rightarrow (Value \rightarrow \mathcal{C})$, and hence $\nu f$ is also a parametrised command. It is assumed that from states satisfying $p_X$, $f$ does not make any recursive calls (i.e. it only uses its base case(s)), which is encoded here by $F$ being unconstrained. The approach corresponds to that of Back and Preoteasa [5, Theorem 23] for the sequential refinement calculus but includes the early termination alternative, which is required for derivation of some concurrent programs (see §4.1).

**Theorem 5 (recursion-early).** *If $p_X$ is a set of states, $\ll$ is a well-founded relation, z is a parametrised variant expression that is type compatible with $\ll$, s is a parametrised command, f is a monotone function from parametrised commands to parametrised commands, and both,*

$$\forall F\,y.\ \{\!\!\{p_X\}\!\!\}\ ;\ s\,y \succeq f\,F\,y \tag{54}$$

$$\forall F\,k.\ (\forall x.\ \{\!\!\{\llcorner z\,x \ll k \lrcorner \cup p_X\}\!\!\}\ ;\ s\,x \succeq F\,x) \Rightarrow (\forall y.\ \{\!\!\{\llcorner z\,y = k \lrcorner\}\!\!\}\ ;\ s\,y \succeq f\,F\,y) \tag{55}$$

*then, $s \succeq \nu f$. See [28] for a proof.*

The proviso (54) is used to handle the case in which $p_X$ holding initially ensures $\nu f$ does not utilise any recursive calls, e.g. taking $f$ to be $(\lambda x.\ \textbf{if}\ b\ \textbf{then}\ c\,;x\ \textbf{else}\ \tau\ \textbf{fi})$, the case in which the guard $b$ is guaranteed to evaluate to false if $p_X$ holds. A special case is if $p_X$ is the empty set, in which case (54) is trivially satisfied and (55) is simplified. Note that the rules for recursion are not specific to rely/guarantee concurrency and can be used in other contexts.

*Related Work.* Schellhorn et al. [47] include recursion in their approach, in which commands are encoded in a variant of interval temporal logic (RGITL) and recursive programs are then defined as recursive formulae in the logic. Sanán et al. [46] allow parameterless procedures and make use of a natural number call depth bound to avoid infinite recursion. Other approaches [11,18,44,54,55] do not consider recursion, instead they define the semantics of while loops via an operational semantics, as do Sanán et al. [46]. □

### 3.1 Example of a Parallel Recursive Search

The task is to search for a value of $i$ in the range $0 \leq i < N$, such that $P\,i$ holds. The variable *found* is set to true if and only if there exists such a value. There may be zero or more occurrences of $i$ for which $P\,i$ holds; any value of $i$ for which $P\,i$ holds is valid. We use a predicative notation for relations, in which a dereferenced l-value expression, $*lve$, stands for its value in the pre-state and a primed dereferenced l-value expression, $*lve'$, stands for its value in the post-state, for example, $\ulcorner *found' = *found \urcorner = \{(\sigma, \sigma').\ \sigma' found = \sigma\, found\}$. Note that we use lower corners, $\llcorner \ldots \lrcorner$ for sets and upper corners, $\ulcorner \ldots \urcorner$ for binary relations.

$$\begin{array}{l} \mathbf{rely}\, \ulcorner *found' = *found \wedge *i' = *i \urcorner \Cap \\ \{\!\!| \llcorner 0 \leq N \lrcorner |\!\!\} \,; found, i : \left(\!\!\left| \begin{array}{l} \ulcorner((\exists j.\ 0 \leq j < N \wedge P\,j) \Rightarrow *found') \wedge \\ (*found' \Rightarrow 0 \leq *i' < N \wedge P(*i'))\urcorner \end{array} \right|\!\!\right) \end{array} \tag{56}$$

The function *search* (specified below) handles searching within a subrange from *lo* to $hi - 1$, inclusive, which may be empty if $lo \geq hi$. The evolve command (25) both relies and guarantees that once a value $*i$ satisfying $P(*i)$ is found, $*found$ remains true. The invariant (27) assumes initially that if $*found$ holds so does $P(*i)$ where $0 \leq *i < N$, it then relies on any environment transitions maintaining this property and guarantees that all program transitions maintain the property. Note that the environment is allowed to change $*i$ but only to a value such that $P(*i)$ holds for $0 \leq *i < N$.

$$\begin{array}{l} search \mathrel{\widehat{=}} \lambda(lo, hi).\ \mathbf{evolve}\, \ulcorner *found \Rightarrow *found' \urcorner \Cap \\ \qquad \mathbf{inv}\, \llcorner *found \Rightarrow 0 \leq *i < N \wedge P(*i) \lrcorner \Cap \\ \qquad \{\!\!| \llcorner 0 \leq lo \leq hi \leq N \lrcorner |\!\!\} \,; found, i : (\!\!| \ulcorner (\exists j.\ lo \leq j < hi \wedge P\,j) \Rightarrow *found' \urcorner |\!\!) \end{array}$$

Note the complete range, from 0 to $N - 1$, is used in the invariant, while the postcondition focuses on the range from *lo* to $hi - 1$. This allows concurrent threads to set $i$ to a value such that $P(*i)$ holds and set *found* to be true. The top level specification (56) is implemented by setting found to false and calling *search* for the range 0 to $N - 1$.

$$(56) \succeq found := \mathsf{false}\,;\, \mathbf{call}\, search\,(0, N)$$

The implementation of *search* uses divide-and-conquer by splitting the range into two halves and recursively searching both halves in parallel. A parallel search is practical if the time complexity of evaluating $P$ is large (relative to the cost of forking threads).

$$
\begin{array}{l}
\mathit{find} \mathrel{\widehat{=}} \lambda F.\ \lambda(lo, hi).\ \{\!\llcorner 0 \le lo \le hi \le N \lrcorner\!\}\ ;\\
\quad \textbf{if}\ \neg{*}\mathit{found} \wedge lo + 1 = hi\ \textbf{then} \quad \text{— range only contains one element, } lo\\
\qquad \textbf{if}\ P\ lo\ \textbf{then}\ i := lo\ ; \mathit{found} := \mathsf{true}\ \textbf{else}\ \textbf{idle}\ \textbf{fi}\\
\quad \textbf{else if}\ \neg{*}\mathit{found} \wedge lo + 2 \le hi\ \textbf{then} \quad \text{— range has size at least 2}\\
\qquad (\textbf{call}\ F\ (lo, \frac{lo+hi}{2}) \parallel \textbf{call}\ F\ (\frac{lo+hi}{2}, hi))\\
\qquad \textbf{else} \quad \text{— have } {*}\mathit{found} \text{ already or the range is empty}\\
\qquad\quad \textbf{idle}\\
\qquad \textbf{fi}\\
\quad \textbf{fi}
\end{array}
$$

Function *search* is implemented recursively as the greatest fixed point of the function *find*,[4] that is, $\mathit{search} \succeq \nu \mathit{find}$, as can be shown by applying Theorem 5 (recursion-early) with $\emptyset$ for $p_X$, $(\lambda(lo, hi).\ hi - lo)$ for the variant function $z$, and *search* for $s$ and *find* for $f$. For the theorem, (54) holds trivially because $p_X$ is empty, and (55) corresponds to the following.

$$
\begin{array}{l}
\forall F\, k.\ (\forall l\, h.\ \{\!\llcorner h - l \ll k \lrcorner\!\}\ ; \mathit{search}(l, h) \succeq F(l, h)) \Rightarrow\\
\qquad (\forall lo\, hi.\ \{\!\llcorner hi - lo = k \lrcorner\!\}\ ; \mathit{search}(lo, hi) \succeq \mathit{find}\ F\ (lo, hi))
\end{array}
\tag{57}
$$

For all $F$ and $k$, we assume the left side of the implication and show the right side holds. Our first steps use Theorem 2 (rely-conditional) twice to introduce the outer conditional and an inner conditional. Note that while ${*}\mathit{found}$ is stable under the rely condition and hence can be assumed in the precondition of (60), $\neg{*}\mathit{found}$ is not stable and hence can not be assumed in the preconditions of (58) and (59).

$$
\begin{array}{ll}
\{\!\llcorner hi - lo = k \lrcorner\!\}\ ; \mathit{search}(lo, hi) \succeq & \\
\textbf{if}\ \neg{*}\mathit{found} \wedge lo + 1 = hi\ \textbf{then} & \\
\quad \{\!\llcorner lo + 1 = hi \lrcorner\!\}\ ; \mathit{search}(lo, hi) & (58)\\
\textbf{else}\ \{\!\llcorner hi - lo = k \lrcorner\!\}; & \\
\quad \textbf{if}\ \neg{*}\mathit{found} \wedge lo + 2 \le hi\ \textbf{then} & \\
\qquad \{\!\llcorner hi - lo = k \wedge lo < \frac{lo+hi}{2} < hi \lrcorner\!\}\ ; \mathit{search}(lo, hi) & (59)\\
\quad \textbf{else} & \\
\qquad \{\!\llcorner {*}\mathit{found} \vee lo = hi \lrcorner\!\}\ ; \mathit{search}(lo, hi) & (60)\\
\quad \textbf{fi} & \\
\textbf{fi} &
\end{array}
$$

For the first alternative (58), the range just contains the single value *lo*, so if $P\ lo$ holds $i$ can be set to *lo* and *found* to true, but it $P\ lo$ does not hold we do nothing (i.e. **idle**).

$$(58) \succeq \textbf{if}\ P\ lo\ \textbf{then}\ i := lo\ ; \mathit{found} := \mathsf{true}\ \textbf{else}\ \textbf{idle}\ \textbf{fi}$$

[4] The programming language Scheme uses the **letrec** notation for such a definition, where $\mathit{fun} = \nu(\lambda F.\ \mathit{body})$ here corresponds to Scheme's $\textbf{letrec}\ \mathit{fun} = \mathit{body}[F \backslash \mathit{fun}]$.

In the **then** branch, $lo$ must be assigned to $i$ before true is assigned to *found* in order to preserve the invariant in the intermediate state (i.e. just after the assignment to $i$). In the **else** branch no action is taken, in particular, *found* is not set to false because it was initialised to false and if another thread has found an element satisfying $P$, it will have set *found* to true and *found* should remain true. The assignment commands in the implementation trivially satisfy the guarantee, $\ulcorner *found \Rightarrow *found' \urcorner$.

For the second alternative (59) when $lo + 2 \leq hi$, a search of the range $(lo, hi)$ needs to establish the postcondition $(\exists j.\ lo \leq j < hi \wedge P\, j) \Rightarrow *found'$, which can be achieved by two parallel searches that establish, $(\exists j.\ lo \leq j < \frac{lo+hi}{2} \wedge P\, j) \Rightarrow *found'$ and $(\exists j.\ \frac{lo+hi}{2} \leq j < hi \wedge P\, j) \Rightarrow *found'$, respectively. The parallel searches use recursive calls on *search*, which are introduced using Theorem 3 (introduce-call).

$$\begin{aligned}(59) \succeq\ & \mathbf{call}\,(\lambda(l,h).\ \{\!\!\{\llcorner h - l \ll k \lrcorner\}\!\!\}\ ; search(l,h))\,(lo, \tfrac{lo+hi}{2}) \parallel \\ & \mathbf{call}\,(\lambda(l,h).\ \{\!\!\{\llcorner h - l \ll k \lrcorner\}\!\!\}\ ; search(l,h))\,(\tfrac{lo+hi}{2}, hi)\end{aligned} \tag{61}$$

We can then apply the assumption from (57) to show,

$$(61) \succeq \mathbf{call}\ F\,(lo, \tfrac{lo+hi}{2}) \parallel \mathbf{call}\ F\,(\tfrac{lo+hi}{2}, hi)$$

Finally, if an element satisfying $P$ has already been found, or the range is empty, the search is satisfied by doing nothing.

$$(60) \succeq \mathbf{idle}$$

Combining the above refinement steps gives,

$$\{\!\!\{\llcorner hi - lo = k \lrcorner\}\!\!\}\ ; search(lo, hi) \succeq find\ F\,(lo, hi), \tag{62}$$

discharging (57), and hence $search \succeq \nu\, find$ by Theorem 5 (recursion-early).

## 4 Introducing a While Loop

For a while loop we derive a law to establish,

$$\mathbf{rely}\ r \Cap \{\!\!\{p\}\!\!\}\ ; (\!| q^* \rhd p_F |\!) \succeq \mathbf{while}\, b\ \mathbf{do}\ c\ \mathbf{od}\,. \tag{63}$$

The while loop should establish the relation $q^*$, between its initial and final states and terminate in a state satisfying $p_F$. The precondition $p$ is also the loop invariant. To show termination we use a variant expression $z$, that is required to strictly decrease according to a well-founded relation $\ll$ on each iteration, unless an iteration establishes an early termination condition $p_X$ that ensures the loop guard $b$ will evaluate to false and hence the loop will exit.

The variant expression $z$ may not be increased by interference from concurrent threads (64). Because the definition of a while loop is based on a conditional command, the law for introducing a while loop inherits the assumptions that evaluating the loop guard $b$ to true from states satisfying $p$ under interference satisfying $r$ establishes

$p_T$ (65), and similarly, evaluating $b$ to false establishes $p_F$ (66), and that the guard must evaluate to a boolean (67). If $b$ is guaranteed not to evaluate to true from states satisfying $p_X \cap p$, the guard evaluation $\langle\!\langle b \rangle\!\rangle_{\mathsf{true}}$ is infeasible and hence establishes $\emptyset$ (68). From initial states satisfying $p_T$ and that the variant $z$ is less than or equal to $k$, the body of the loop $c$ must establish $q^*$ between its pre and post states, and its post state must re-establish the loop invariant $p$ and either strictly decrease the variant $z$ or establish $p_X$, from which the loop is guaranteed to terminate on the next iteration (69). The bound variable $k$ can be thought of as the value of $z$ before guard evaluation; after guard evaluation only $z \lll k$ can be assumed because interference may have decreased $z$, where $\lll$ is the reflexive closure of $\ll$. Note that, commonly, $q$ is reflexive and transitive, i.e. $q = q^*$.

**Theorem 6 (intro-while).** *If b is a boolean expression, r is a relation, p, $p_T$, $p_F$ and $p_X$ are sets of states, $\ll$ is a transitive, well-founded relation, z is a variant expression that is type compatible with $\ll$, q is a relation, such that $q^*$ tolerates r from p, and,*

$$r \subseteq \ulcorner z' \lll z \urcorner \tag{64}$$
$$\{p\}\ \mathbf{rely}\ r \Cap \langle\!\langle b \rangle\!\rangle_{\mathsf{true}}\ \{p_T\} \tag{65}$$
$$\{p\}\ \mathbf{rely}\ r \Cap \langle\!\langle b \rangle\!\rangle_{\mathsf{false}}\ \{p_F\} \tag{66}$$
$$\forall k.\ \{p\}\ \mathbf{rely}\ r \Cap \langle\!\langle b \rangle\!\rangle_{k}\ \{\llcorner k \in \mathbb{B} \lrcorner\} \tag{67}$$
$$\{p_X \cap p\}\ \mathbf{rely}\ r \Cap \langle\!\langle b \rangle\!\rangle_{\mathsf{true}}\ \{\emptyset\} \tag{68}$$
$$\forall k.\ \mathbf{rely}\ r \Cap \{\!\!\{ p_T \cap \llcorner z \lll k \lrcorner \}\!\!\}\ ;\ (\!| q^* \rhd ((\llcorner z \ll k \lrcorner \cup p_X) \cap p) |\!) \succeq c \tag{69}$$

*then* $\mathbf{rely}\ r \Cap \{\!\!\{p\}\!\!\}\ ;\ (\!| q^* \rhd p_F |\!) \succeq \mathbf{while}\ b\ \mathbf{do}\ c\ \mathbf{od}$ . *See [28] for a proof.*

A reflexive guarantee distributes into a while loop, that is, a while loop satisfies a guarantee provided its body does.

## 4.1 Example Using the Early Termination Version of the While Loop Law

To implement an atomic specification command that updates $m$ to the minimum of $m$ and the constant $lo$ under interference that may decrease $m$ but cannot increase $m$, we can make use of a compare-and-swap instruction, $CAS(m, old, new)$, that atomically both checks if the current value of the variable $m$ is $old$ and succeeds in updating $m$ to be $new$ but if $m$ is not equal to $old$ it fails and has no effect.

$$CAS \mathrel{\widehat{=}} \lambda m\, old\, new.\ m : \langle (*m = old \Rightarrow *m' = new) \wedge (*m \neq old \Rightarrow *m' = *m) \rangle$$

Because the $CAS$ may fail to update $m$ if the value of $m$ is changed (decreased) between its sampling into $old$ and the atomic action of the $CAS$ taking place, a while loop is required to repeat the $CAS$ until it succeeds in updating $m$ to the minimum of $old$ and $lo$, each time based on a fresh sample of $*m$.[5]

$$\mathbf{rely}\ \ulcorner *m \geq *m' \urcorner \Cap m : \langle \ulcorner *m' = min\{lo, *m\} \urcorner \rangle$$
$$\succeq \mathbf{while}\ lo < *m\ \mathbf{do}\ \textstyle\bigvee old.\ \langle\!\langle *m \rangle\!\rangle_{old}\ ;\ \mathbf{call}\ CAS\,(m, old, min\{lo, old\})\ \mathbf{od}$$

[5] The body of the loop corresponds to $\mathbf{let}\ old = *m\ \mathbf{in}\ \mathbf{call}\ CAS\,(m, old, min\{lo, old\})$ in other languages.

Without interference, an obvious loop variant to show the termination of the loop is $*m$ because (without interference) $*m$ is reduced to *lo* by the *CAS* and the loop terminates after one iteration. However, interference may at any point decrease the value of $*m$. If that interference decreases $*m$ to a value less than *lo* after the guard evaluation, the *CAS* will fail to decrease $*m$, and hence the loop body will fail to decrease the variant $*m$. However, because $*m$ has been reduced below *lo*, the guard evaluation on the next iteration gives false and the loop terminates, which implies we need to utilise the early exit case of the while loop law. For the application of Theorem 6 (intro-while) we take $p_X$ as $\llcorner *m \leq lo \lrcorner$, $p_T$ as $\llcorner \mathsf{true} \lrcorner$, $p_F$ as $\llcorner *m \leq lo \lrcorner$, $p$ as the type invariant $\llcorner *m \in int \wedge lo \in int \lrcorner$, $q$ as the universal relation $\mathsf{univ}$, which is both reflexive and transitive, and $z$ as $*m$. Provisos (64), (65), (66) and (68) hold trivially, and (67) follows from the type invariant $p$. Finally the body of the loop satisfies (69) because if the *CAS* succeeds, $p_X$ is stably established and guarantees both the postcondition and termination of the loop, whereas if the *CAS* fails, interference must have decreased $*m$, that is, it has reduced the variant.

### 4.2 Fair Termination

The command **fair** disallows an infinite contiguous sequence of environment transitions [24].

$$\mathbf{fair} \mathrel{\widehat{=}} (\epsilon^\star \,;\, \pi)^\omega \,;\, \epsilon^\star \tag{70}$$

Fair execution of a command $c$ can be represented as $c \Cap \mathbf{fair}$, which rules out an infinite contiguous sequence of environment transitions when executing $c$, unless $c$ aborts. The command $\mathbf{term}$ allows only a finite number of program transitions but does not rule out an infinite contiguous sequence of environment transitions, however, $\mathbf{term} \Cap \mathbf{fair} = \boldsymbol{\alpha}^\star$ and hence allows only a finite number of transitions. Thus if a command $c$ refines $\mathbf{term}$, then $c \Cap \mathbf{fair}$ only performs a finite number of transitions, i.e.

$$c \Cap \mathbf{fair} \preceq \mathbf{term} \Cap \mathbf{fair} = \boldsymbol{\alpha}^\star. \tag{71}$$

Hence it is sufficient to show that a command $c$ refines $\mathbf{term}$ in order to show fair execution of $c$ only makes a finite number of transitions. The reader is referred to [24] for a more thorough treatment of fairness in our theory.

*Related Work.* Dingel [18] handles fairness by defining the trace semantics of his parallel operator to only allow fair interleaving. Because the semantics of Schellhorn et al. [47] explicitly alternates between a program transition and an environment transition (corresponding to any number of our environment transitions), it implicitly corresponds to fair execution. Our approach allows one to decouple fair execution and allows a simpler definition of the parallel operator [24]. □

## 5 Conclusion

The main contributions of this work are to provide general laws for reasoning about recursion and while loops in the context of interference from concurrent threads, including termination arguments based on a variant and a well-founded relation. Our laws cover early termination because this is useful in the context of concurrency, and in this context (unlike the sequential context) they do not follow from a version of a law that does not handle the early termination case. Our approach handles reasoning about fair termination in the context of concurrency, that is, termination provided the thread is executed fairly [24].

We do not assume either expression evaluations or assignment commands are executed atomically but employ a fine-grained semantics for expressions to justify a set of inference rules that allow compositional reasoning about expressions, including guards [26]. The fine-grained theory has been used to develop laws for assignment and conditional commands in [26] and for procedure calls, recursion and while loops in the current paper. We only support call-by-constant parameter passing where formal parameters act as constants and hence may not be modified within the procedure body but because we allow an l-value to be passed (by constant) as a parameter, we effectively support call-by-reference parameters. More general call-by-value parameter passing where the formal parameter acts as a local variable that can be modified within the procedure body, and call-by-result parameters and combined call-by value-result parameters could be supported in future work by combining the theories developed here with our theories for handling local variables [38].

Our concurrency theory has been formalised within the Isabelle/HOL theorem prover [42], and the results presented in this paper have been verified in that theory.

**Acknowledgements.** Our collaboration has been supported by the Australian Research Council under their Discovery Program Grant DP190102142. Hayes and Meinicke were also supported by funding from the Department of Defence, administered through the Advanced Strategic Capabilities Accelerator grant *Verifying Concurrent Data Structures for Trustworthy Systems*. Jones was supported by Leverhulme Trust RPG-2019-020 and would like to acknowledge the stimulus of the *Big Specification* programme at the Cambridge *Isaac Newton Institute*.

## References

1. Aczel, P.H.G.: On an inference rule for parallel composition (1983). Private communication to Cliff Jones. http://homepages.cs.ncl.ac.uk/cliff.jones/publications/MSs/PHGA-traces.pdf
2. Andrews, G.R.: Concurrent Programming: Principles and Practice. Benjamin/Cummings (1991)
3. Back, R.-J.R., von Wright, J.: Refinement Calculus: A Systematic Introduction. Springer, New York (1998). https://doi.org/10.1007/978-1-4612-1674-2
4. Back, R.-J.R., von Wright, J.: Reasoning algebraically about loops. Acta Informatica **36**, 295–334 (1999). https://doi.org/10.1007/s002360050163
5. Back, R.-J., Preoteasa, V.: An algebraic treatment of procedure refinement to support mechanical verification. Formal Aspects Comput. **17**, 69–90 (2005). https://doi.org/10.1007/s00165-004-0060-7
6. Bauer, F.L., Broy, M., Gnatz, R., Hesse, W., Krieg-Brückner, B.: A wide spectrum language for program development. In: 3rd International Symposium on Programming, Paris, pp. 1–15 (1978). https://doi.org/10.1145/954587.954588
7. Ben-Ari, M.: Principles of Concurrent and Distributed Programming, 2nd edn. Addison Wesley (2005)

8. Bornat, R., Amjad, H.: Inter-process buffers in separation logic with rely-guarantee. Formal Aspects Comput. **22**(6), 735–772 (2010). https://doi.org/10.1007/s00165-009-0141-8
9. Bornat, R., Amjad, H.: Explanation of two non-blocking shared-variable communication algorithms. Formal Aspects Comput. **25**(6), 893–931 (2011). https://doi.org/10.1007/s00165-011-0213-4
10. Brookes, S., O'Hearn, P.W.: Concurrent separation logic. ACM SIGLOG News **3**(3), 47–65 (2016). https://doi.org/10.1145/2984450.2984457
11. Coleman, J.W., Jones, C.B.: A structural proof of the soundness of rely/guarantee rules. J. Log. Comput. **17**(4), 807–841 (2007). https://doi.org/10.1093/logcom/exm030
12. Coleman, J.W.: Constructing a tractable reasoning framework upon a fine-grained structural operational semantics. Ph.D. thesis, Newcastle University, January 2008. http://theses.ncl.ac.uk/jspui/handle/10443/898
13. Collette, P., Jones, C.B.: Enhancing the tractability of rely/guarantee specifications in the development of interfering operations, chap. 10. In: Plotkin, G., Stirling, C., Tofte, M. (eds.) Proof, Language and Interaction, pp. 277–307. MIT Press (2000). https://doi.org/10.7551/mitpress/5641.003.0016.
14. Colvin, R.J., Hayes, I.J., Meinicke, L.A.: Designing a semantic model for a wide-spectrum language with concurrency. Formal Aspects Comput. **29**(5), 853–875 (2017). https://doi.org/10.1007/s00165-017-0416-4
15. de Roever, W.-P.: Concurrency Verification: Introduction to Compositional and Noncompositional Methods. Cambridge University Press (2001)
16. Dijkstra, E.W.: Guarded commands, nondeterminacy and formal derivation of programs. CACM **18**(8), 453–458 (1975). https://doi.org/10.1145/360933.360975
17. Dijkstra, E.W.: A Discipline of Programming. Prentice-Hall (1976)
18. Dingel, J.: A refinement calculus for shared-variable parallel and distributed programming. Formal Aspects Comput. **14**(2), 123–197 (2002). https://doi.org/10.1007/s001650200032
19. Fell, J., Hayes, I.J., Velykis, A.: Concurrent refinement algebra and rely quotients. Arch. Formal Proofs, pp. 1–44 (2016). http://isa-afp.org/entries/Concurrent_Ref_Alg.shtml
20. Feng, X., Ferreira, R., Shao, Z.: On the relationship between concurrent separation logic and assume-guarantee reasoning. In: De Nicola, R. (ed.) ESOP 2007. LNCS, vol. 4421, pp. 173–188. Springer, Heidelberg (2007). https://doi.org/10.1007/978-3-540-71316-6_13
21. Gries, D.: The Science of Programming. Springer, New York (1981). https://doi.org/10.1007/978-1-4612-5983-1
22. Hayes, I.J.: Generalised rely-guarantee concurrency: an algebraic foundation. Formal Aspects Comput. **28**(6), 1057–1078 (2016). https://doi.org/10.1007/s00165-016-0384-0
23. Hayes, I.J., Colvin, R.J., Meinicke, L.A., Winter, K., Velykis, A.: An algebra of synchronous atomic steps. In: Fitzgerald, J., Heitmeyer, C., Gnesi, S., Philippou, A. (eds.) FM 2016. LNCS, vol. 9995, pp. 352–369. Springer, Cham (2016). https://doi.org/10.1007/978-3-319-48989-6_22
24. Hayes, I.J., Meinicke, L.A.: Encoding fairness in a synchronous concurrent program algebra. In: Havelund, K., Peleska, J., Roscoe, B., de Vink, E. (eds.) FM 2018. LNCS, vol. 10951, pp. 222–239. Springer, Cham (2018). https://doi.org/10.1007/978-3-319-95582-7_13
25. Hayes, I.J., Meinicke, L.A.: Developing an algebra for rely/guarantee concurrency: design decisions and challenges. In: Ribeiro, P., Sampaio, A. (eds.) UTP 2019. LNCS, vol. 11885, pp. 176–197. Springer, Cham (2019). https://doi.org/10.1007/978-3-030-31038-7_9
26. Hayes, I.J., Jones, C.B., Meinicke, L.A.: Reasoning about expression evaluation under interference. Formal Aspects Comput. 38(3), Article 29, 1–36 (2026). https://doi.org/10.1145/3801150
27. Hayes, I.J., Meinicke, L.A., Evangelou-Oost, N.: Restructuring a concurrent refinement algebra. In: Fahrenberg, U., Fussner, W., Glück, R. (eds.) Relational and Algebraic Methods in

Computer Science. LNCS, vol. 14787, pp. 135–155. Springer, Cham (2024). https://doi.org/10.1007/978-3-031-68279-7_9
28. Hayes, I.J., Meinicke, L.A., Jones, C.B.: Reasoning about concurrent loops and recursion with rely-guarantee rules. arXiv arXiv:2512.06242 (2026)
29. Hayes, I.J., Meinicke, L.A., Meiring, P.A.: Deriving laws for developing concurrent programs in a rely-guarantee style, pp. 1–80. arXiv (2021). https://doi.org/10.48550/arXiv.2103.15292.
30. Hayes, I.J., Meinicke, L.A., Winter, K., Colvin, R.J.: A synchronous program algebra: a basis for reasoning about shared-memory and event-based concurrency. Formal Aspects Comput. **31**(2), 133–163 (2018). https://doi.org/10.1007/s00165-018-0464-4
31. Hoare, C.A.R.: An axiomatic basis for computer programming. Commun. ACM **12**(10), 576–580, 583 (1969). https://doi.org/10.1145/363235.363259.
32. Jones, C.B.: Development methods for computer programs including a notion of interference. Ph.D. thesis, Oxford University, June 1981. Oxford University Computing Laboratory (now Computer Science) Technical Monograph PRG-25. https://www.cs.ox.ac.uk/files/9025/PRG-25.pdf
33. Jones, C.B.: Specification and design of (parallel) programs. In: Proceedings of IFIP'83, pp. 321–332. North-Holland (1983)
34. Jones, C.B.: Tentative steps toward a development method for interfering programs. ACM ToPLaS **5**(4), 596–619 (1983). https://doi.org/10.1145/69575.69577
35. Jones, C.B.: Systematic Software Development Using VDM, 2nd edn. Prentice Hall International (1990). http://homepages.cs.ncl.ac.uk/cliff.jones/publications/Books/vdm_tn.pdf
36. Jones, C.B., Hayes, I.J.: Possible values: exploring a concept for concurrency. J. Log. Algebraic Meth. Program. **85**(5, Part 2), 972–984 (2016). https://doi.org/10.1016/j.jlamp.2016.01.002
37. Jones, C.B., Yatapanage, N.: Reasoning about separation using abstraction and reification. In: Calinescu, R., Rumpe, B. (eds.) SEFM 2015. LNCS, vol. 9276, pp. 3–19. Springer, Cham (2015). https://doi.org/10.1007/978-3-319-22969-0_1
38. Meinicke, L.A., Hayes, I.J.: Using cylindric algebra to support local variables in rely/guarantee concurrency. In: 2023 IEEE/ACM 11th International Conference on Formal Methods in Software Engineering (FormaliSE), pp. 108–119. IEEE (2023). https://doi.org/10.1109/FormaliSE58978.2023.00019
39. Meinicke, L.A., Hayes, I.J.: Reasoning about distributive laws in a concurrent refinement algebra. In: Cavalcanti, A., Baxter, J. (eds.) The Practice of Formal Methods: Essays in Honour of Cliff Jones. LNCS, Part II, vol. 14781, pp. 1–22. Springer, Cham (2024). https://doi.org/10.1007/978-3-031-66673-5_1
40. Milner, R.: Calculi for synchrony and asynchrony. Theoret. Comput. Sci. **25**(3), 267–310 (1983). https://doi.org/10.1016/0304-3975(83)90114-7
41. Morgan, C.C.: Programming from Specifications, 2nd edn. Prentice Hall (1994)
42. Nipkow, T., Wenzel, M., Paulson, L.C. (eds.): Isabelle/HOL. LNCS, vol. 2283. Springer, Heidelberg (2002). https://doi.org/10.1007/3-540-45949-9
43. O'Hearn, P.W.: Resources, concurrency and local reasoning. Theoret. Comput. Sci. **375**(1–3), 271–307 (2007). https://doi.org/10.1016/j.tcs.2006.12.035
44. Prensa Nieto, L.: The rely-guarantee method in Isabelle/HOL. In: Degano, P. (ed.) ESOP 2003. LNCS, vol. 2618, pp. 348–362. Springer, Heidelberg (2003). https://doi.org/10.1007/3-540-36575-3_24
45. Reynolds, J.C.: Separation logic: a logic for shared mutable data structures. In: IEEE Symposium on Logic in Computer Science (LICS), pp. 55–74. IEEE Computer Society (2002). https://doi.org/10.1109/LICS.2002.1029817

46. Sanan, D., Zhao, Y., Lin, S.-W., Yang, L.: CSim$^2$: compositional top-down verification of concurrent systems using rely-guarantee. ACM Trans. Program. Lang. Syst. **43**(1), 1–46 (2021). https://doi.org/10.1145/3436808
47. Schellhorn, G., Tofan, B., Ernst, G., Pfähler, J., Reif, W.: RGITL: a temporal logic framework for compositional reasoning about interleaved programs. Ann. Math. Artif. Intell. **71**, 131–174 (2014). https://doi.org/10.1007/s10472-013-9389-z
48. Stølen, K.: Development of parallel programs on shared data-structures. Ph.D. thesis, Manchester University (1990). Published as technical report UMCS-91-1-1. https://doi.org/10.48550/arXiv.2404.16624
49. Stølen, K.: A method for the development of totally correct shared-state parallel programs. In: Baeten, J.C.M., Groote, J.F. (eds.) CONCUR 1991. LNCS, vol. 527, pp. 510–525. Springer, Heidelberg (1991). https://doi.org/10.1007/3-540-54430-5_110
50. Stølen, K.: Shared-state design modulo weak and strong process fairness. In: Diaz, M., Groz, R. (eds.) Formal Description Techniques, V, Proceedings of the IFIP TC6/WG6.1 Fifth International Conference on Formal Description Techniques for Distributed Systems and Communication Protocols, FORTE '92. IFIP Transactions, Perros-Guirec, France, 13–16 October 1992, vol. C-10, pp. 479–498. North-Holland (1992)
51. Vafeiadis, V.: Modular fine-grained concurrency verification. Ph.D. thesis, University of Cambridge (2007). https://doi.org/10.48456/tr-726
52. von Wright, J.: Towards a refinement algebra. Sci. Comput. Program. **51**(1–2), 23–45 (2004). https://doi.org/10.1016/j.scico.2003.09.002
53. Wickerson, J., Dodds, M., Parkinson, M.J.: Explicit stabilisation for modular rely-guarantee reasoning. Technical Report 774, Computer Laboratory, University of Cambridge, March 2010. Extended technical report version of [54]. https://doi.org/10.48456/tr-774
54. Wickerson, J., Dodds, M., Parkinson, M.: Explicit stabilisation for modular rely-guarantee reasoning. In: Gordon, A.D. (ed.) ESOP 2010. LNCS, vol. 6012, pp. 610–629. Springer, Heidelberg (2010). https://doi.org/10.1007/978-3-642-11957-6_32
55. Qiwen, X., de Roever, W.-P., He, J.: The rely-guarantee method for verifying concurrent programs. Formal Aspects Comput. **9**(2), 149–174 (1997). https://doi.org/10.1007/BF01211617

# Consistency Proofs for Axiomatic Extensions: Translating VerCors' Axiomatic Data Types Into Isabelle

Edoardo Putti(✉) and Alexander Stekelenburg

Formal Methods and Tools (FMT), University of Twente, Enschede, The Netherlands
e.putti@utwente.nl

**Abstract.** A challenge in software verification is that we may start from inconsistent axiomatizations. This is a concrete problem when verifiers let the user extend the axioms and specification language and do not guard against inconsistencies explicitly. The VerCors deductive verifier assumes any user extension is consistent and does not support a workflow for establishing consistency. We implemented a translation for VerCors' Axiomatic Data Types (ADTs) to the Isabelle theorem prover and created a workflow to prove them consistent. The translation allowed us to prove consistency of the 12 ADTs distributed with VerCors. During the proofs we found and investigated three consistency problems that led to one true consistency bug. We have also used the same workflow to prove consistent a more complex pointer arithmetic ADT. The manual effort in the Isabelle prover depends on the complexity of the input Axiomatic Data Type (ADT) but simple automation eliminates most manual work for straightforward cases.

**Keywords:** Cooperative Verification · Axiomatic Data Types · Consistency Checking · Deductive Software Verification · Interactive Theorem Proving

## 1 Introduction

Software controls for industrial systems must operate safely. This is particularly important in safety-critical systems where errors have catastrophic consequences such as loss of lives [16] and economic damages [13]. *Formal verification* offers one way to prevent these errors by mathematically proving that the control software satisfies a specification [4]. This procedure guarantees that all possible behaviors of a given program satisfy a formally defined property, e.g., that the program will never reach an error state.

Verification tools like deductive verifiers [8] can achieve this goal by implementing logical inference in software. An example of one such tool is the VerCors deductive verifier [3]. VerCors has been used to verify software correctness

This work was supported by the NWO OCENW.M.21.291 "VESPA" grant
This work was supported by the NWO OCENW.M.22.194 "Pallas" grant.


P. Gorm Larsen and K. Y. Rozier (Eds.): FMICS 2026, LNCS 16967, pp. 80–97, 2027.
https://doi.org/10.1007/978-3-032-36849-2_5

in tunnel controls [9], automotive control systems [24], and real-time embedded systems [23], and it allows developers to verify that their concrete programs satisfy specifications of memory safety and functional correctness. Specifications in VerCors are written as function pre/post-conditions using the language of first-order fractional separation logic [6] – a logic for sharing resources – and users can extend the specification language and introduce axioms. This flexibility is highly desirable, as users can adapt VerCors to novel use-cases without having to change its original implementation.

However, blindly trusting axiomatizations may result in silently verifying programs that should not: inconsistent axioms allow VerCors to verify *any* program against *any* specification, losing formal guarantees of correctness. This is a known problem in software verification [10] but no concrete solution has been proposed when specifically working with the VerCors verifier. We want to keep VerCors extensible but the only extension mechanism is axiomatization (see related works). We want axiomatizations to be consistent but VerCors cannot check for its own consistency.

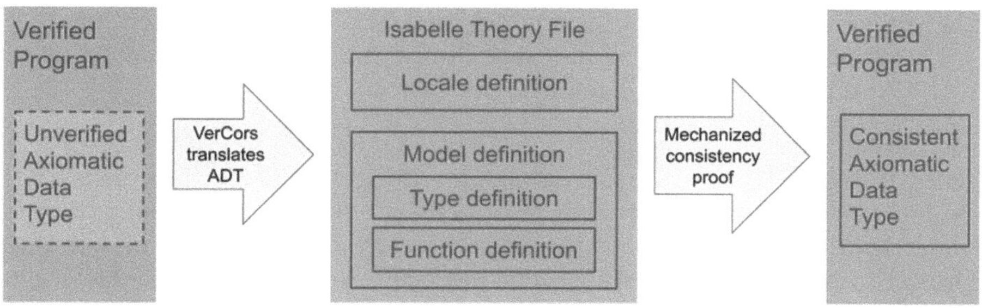


**Fig. 1.** Our workflow automatically translates an unverified Axiomatic Data Type into an Isabelle theory file. The file contains definitions for an equivalent locale and templates for the models to use in the consistency proofs. The user manually performs the consistency check within the interactive theorem prover by proving the model satisfies the axioms. This proof is mechanically checked by the interactive theorem prover which guarantees its correctness.

To solve this problem we propose a new workflow (see Fig. 1) based on a second verifier – the Isabelle theorem prover [17] – to formally verify the consistency of a new axiomatization specified in the VerCors toolset. This workflow preserves axiomatizations as VerCors extension point – leaving extensibility intact – and allows the user to formally verify consistency of an axiomatic extension. In the Isabelle theorem prover the user can check consistency of an axiomatization by defining a model and deriving the axioms (see related works). This solution guarantees consistency of axiomatizations, but nevertheless leaves something to be desired. In particular – in spite of the features of both VerCors and Isabelle – there is no clear path for VerCors-to-Isabelle interaction, and a naive approach would require extensive working knowledge of a second verifier and non-negligible manual work. Specifically, the user would need to manually translate the axiomatization between VerCors and Isabelle, manually define the models in the Isabelle verifier, and prove the models satisfy the translated axioms to show that the original axiomatization is consistent.

To make this solution viable and more streamlined, we implement automatic support for this workflow in the VerCors verifier. From an axiomatic extension in VerCors we automatically generate 1) an Isabelle theory, 2) templates for the models, and 3) templates for the consistency proof. Concretely, we achieve this objective via the following contributions:

- We propose a concrete workflow (Fig. 1) for translating VerCors' Axiomatic Data Types (ADTs) to the Isabelle theorem prover, i.e. we show how to translate concrete specifications between the two verifiers, and describe the work required to prove an ADT consistent in the Isabelle theorem prover.
- We implement this translation in VerCors, by making VerCors output an Isabelle theory containing the axiomatization, and implement automation to help the user follow the workflow by pre-defining the models for them.
- We evaluate the effectiveness of our workflow and implementation by:
  1. proving that the ADTs distributed with VerCors are consistent, and
  2. conducting a non-trivial case study involving ADTs for reasoning about pointer arithmetic, as a realistic use case analysis.

*Related Work.* In [5] the authors combine the Boogie verifier with Isabelle/HOL in a new proof environment that is also used to verify the consistency of background theories. Their implementation is extensive compared to ours but their approach to verifying axiomatizations is the same. An Isabelle theory file is generated by the Boogie verifier but there is no support for templates and they report that – for their use case – the effort is measured in person-months. Our scope is much smaller and the workflow described can be completed in hours. In [14] the authors report using an SMT solver to prove consistency of axiomatizations in the Spec# verifier. Their solution is fully automatic but trusted (see Sect. 6). An alternative to verifying consistency of axiomatizations is to test them: in [2] ideas from model-based testing are used to find soundness issues in axioms from the AutoCert verifier. Finally, conservative extensions [20] are an alternative to axiomatizations that have found success in interactive theorem provers [12]. Unfortunately, this technique cannot be used for VerCors because the underlying verifier – the Viper toolchain [7] – only supports axiomatizations.

*Structure of the Paper.* The rest of this paper is structured as follows: Sect. 2 contains background knowledge of VerCors, Isabelle, and their specification language, Sect. 3 describes the translation from a VerCors ADT to an Isabelle theory, Sect. 4 describes the implementation of this transformation in VerCors itself, Sect. 5 describes our evaluation and the inconsistency we found in VerCors' ADTs, Sect. 6 concludes this paper and discusses future work.

# 2 Background

## 2.1 VerCors

VerCors is a deductive verifier for imperative, concurrent programs with shared memory [3]. It can verify functional correctness and memory safety of concrete programs written in C/C++/Java and more. To verify a program VerCors requires that the user annotates the functions to verify using *function contracts* consisting of pre/post-conditions. If VerCors successfully verifies the function implementation against this specification, we know that all possible executions of the function where the pre-condition holds initially are such that the post-condition holds if the program terminates.

*Axiomatic Data Types.* In this paper we will focus on Axiomatic Data Types (ADTs). ADTs are a VerCors extension point for introducing new types and their specification introduces a type, functions, and axioms together. In Fig. 2 the `SquareRoot` ADT specifies a function `sqrt` from integers to integers and that `sqrt` it a total function and it computes the square root of an integer number. We know this function cannot exist because the square root is a partial function – it is undefined for negative values – and its result is not guaranteed to be an integer number as its signature specifies, but VerCors assumes the specification is consistent. This is a toy example but it shows an important lesson: it is easy to forget about partiality, especially when writing axioms.

```
adt SquareRoot {
    pure int sqrt(int n);
    axiom (forall int n; sqrt(n) * sqrt(n) = n);
}
```

**Fig. 2.** An inconsistent ADT introducing a overspecified square root function. The axiom specifies `sqrt` to be total and the signature constrains the results to be an integer.

## 2.2 Isabelle

Isabelle/HOL is an implementation of *higher-order logic* [15] in an interactive theorem prover [17]. As the user writes specifications and proofs, Isabelle checks each step and reports to the user *goals* to be proved. This interaction happens through a series of commands to write specifications (`datatype`, `definition`, `fun`, `theorem`, `typedecl`, `typedef`) or to write proofs, e.g. `apply auto`. Once a proof is completed, Isabelle certifies the proof through a small trusted kernel [18] which means certified proofs are highly unlikely to contain mistakes.

Figure 3 explains the main relevant Isabelle commands (`datatype`, `definition`, `fun`, and `theorem`) by example. We define the list datatype and the recursive functions `length` and `tail` by pattern matching. We then state and prove two theorems. The theorems state that the functions `length` and `tail` act as expected, linking the length of a list to its structure as a repeated application of a constructor. After stating a theorem, the tool gives us goals to prove (omitted in the example) that we can solve using the proof method `auto`. As an alternative to `datatype` we can use `typedecl` when the data constructors are not known, e.g. line 18 axiomatizes the type of maps from keys of type 'k to values of type 'v without specifying the constructors, or `typedef` when we create a type from a non-empty set of values [12], e.g. line 19 introduces the type of non-empty lists.

Throughout our example we provided specifications to the commands by writing mathematical formulas in double quotes, e.g. the equation on line 5 in Fig. 3. Practically, we think of these formulas as terms in the language of higher-order logic implemented in a pure functional programming language.

```
1   datatype 'a list = Nil | Cons "'a" "'a list"
2   definition "isEmpty xs ≡ xs = Nil"
3   fun tail
4     where
5  "tail (Cons x xs) = xs"
6   fun length
7     where
8    "length Nil = 0"
9  | "length (Cons x xs) = 1 + length xs"
10  theorem
11   "isEmpty xs ⟶ length xs = 0"
12  unfolding isEmpty_def
13  by auto
14  theorem
15   "¬ isEmpty xs ⟶ length xs = 1 + length (tail xs)"
16  unfolding isEmpty_def
17  by auto
18  typedecl ('k, 'v) map
19  typedef 'a nonemptylist = "{ xs . ¬ isEmpty xs }"
```

**Fig. 3.** Example Isabelle specification.

The last command that we need is `locale` (see Fig. 4). Locales are best understood as modules [11]: definitions and proofs inside the locale are abstracted over the parameters and assumptions of the locale. As Isabelle makes no guarantees that a locale's assumptions are consistent, we can only reuse proofs from a locale after we show that the locale assumptions are satisfied using the `interpretation` command. Proving the goals of the `interpretation` command shows that the axioms of the locale are satisfied, i.e. the user provided a model for the locale and showed it consistent.

```
1  locale list_signature =
2    fixes lisEmpty :: "'a list"
3      and ltail :: "'a list ⇒ 'a list"
4      and llength :: "'a list ⇒ int"
5  assumes "lisEmpty xs ⟶ llength xs = 0"
6      and "¬ lisEmpty xs ⟶ llength xs = 1 + llength (ltail xs)"
7  begin
8  end
9
10 interpretation list_signature isEmpty tail length
```

**Fig. 4.** Locale declaration and interpretation corresponding to the theory of Fig. 3. On line 10 we used the `interpretation` command on the `list_signature` locale: the names `isEmpty`, `tail`, `length` from Fig. 3 are mapped to `lisEmpty`, `ltail`, and `llength` from the locale. Isabelle then shows one goal for each locale assumption (omitted), where it replaces the locale names with the interpretation names.

## 3 Translating ADT Specifications to Isabelle

We describe by means of examples a translation between VerCors' ADTs and Isabelle's locales. First we provide a high-level description of the translation and comment on its validity. Then we give example (Sect. 3.2) input-output pairs and finally we discuss limitations of this approach.

### 3.1 Translation and Semantic Preservation

*Translating an ADT.* An ADT introduces a type, functions, and axioms to VerCors' logical context. To translate it to Isabelle we split it into a type declaration to represent the type and a locale declaration to group the ADT functions and axioms. Each function declared in the ADT is mapped to a locale parameter and each axiom is mapped to a locale assumption.

*Semantic Preservation.* The translation we describe is purely syntactical and straightforward but we do not present a semantics preservation argument. This is not a problem in practice because the user of our implementation (Sect. 4) can (and should) always inspect the output locale. As such, our informal argument for semantic preservation is that we map between the same concepts in the two verifiers. An ADT in VerCors is a pair of a new type and a parametric theory. We map it to a pair in Isabelle of new type declaration and locale. Assertions in axioms are terms in typed first-order logic which we map into Isabelle's typed higher-order logic. This mapping is faithful as the two logics agree on the semantics of the first-order fragment.

### 3.2 Translation Examples

In the following translations, we introduce the type associated with an ADT using the command `typedecl`. This axiomatizes the type and therefore needs to be changed later into a `datatype` or `typedef` before an `interpretation` is attempted. This makes the description of our examples simple and aligns with the axiomatic semantics of ADTs in VerCors but we will describe basic automation (Sect. 4) that defaults to using a `typedecl` only when it fails. Because the translation is mostly syntactical and straightforward, we only comment on what makes these example ADTs interesting for our workflow and what issue we will face during the interpretation proof.

*Option ADT.* The `Option` ADT (Fig. 5a) introduces the canonical type for partial values, its translation is in Fig. 5b. The functions `None` and `some` can be used as constructors for partial values, describing respectively an undefined or defined value. `option_get` is a partial function that is used as total in the axioms, in Sect. 5.1 we will see that this is the first example of *overspecified* ADT and we will comment on how VerCors uses this ADT soundly.

```
adt option<T> {
  pure option<T> None();
  pure option<T> some(T x);

  pure T option_get(option<T> opt);

  axiom (forall T x; None() != some(x));
  axiom (forall T x; option_get(some(x)) == x);
  axiom (forall option<T> opt; some(option_get(opt)) == opt);
}
```

(a) Input `Option` ADT.

```
typedecl "'t option"
locale option_signature =
fixes None :: "'t option"
  and some :: "'t ⇒ 't option"
  and option_get :: "'t option ⇒ 't"
assumes "∀ x. None ≠ some x"
    and "∀ x. option_get (some x) = x"
    and "∀ opt. some (option_get opt) = opt"
begin
end
```

(b) Output `option_signature` locale for `Option` ADT.

**Fig. 5.** Example: translation of `Option` ADT into a locale.

*Example: Fractional.* The `Frac` ADT (Fig. 6a) introduces the type of rational numbers between 0 (exclusive) and 1 (inclusive) for the purpose of specifying *fractional permissions* [6], its translation is in Fig. 6b. The function `frac_val` maps fractional permissions into the rational numbers and is injective. In the translation we replace the syntactic sugar `none` and `write` with their respective values 0 and 1. The novelty of `Frac` compared to `Option` is that it introduces a constraint on the values it describes: *fractional permissions* are rational numbers in $\mathbb{Q} \cap (0, 1]$ instead of all rational numbers.

*Example: Block of Memory.* The `block` ADT (Fig. 7a) introduces the type of contiguous memory in a C program, its translation is in Fig. 7b. Because VerCors' built-in datatype for memory locations is a *reference*, values of the `block` type are in bijection with a set of contiguous *references*. This makes the `block` ADT not self-contained: it depends on a second type. This means that its consistency proof will required two models: one for *references* and one for *blocks*.

### 3.3 Limitations

A naive translation would output one locale per ADT, but axioms in an ADT can reference any function, not just the ones defined by the ADT. This translation can introduce free variables if referenced names are not introduced in the locale lexical scope. In practice, if ADT `A` references a function `f` that is not defined in ADT `A` we need to add `f` to the lexical scope in the translation. To do so we introduce one limitation on the input ADTs. Their axioms can only contain functions defined in ADTs. This allows us to link the lexical scopes during the translation. In practice, if ADT `A` references a function defined in ADT `B` we declare the translation of `A` to be a locale extending the translation of `B`. All names declared in `B` are then visible in the lexical scope of `A`.

## 4 Implementation

We implemented the translation described in Sect. 3 in VerCors itself [19]. As a result, VerCors can now output an Isabelle theory containing the concrete locale syntax associated with an input Axiomatic Data Type. The implementation corresponds to the left arrow in Fig. 1 and is completely automatic. The output is a theory file that can be inspected in the Isabelle theorem prover and is the basis for our workflow. With the commands presented in Sect. 2.2, the user defines models for the locales and proves they satisfy the axioms by completing an *interpretation proof.* This proof is then mechanically checked by Isabelle to certify that the input ADT is consistent (right arrow in Fig. 1).

To help the user succeed in this task we predefine models for them by generating commands like `datatype` and `definition` from templates. The argument to these commands are chosen through syntactic analysis of the input ADT under the assumption that the input ADT does not describe a recursive type, i.e.

recursive constructors will not be selected as arguments of datatype and will be introduced as definition. This heuristic is enough for simple cases and – when it fails because it found no constructors – is reverted to a typedecl. We explain the templates by example in Fig. 8 using the block ADT from Fig. 7a as input. The locInv1 function from Fig. 7a is selected as constructor in the datatype command (line 1 in Fig. 8) for the raw_block type because its return type is block. The rest of the functions – blockLength, blockAddress – use a different template based on the command definition. From the axioms in Fig. 7a we select two (lines 8, 10 in Fig. 7a) as the constraints for the block type. The constraints are found by looking for a universal quantification over values of the type block and conjoined under the name block_axioms (line 8) and used in the construction of a new type block (line 11) with the typedef command. Because the functions in 7a do not have an associated function body we leave the definition commands to be filled in, e.g. we use the constant undefined (line 4 in Fig. 7a).

```
adt frac {
  pure rational frac_val(frac f);

  axiom (forall frac f, frac g;
                frac_val(f) == frac_val(g) ==> f == g);

  axiom (forall frac f; true;
                none < frac_val(f) && frac_val(f) <= write);
}
```

(a) Input Frac ADT.

```
typedecl frac
locale frac_signature =
fixes frac_val :: "frac ⇒ rat"
assumes "∀ f. ∀ g. frac_val f = frac_val g ⟶ f = g"
    and "∀ f. 0 < frac_val f ∧ frac_val f ≤ 1"
begin
end
```

(b) Output frac_signature locale for Frac ADT.

**Fig. 6.** Example: translation of frac ADT into a locale.

```
adt block {
  pure int block_length(block b);
  pure ref loc(block b, int i);
  pure int block_address(block b);

  pure block loc_inv_1(ref r);
  pure int loc_inv_2(ref r);

  axiom (\forall block b; block_length(b) >= 0);

  axiom (\forall block b, int i;
    loc_inv_1(loc(b, i)) == b && loc_inv_2(loc(b, i)) == i);

  axiom (\forall block b; block_address(b) > 0);
}
```

(a) Input `block` ADT.

```
typedecl block
locale block_signature  =
    fixes blockLength :: "block ⇒ int"
    fixes loc :: " block ⇒ int ⇒ ref"
    fixes blockAddress :: " block ⇒ int"
    fixes locInv1 :: "ref ⇒  block"
    fixes locInv2 :: "ref ⇒ int"
    assumes "∀ b . (blockLength b) ≥ 0"
    assumes "∀ b i . (locInv1 (loc b i)) = b ∧ (locInv2 (loc b i)) = i"
    assumes "∀ b . (blockAddress b) > 0"
begin
end
```

(b) Output `block_signature` locale for `block` ADT.

**Fig. 7.** Example: translation of `block` ADT into a locale.

## 5 Evaluation

We evaluate our translation and its implementation on the following criteria.

*Correctness of Translation.* We evaluate the output of our implementation for its syntactic and semantic correctness. To do so we inspect the output manually to assess correctness of the translation and the output of the automation. We also load it into Isabelle to assess that it produced a valid theory file.

*Detect Inconsistency.* The most important task of our evaluation is to assess if this translation helps us prove consistency, and find inconsistencies, in the input ADTs. To do so, we use as input the ADTs that are listed in the VerCors tutorial [25] and manually attempt to prove them consistent.

*Quantify Effort.* The templates from Sect. 4 are only useful if they reduce the user effort in proving consistency of an ADT. We quantify how much effort is required from the user (with and without the templates) in the *model definition* phase from Fig. 1 and show it proportional to how complex the ADT is.

```
1  datatype raw_block = locInv1 ref
2  definition blockLength :: "raw_block ⇒ int"
3    where
4  "blockLength b ≡ undefined"
5  definition blockAddress :: "raw_block ⇒ int"
6    where
7  "blockAddress b ≡ undefined"
8  definition block_axioms :: "raw_block ⇒ bool"
9    where
10 "block_axioms b ≡ (blockLength b) ≥ 0 ∧ (blockAddress b) > 0"
11 typedef block = "{ b . block_axioms b }"
```

**Fig. 8.** Templates for the `block` ADT. These definitions are added to the theory file together with the locale definition from Fig. 7b. Function `locInv1` (line 6 in Fig. 7a) has been selected as constructor for the datatype (line 1), `block_axioms` (line 8) has been generated from lines 8 and 10 in Fig. 7a. The `block` type (line 11) is the set of blocks satisfying the axioms.

As a separate case study, we show that our translation can also help VerCors developers by showing consistent the `block` and `pointer` ADTs. These ADTs are used internally by VerCors to reason about pointer arithmetic and are not part of the tutorial [25]. The associated artifact for our evaluation can be found at [1].

### 5.1 Consistency of VerCors' Axiomatic Data Types

For each ADT in the VerCors tutorial [25] we generated a locale declaration, models from templates, and an interpretation command using VerCors. Every ADT translated to a locale as expected and the resulting theories were syntactically correct and could be loaded into Isabelle. The templates also produced the expected definitions as described in Sect. 4.

*Detecting Inconsistency.* To quantify the manual effort required, we defined the models and proved the models satisfy the locale axioms for each of the ADTs except for `Option`, `ConstPointer`, and `MapCompat` as they have inconsistent axioms. We explain why using the `Option` ADT from Fig. 9a. On line 3 the axiom can be instantiated as follows `some(option_get(None())) == None()`, then using the axiom on line 2 we derive false. This happens because `option_get` is a partial function – `option_get(None())` is undefined – but is used as if it is total in the axioms, i.e. without assumptions on the input. The same issue happens with the `ConstPointer` ADT. In the `MapCompat` ADT the two axioms in Fig. 9b were inconsistent because of a typo. The two axioms characterize how the function `remove` changes a map size. Line 3 specifies that removing a key from the map reduces the size of the map and line 5 specifies that removing a key from the map does not change the size. This bug was fixed in [21] and was not theoretical: we were able to derive false (line 4 in Fig. 9c) starting from a satisfiable assumption and using `remove` on the input map `m`.

```
1 adt option<T> {
2   axiom (\forall T x; None() != some(x));
3   axiom (\forall option<T> opt; some(option_get(opt)) == opt);
4 }
```

(a) Inconsistent axioms for `Option` ADT. Line 3 is missing a the guard `opt != None` as an assumption.

```
1 adt MapCompat<K, V> {
2     axiom (\forall map<K, V> m, K k;
3               k \in m ==> map_remove(m, k).size == m.size - 1);
4     axiom (\forall map<K, V> m, K k;
5               (k \in m) ==> map_remove(m, k) == m);
6 }
```

(b) Inconsistent axioms from the `MapCompat` ADT. The assumption `k \in m` on line 5 is missing a logical negation.

```
requires 10 \in m;
void oops(map<int, int> m) {
    assert |m| == |m.remove(10)|;
    assert false;
}
```

(c) Reproducer for the consistency bug. VerCors verifies successfully that this program derives `false` just from removing the key `10` from the map `m`.

**Fig. 9.** .

*Guarding Partiality.* The issues we found, axioms using partial functions as if they were total, do not influence VerCors' soundness claim in practice. A user cannot write `option_get(o)` in a specification – it raises a syntax error – and must use an alias `opt_get(o)` with preconditions `o != None()`. This prevents the underlying verifier from instantiating the axiom on line 3 in two ways: the goal `option_get(None())` cannot be sent to the SMT solver because the precondition for the alias does not hold and the verifier is configured to only instantiate a universal quantifier with values present in goals. As such, we changed the axioms of the input ADTs to include these preconditions for each partial function and were able to show the ADTs consistent. This means that VerCors' use of these ADTs is sound and that the preconditions of the aliases are correct.

This shows that our approach works in practice. A user can translate their ADTs into an Isabelle theory and attempt a manual consistency proof. Just like in our evaluation, they can detect the inconsistency of their ADT, e.g. that the axioms of the ADT are overspecified or contain contradictions.

## 5.2 Manual Effort and Templates

To quantify the manual effort of this workflow and how the templates (Sect. 4) reduce it we focus on three metrics: count of new definitions (type and function), lines of code added (both specifications and proof steps), total lines required (including the locale declaration). These metrics are a useful proxy for the effort put in the formalization. Type and function definitions introduce concepts and abstractions that need to be linked to the current theory through their properties. This requires work from the user in coming up with the definitions and properties required for the verification of the axioms. Lines added and total lines added are a more concrete proxy for the user effort. We decided to use them as a measure of efforts because while definitions are usually a few lines of formalization, the resulting proofs of the axioms from the definitions can be arbitrarily long and complicated. In Table 1 we report the metrics for two scenarios: a baseline with no templates and one with templates.

*Baseline Scenario.* In this scenario the user defines the models and completes the interpretation manually. ADTs that have a predefined model in Isabelle/HOL (e.g. the `Option` ADT has a model in the `option` type) had the lowest effort: no new definitions were required and very few proof steps were necessary. ADTs without a predefined model – `Frac` and `ZFrac` describe a subset of rational numbers within a bound, `Array` and `ConstPointer` describe fixed length lists of values – required more work. In general, an ADT with constraints will not have a predefined model in Isabelle/HOL. Choosing the correct model for it translates to manual effort but our results show that the effort is proportional to the complexity of the input ADT, i.e. the number of functions and axioms it describes as well as if these functions are partial or total.

*Templates Scenario.* In this scenario the user obtains an Isabelle theory containing the translated ADT as a locale as well as templates for the models (see Sect. 4). The manual work is in completing definitions and finishing the interpretation proof. For most of the ADTs the effort was minimal and required filling in the definitions. For the rest, the effort required was reduced (with the exception of `MapCompat`, the most complex ADT) as the user only introduces a new definition when the templates cannot generate a type definition. For the number of lines added, we counted filling in a templated definition, creating a new definition, and manual proof steps required.

*Conclusion.* Table 1 shows that our approach has low effort, even though it requires a second verifier, and that templates can reduce the manual effort for simple cases. The effort required for proving an ADT consistent is proportional to its complexity in terms of number of axioms and functions introduced and, most importantly, whether it describes partial functions. The templates reduce the number of lines added by the user in almost all cases but result in longer formalizations. This is expected as the user only needs to fill in some information that is missing in the templates for the definitions (Sect. 4) but the proof involving these definitions grow in size. Because a `definition` command introduces an abstraction, there is a tradeoff between helping the user by guiding the definitions through the templates and having the user do more work, i.e. the user unwraps definitions manually in proof more frequently or they prove intermediate properties of their definitions and link them to the automatic proof methods.

**Table 1.** Effort metric for each of the input ADTs. Most complex ADTs (by axiom count) are listed first.

| Axiomatic Data Type | New definitions | | Lines added | | Total lines of formalization | |
|---|---|---|---|---|---|---|
| | Manual | Automated | Manual | Automated | Manual | Automated |
| `MapCompat<K,V>` | 4 | 4 | 83 | 83 | 112 | 112 |
| `Either<K,V>` | 0 | 0 | 5 | 3 | 20 | 33 |
| `Option<V>` | 0 | 0 | 4 | 3 | 13 | 19 |
| `Tuple<A, B>` | 0 | 0 | 5 | 2 | 14 | 23 |
| `Array` | 9 | 6 | 64 | 45 | 87 | 84 |
| `ConstPointer` | 6 | 0 | 59 | 19 | 77 | 55 |
| `Frac` | 2 | 1 | 15 | 11 | 27 | 35 |
| `Zfrac` | 2 | 1 | 16 | 6 | 26 | 30 |
| `Void` | 0 | 0 | 5 | 3 | 7 | 10 |
| `Null` | 0 | 0 | 5 | 1 | 10 | 10 |
| `Any` | 0 | 0 | 0 | 0 | 6 | 6 |
| `Vector` | 0 | 0 | 3 | 0 | 7 | 1 |
| `Nothing` | 0 | 0 | 2 | 1 | 6 | 6 |

### 5.3 Consistency of Pointer Arithmetic

VerCors supports verification of pointer-arithmetic programs by translating pointer arithmetic into operations defined by the `pointer` ADT (omitted because of space). The ADT axioms then relate pointer operations to *references*, the built-in type for VerCors' memory model. This makes it possible to reason about pointer aliasing and pointer arithmetic using VerCors's own aliasing notion. Consistency of the pointer arithmetic axioms then becomes an interesting case study on its own because of two reasons. First, we want to derive a model of pointers from a model of references to justify pointer arithmetic reasoning using aliasing, and second we want to prove consistency of the `pointer` ADT that, during development, was bound to be inconsistent because of human errors.

*Models for Reference, Block, and Pointer.* The model for the `pointer` ADT requires us to provide two additional models: a model for references, VerCors' built-in type for memory locations, and one for blocks, a contiguous region of memory. A pointer value is then defined as an offset into a block of memory. We defined 3 datatypes in Isabelle/HOL to represent references, blocks and pointers as in Fig. 10. The model for references (line 1) is a triple of *length*, *address*, and *offset* and is ad-hoc for supporting pointer arithmetic in the C programming language. The model for blocks (line 11), contiguous locations of memory, is a tuple of *base address* and *length*. In the axioms for the pointer datatype (line 27) we used the function `block_length` (definition omitted) to access the length of the block. Each Isabelle/HOL type definition for the model is split into three parts: a datatype without constraints on the values (lines 1, 11, 21), the constraint (lines 3-7, 13-17, 23-27), and a `typedef` to create the type with constraints as a set enumeration (lines 9, 19, 29). The `block` type is not defined in terms of `ref` because it was simpler to treat it as a pair of base address and length and relate those to `ref` as specified by the `block` locale axioms.

```
1   datatype raw_ref = RRef nat nat int
2
3   fun ref_axioms :: "raw_ref ⇒ bool"
4     where
5   "ref_axioms (RRef length address offset) =
6                length > 0 ∧ address > 0 ∧
7                offset ≥ 0 ∧ offset < int length"
8
9   typedef ref = "{ r . ref_axioms r }"
10
11  datatype raw_block = RBlock nat nat
12
13  fun block_axioms :: "raw_block ⇒ bool"
14    where
15  "block_axioms (RBlock length base_address) =
16                 length > 0  ∧
17                 base_address > 0"
18
19  typedef block = "{ b . block_axioms b}"
20
21  datatype pointer_raw = RPointer block int
22
23  fun pointer_axioms :: "pointer_raw ⇒ bool"
24    where
25  "pointer_axioms (RPointer b offset) =
26                    offset ≥ 0 ∧
27                    offset ≤ block_length b"
28
29  typedef pointer = "{ p . pointer_axioms p }"
```

**Fig. 10.** Type definitions for the models of *references*, `block`, and `pointer`.

*Outcome and Effort.* We were able to manually define models for *references*, `blocks` of memory, and `pointers` in Isabelle/HOL and conclude the interpretation proofs for the `block` and `pointer` ADTs. These models were developed manually as they are complex and require domain specific knowledge of VerCors' internals. This makes them the ADTs with the highest effort so far in our evaluation: the resulting theory contains 43 definitions, 565 lines, and required about 6 hours of work.

*Conclusion.* With this case study we showed that our approach scales to complex, domain-specific ADTs and it allowed us to achieve both our goals: proving the ADTs consistent and relating pointer arithmetic reasoning to references. This means that our workflow can apply to more general classes of ADTs than the basic one from Sect. 5.1, even if the user may need to sacrifice the automation and manually define the models. Additionally, this work required only basic Isabelle knowledge, at a level accessible to a master's student, demonstrating that it's an accessible technique.

## 6 Conclusion

We presented a workflow and associated tooling for VerCors users and developers to prove consistency of their axiomatizations in the Isabelle theorem prover. This workflow allowed us to find a consistency bug (Fig. 9c) which was fixed in [21]. We also investigated two more issues related to axiomatized partial functions and confirmed that VerCors is using them soundly. As an additional case study, we derived a model for reasoning about aliasing in pointer-arithmetic programs from VerCors' internal heap model and used it to prove an axiomatization of pointer-arithmetic reasoning consistent. This shows that our approach works in practice: our workflow can detect inconsistency and prove consistency of an axiomatization. We evaluated the user effort required by our workflow and showed it to be manageable by users with basic interactive theorem proving experience.

*Future Work.* We investigated two potential consistency issues that were related to axiomatizing partial functions and using them as if they were total. We found no inconsistency (Sect. 5.1) but it required manual changes to the input ADT. These changes can be automated for every ADT that declares a partial function, a guarded alias outside of the ADT, and uses the partial function as total in the axioms. Moreover, supporting this use case would prove not only that the ADT is consistent but also that the alias preconditions are correct.

Our approach involved the use of templates for the definition of the models as a simple solution to a more fundamental problem. There is no formal semantics of Axiomatic Data Types as used by VerCors and therefore the only analyses that can be reliably done are syntactic in nature. This opens up two directions, either introducing concrete syntax to instruct the syntactic analyses or defining a semantics for ADTs. Concrete syntax for a `datatype`, `constructor`, or `constrain` command in VerCors would simplify the translation between VerCors and Isabelle bypassing the need for a syntactic analysis altogether. A semantics of ADTs instead would allow the precise characterization of the ADTs whose model can be found automatically.

The automatic approach of [14] is an appealing extension for VerCors. It is possible to automatically prove consistent ADTs by translating them to SMT and the implementation is reasonably simple. This approach would be enough for simple ADTs but has two drawbacks. First, the translation to SMT would be automatic and unverified and second, the SMT solver is not guaranteed to find a model. The automation is appealing but, without a user in the loop to catch mistakes, this solution does not address the problem of trusting VerCors and the axiomatizations.

The pointer arithmetic case study uses a general encoding and model of pointers for the C programming language. While this encoding can be used for other languages it may be desirable to explicitly support features such as *smart pointers* [22]. Smart pointers implement user-defined semantics for pointer dereference operations which in turn may decouple pointer operations from the heap altogether. A consistent axiomatization of a smart pointer and its operations would allow VerCors users to more easily specify and verify complex programs.

**Acknowledgments.** The authors would like to thank Marieke Huisman and Peter Lammich for reviewing drafts of this paper and providing their feedback.

## References

1. [Artifact] Consistency proofs for axiomatic extensions: translating VerCors' Axiomatic Data Types into Isabelle. https://doi.org/10.5281/zenodo.19960874
2. Ahn, K.Y., Denney, E.: Testing First-Order Logic Axioms in Program Verification. In: Fraser, G., Gargantini, A. (eds.) TAP 2010. LNCS, vol. 6143, pp. 22–37. Springer, Heidelberg (2010). https://doi.org/10.1007/978-3-642-13977-2_4
3. Armborst, L., et al.: The VerCors Verifier: A Progress Report. In: Gurfinkel, A., Ganesh, V. (eds.) Computer Aided Verification, pp. 3–18. Springer, Cham (2024). https://doi.org/10.1007/978-3-031-65630-9_1
4. Baier, C., Katoen, J.-P.: Principles of Model Checking, MIT Press (2008)
5. Böhme, S., Leino, K.R.M., Wolff, B.: HOL-Boogie — An Interactive Prover for the Boogie Program-Verifier. In: Mohamed, O.A., Muñoz, C., Tahar, S. (eds.) TPHOLs 2008. LNCS, vol. 5170, pp. 150–166. Springer, Heidelberg (2008). https://doi.org/10.1007/978-3-540-71067-7_15
6. Boyland, J.: Checking Interference with Fractional Permissions. In: Cousot, R. (ed.) SAS 2003. LNCS, vol. 2694, pp. 55–72. Springer, Heidelberg (2003). https://doi.org/10.1007/3-540-44898-5_4
7. Eilers, M., Schwerhoff, M., Summers, A.J., Müller, P.: Fifteen Years of Viper. In: Piskac, R., Rakamarić, Z. (eds.) Computer Aided Verification, pp. 107–123. Springer, Cham (2025). https://doi.org/10.1007/978-3-031-98668-0_6
8. Hähnle, R., Huisman, M.: Deductive Software Verification: From Pen-and-Paper Proofs to Industrial Tools. In: Steffen, B., Woeginger, G. (eds.) Computing and Software Science. LNCS, vol. 10000, pp. 345–373. Springer, Cham (2019). https://doi.org/10.1007/978-3-319-91908-9_18
9. Huisman, M., Monti, R.E.: On the Industrial Application of Critical Software Verification with VerCors. In: Margaria, T., Steffen, B. (eds.) Leveraging Applications of Formal Methods, Verification and Validation: Applications, pp. 273–292. Springer, Cham (2020). https://doi.org/10.1007/978-3-030-61487-4_18

10. Huth, M., Ryan, M.: Logic in computer science: modelling and reasoning about systems. Cambridge University Press, Cambridge [U.K.] ; New York (2004)
11. Kammüller, F., Wenzel, M., Paulson, L.C.: Locales A Sectioning Concept for Isabelle. In: Bertot, Y., Dowek, G., Théry, L., Hirschowitz, A., Paulin, C. (eds.) TPHOLs 1999. LNCS, vol. 1690, pp. 149–165. Springer, Heidelberg (1999). https://doi.org/10.1007/3-540-48256-3_11
12. Kunčar, O., Popescu, A.: Safety and conservativity of definitions in HOL and Isabelle/HOL. Proc. ACM Program. Lang. **2**(POPL), 24:1–24:26 (2017). https://doi.org/10.1145/3158112
13. Le Lann, G.: An analysis of the Ariane 5 flight 501 failure-a system engineering perspective. In: Proceedings International Conference and Workshop on Engineering of Computer-Based Systems, pp. 339–346 (1997). https://doi.org/10.1109/ECBS.1997.581900
14. Leino, K.R.M., Middelkoop, R.: Proving Consistency of Pure Methods and Model Fields. In: Chechik, M., Wirsing, M. (eds.) FASE 2009. LNCS, vol. 5503, pp. 231–245. Springer, Heidelberg (2009). https://doi.org/10.1007/978-3-642-00593-0_16
15. Levant, D.: Higher order logic. In: Handbook of Logic in Artificial Intelligence and Logic Programming, pp. 229–321. Oxford University Press Inc, USA (1994)
16. Leveson, N., Turner, C.: An investigation of the Therac-25 accidents. Computer **26**(7), 18–41 (1993). https://doi.org/10.1109/MC.1993.274940
17. Nipkow, T., Wenzel, M., Paulson, L.C., Goos, G., Hartmanis, J., Van Leeuwen, J. (eds.): Isabelle/HOL. Springer, Berlin, Heidelberg (2002)
18. Paulson, L.C.: Computational logic: its origins and applications. In: Proceedings of the Royal Society A: Mathematical, Physical and Engineering Sciences, Vol. 474, no. (2210), 20170872 (2018). https://doi.org/10.1098/rspa.2017.0872
19. Putti, E.: Add Isar output mode by edoput · Pull Request #1391 · utwente-fmt/vercors. https://github.com/utwente-fmt/vercors/pull/1391, Visited 18 Jan 2026
20. Shoenfield, J.R.: Mathematical logic, AK Peters/CRC Press (2018)
21. Stekelemburg, A.: Merge pull request #1416 from utwente-fmt/unsound-map-compat · utwente-fmt/vercors@8096f5b. https://github.com/utwente-fmt/vercors/commit/8096f5b7d11837deb3eef01a49e15a1e1ad65ead, Visited 13 Apr 2026)
22. Stroustrup, B.: The Evolution of C++ 1985 to 1987. In: Proceedings of the C++ Workshop. Santa Fe, NM, USA, November 1987, pp. 1–22. USENIX Association (1987)
23. Tasche, P., Herber, P., Huisman, M.: Deductive Verification of Cooperative RTOS Applications. ACM Trans. Embed. Comput. Syst. **24**(5s), 131:1–131:25 (2025). https://doi.org/10.1145/3759251
24. Tasche, P., Monti, R.E., Drerup, S.E., Blohm, P., Herber, P., Huisman, M.: Deductive Verification of Parameterized Embedded Systems Modeled in SystemC. In: Verification, Model Checking, and Abstract Interpretation: 25th International Conference, VMCAI 2024, London, United Kingdom, January 15–16, 2024, Proceedings, Part II, pp. 187–209. Springer, Cham (2024). https://doi.org/10.1007/978-3-031-50521-8_9
25. Tutorial · VerCors Tool FMT — UTwente, en. https://utwente.nl/vercors, Visited 14 Apr 2026

# Exploiting the Layout of a Railway Interlocking System for Path Reliability Evaluation

Alessandro Fantechi, Gloria Gori(✉), and Jacopo Zecchi

DINFO, University of Florence, Florence, Italy
{alessandro.fantechi,gloria.gori}@unifi.it

**Abstract.** Railway interlocking systems are subject to strict reliability requirements under EN 50126, yet automating reliability evaluation remains a non-trivial task. This paper proposes two workflows that exploit the same formal representation of a railway interlocking layout to produce exact reliability curves for paths in a station. The first workflow is monolithic: it extracts the required physical components from the route table and constructs an exact fault tree for analysis with FaultFlow. The second is compositional: it decomposes the interlocking into elementary networks, applies a virtualisation rule to handle shared components correctly, evaluates each network independently using FaultFlow, and composes the results. We prove that the two workflows yield identical reliability functions. Both are validated on realistic interlocking layouts, where the compositional approach is faster on all evaluated paths, with speedup increasing with path length.

**Keywords:** railway interlocking systems · reliability evaluation · compositional analysis · elementary networks

## 1 Introduction

Railway Interlocking Systems (RIS) are safety-critical components of modern railway infrastructure. Their function—ensuring that trains are routed through a network without collision or derailment—demands not only correct behaviour under normal conditions but also a rigorous quantitative characterisation of dependability under component failure and under operational constraints. Increasing traffic density and network complexity place ever-greater demands on both routing decisions and maintenance planning. Standards such as EN 50126 [7] provide a systematic process for managing reliability, availability, maintainability, and safety (RAMS) targets on railway systems throughout their lifecycle. To achieve these targets, dependability analysis of a railway station or yard can be effectively performed at the level of operational paths: the sequences of routes, each composed of the track sections, points, and signals that a train traverses from a source signal to a destination signal [18,21,30].


P. Gorm Larsen and K. Y. Rozier (Eds.): FMICS 2026, LNCS 16967, pp. 98–117, 2027.
https://doi.org/10.1007/978-3-032-36849-2_6

Path-level reliability evaluation is a computationally demanding problem, and any solution must address a fundamental challenge: routes within a path share physical components at least at their boundaries. Any reliability model that fails to account for this sharing will either double-count failure contributions or produce incorrect composition. Two broad strategies are conceivable. A monolithic approach constructs a single reliability model for all components involved in a path. For realistic station layouts, which may contain dozens of points and hundreds of track sections, the state space grows rapidly with the number of components [26], making this approach increasingly expensive for large networks. Alternatively, one might attempt to decompose the path, evaluate sub-problems independently, and compose the results, but a naive decomposition into constituent routes and independent composition is mathematically incorrect precisely because of the shared components at route boundaries.

We address this problem by exploiting the operational structure of the interlocking formalised in the RobustRailS[1] XML representation, which captures both the physical layout and the route table of an interlocking. We propose two automated workflows that take this representation as input and produce a path reliability curve as output. The first is *monolithic*: it constructs an overall Fault Tree (FT) directly from the route table and analyses it with FaultFlow [4]. The second workflow is *compositional* and conceptually similar to the one in [5]: it decomposes the interlocking layout into a set of elementary networks [16], assigns each shared boundary component to exactly one elementary network via a virtualisation rule, evaluates each elementary network independently using FaultFlow, and composes the resulting reliability curves leveraging *librbd* [13]. Because elementary networks are independent under the virtualisation rule, their FaultFlow evaluations can be parallelised with the total compositional time further reduced.

We show that both strategies can be defined from the same RobustRailS representation, that the compositional workflow is provably exact under the virtualisation rule, and that both yield identical reliability functions on realistic case studies. Our specific contributions are as follows.

1. **An automated monolithic workflow for path reliability evaluation.** Starting from the RobustRailS XML representation of an interlocking, the workflow automatically enumerates the path, extracts the allocation conditions from the route table, removes duplicate components shared between different routes in the path, and constructs an exact fault tree for FaultFlow analysis.
2. **A compositional workflow with a correctness guarantee.** We extend the elementary network decomposition of [16] to the reliability domain by introducing a virtualisation rule that assigns each shared boundary component to exactly one elementary network. We prove that under this assignment the product-form composition of elementary network reliability functions yields the exact path reliability (Proposition 1).

[1] https://orbit.dtu.dk/en/projects/robustrails-robustness-in-railway-operations/.

3. **Empirical validation on real interlockings.** We apply both workflows to two realistic cases studies taken by [15], namely the layout of the Belgian Leval-Blanche station (Lvr1) and a more complex layout inspired by the Florence tramway network (a single track tramway line with several branches - not shown here for size limits), evaluating a total of four representative paths. In both cases, the two methods yield identical reliability functions, confirming the correctness of the composition rule.

The remainder of this paper is organised as follows. Section 2 reviews related work, Sect. 3 provides the necessary background on the RobustRailS framework and decomposition algorithm. Section 4 presents the two automated workflows. Section 5 describes the experiments run on the case studies and their results. Section 6 concludes the paper and outlines directions for future work.

## 2 Related Works

*Reliability and Risk Analysis for Railway Infrastructure.* Quantitative dependability assessment of railway systems has received growing attention in the context of EN 50126 [7] compliance, yet the majority of contributions focus on individual subsystems rather than on path- or network-level metrics [6]. Weik et al. [30] propose a Dynamic FT (DFT) modelling approach for operational risk assessment of railway infrastructure, explicitly addressing the challenge of capturing dependencies among track-side components; their work is the closest in spirit to ours, but targets risk metrics at the infrastructure level rather than focusing on interlocking logic's impact on path success. Meier-Hirmer et al. [24] address maintenance optimisation for railway infrastructure using reliability models fitted to inspection data, demonstrating the importance of component-family failure distributions – an assumption we adopt explicitly in our component model. At the system level, the survey by Ruijters and Stoelinga [26] provides a comprehensive overview of FT analysis methods and tools, establishing the state of the art against which our compositional approach is positioned.

*Dependability Evaluation Tools.* A broad range of tools has been developed for quantitative dependability evaluation using several dependability models. Among those tools supporting DFTs, which manage dependencies among component behaviours, we mention *DFTCalc* [1], *SAFEST* [28], *DFTRES* [2] and *SHyFTOO* [8]. Among tools supporting Stochastic FTs (SFTs), we mention the *FaultFlow* library [4], a tool that performs complete state-space analysis via Stochastic Time Petri Nets and supports non-Markovian failure distributions. A common limitation when applying these tools directly to large interlockings is that they treat the system as a monolithic model: for such networks, the state-space complexity of the resulting stochastic process becomes intractable. Among tools supporting an extension of Reliability Block Diagram (RBD), RBDs with Repeated Blocks (RBDRBs), we mention *rbdEngine*, a tool that leverages *librbd* library [13] to numerically evaluate complex RBDs in which each block can appear more than once. Finally, we mention *SHARPE* [27], a framework supporting the hierarchical definition of a dependability model exploiting both FTs, RBDs and stochastic approaches. For our analysis we selected both the *FaultFlow* library and the *rbdEngine*. *FaultFlow* has been selected to evaluate the path reliability, while the latter has been chosen for the composition operation.

*Compositional Verification of Interlocking Systems.* Model checking has been extensively applied to the safety verification of RISs [9,14,19,31]. However, the state-space explosion problem limits its scalability to large networks [12]. Compositional approaches address this by dividing the network into sub-networks, verifying each independently, and exploiting compositionality theorems to conclude safety for the whole. Several such approaches have been proposed, including those based on CSP||B [19], OCRA [20], and the RobustRailS framework [17,22,23]. The latter is of particular relevance here: we have already mentioned that this approach allows any well-formed interlocking network to be decomposed into a library of pre-verified *elementary networks*, reducing safety verification to a structural check. The cited compositional verification approaches address *qualitative* safety properties, but do not consider *quantitative* dependability metrics such as reliability or availability.

# 3 RIS Decomposition in Elementary Networks

## 3.1 Railway Interlocking System (RIS)

A Railway Interlocking System (RIS) is a signalling system that is responsible for safe routing of trains through (a fraction of) a railway network under its control. An interlocking system is traditionally specified by a layout of the railway network that it controls, and a so-called *interlocking table* that specifies allowed routes through the network, and conditions for these routes to be exclusively reserved by a train. In the following, the definitions and graphs follow the conventions and terminology of the RobustRailS research project [17,29].

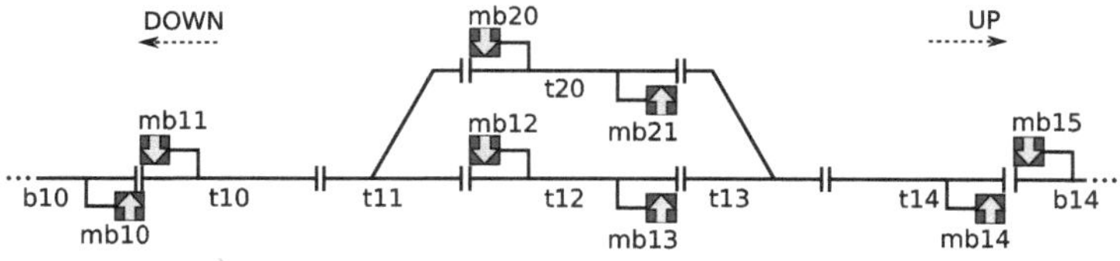


**Fig. 1.** A railway network layout example.

In Fig. 1 an example of a railway network layout for a small station is given, consisting of: (1) train detection sections that are either linear sections (like `t10`) or switchable points (like `t11`) having a stem side and two branching sides (e.g.

`t11` has its stem next to `t10` and its branches next to `t20` and `t12`, respectively) and (2) signals[2] (like `mb10`) placed at the ends of linear sections and only visible in one direction (e.g. `mb10` is visible in direction UP). As a general rule for the networks considered in this paper, there is at most one signal in each end of a linear section and it can only be seen when leaving the section. Furthermore, at the borders of a network, there are always two linear sections (like `b10` and `t10`) with a signal configuration having an *entry signal* on the border section and an *exit signal* on the section next to the border section.

In this context, a *route* is defined as the sequence of elements that a train shall follow for travelling from a signal in a given direction to the next one in the same direction. For example, in Fig. 1 the route from signal `mb10` to signal `mb13` (in direction UP) is made of elements `mb10,t10,t11,mb12,t12,mb13`.

We also define as a *path* a concatenation of routes from an entry signal to an exit signal of the network. The path from `mb10` to `mb14` is made of two consecutive routes. Note that the routes that compose a path share some elements (that is `mb12,t12,mb13` in the example.

### 3.2 Compositional Interlocking Verification Methods

In this paper, we refer to the compositional approach of [17], developed within the RobustRailS project, which defines a specific notion of *legal cut* such that, if the two subnetworks separated by a legal cut are independently verified as safe, it is proved that the whole network is safe as well.

Figure 2 shows how this approach decomposes a network into two subnetworks $N_1$ and $N_2$ by a *single cut* between $t1$ and $t2$. $N_1$ is obtained from the sub-network $N_{-1}$ on the left-hand side of the cut by adding a border linear section $b1$ and border signals $s_{entry_1}$ and $s_{exit_1}$. $N_2$ is obtained in a similar way. The added border elements restore the well-formedness of the sub-network and act as interfaces abstracting the behaviour of the other subnetwork for what concerns safety verification. A *cluster cut* consisting of several single cuts is also defined in [17].

The decomposition process is fully automated: once a cut is identified, the algorithm generates two separate XML files representing the resulting subnetworks. At the boundaries of these subnetworks, specific interface components are introduced, namely border track circuits and border signals, which act as the connection points.

A crucial distinction must be made between *virtual signals*, added solely to preserve the interface logic during the cut, and *physical signals*, which belong to the actual station layout. The distinction between physical and virtual signal is automatized, according to the naming rules adopted by the decomposition

[2] RobustRails considers modern ERTMS level 2 based RISs for which there are no physical signals, which are replaced by *markerboards*, and the movement authority at their location is communicated to the train by radio. For generality, we consider only physical signals, whose reliability has an impact on the overall reliability of a station, although we maintain in the figures the graphic appearance of a markerboard.

algorithm. While both types are included in the generated elementary networks to maintain structural consistency, virtual signals do not impact the overall reliability evaluation; they are assigned a functional reliability value of $R = 1$. Conversely, physical signals retain their stochastic properties.

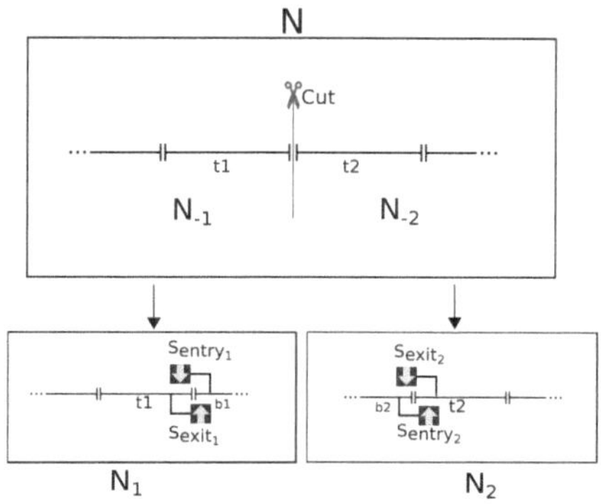


**Fig. 2.** An example decomposition of a network into sub-networks. From [17].

### 3.3 Elementary Networks

In [16] the question on which cuts should be made in order to effectively decompose a network is answered by proposing a library of pre-verified elementary networks and a strategy for dividing a given network into subnetworks of which as many as possible are elementary.

As elementary networks, [16] defines the network patterns shown in Fig. 3:*a*-*d*. Patterns *b* and *d* admit an unbounded number of linear elements at the indicated positions. Model instances of the networks of Fig. 3 have been model checked to be safe, for all the admitted combinations of presence of signals, but without the presence of the admitted extra linear sections. Moreover, a result from [17] allows an unbounded number of linear sections to be added at the indicated specific positions without impacting safety. Hence, we can conclude that *model instances for all elementary networks are safe.*

### 3.4 Decomposing a Network in Elementary Networks

In [16] a strategy is defined to search for places to make legal cuts, one by one, such that the network can be divided into parts that are either *elementary* networks or *nondecomposable* networks (that is, non-elementary networks that cannot be decomposed by any legal cut(s) ). In the ideal case that the decomposition leads to networks that are all elementary, no additional model checking is needed for verifying the safety of the whole network.

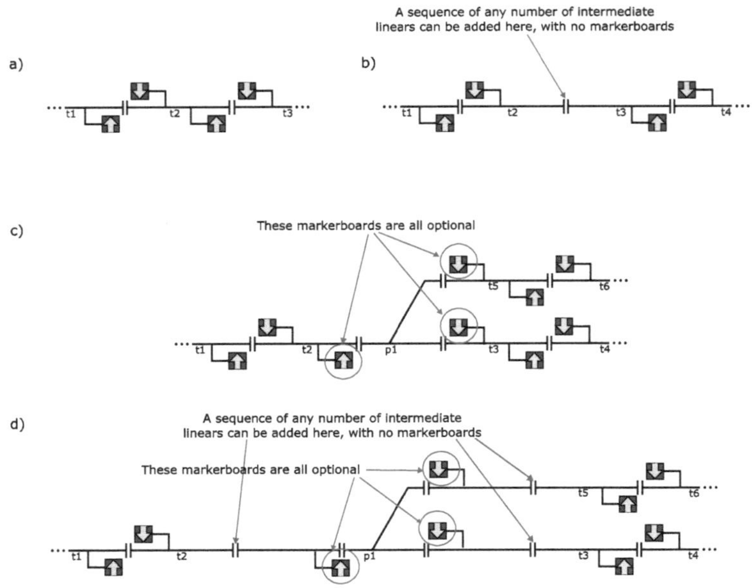


**Fig. 3.** Patterns for elementary networks (from [17])

As an example, consider the network shown in Fig. 4, representing the Leval-Blanche interlocking. By making the three cuts (two single cuts $(083, PM02U)$ and $(PM02U, PM03U)$ and the cluster cut $\{(802, PM04U), (801, PM04U)\}$) shown by green lines, one by one, it yields four elementary networks of type $c$, each containing just one point (respectively, PM01U, PM02U,PM03U, PM04U).

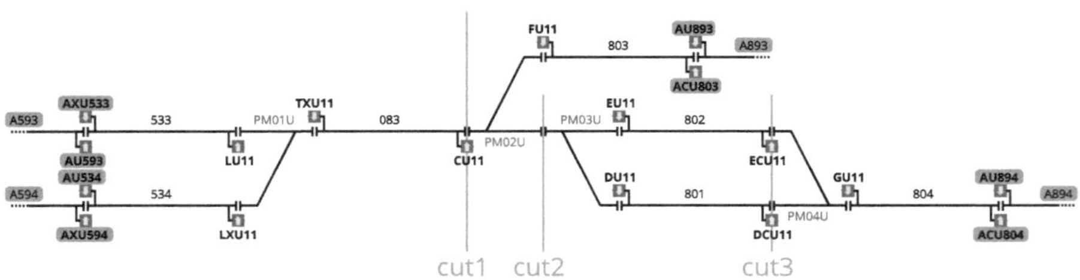


**Fig. 4.** Cuts shown on the Leval-Blanche (Lvr1) case study (from [16])

A decomposition procedure is proposed in [16] to find such cuts, visiting a network $N$ starting from one of its borders $b$. The visit can either find a cut which divides $N$ so that the subnetwork $N_1$ containing $b$ is elementary, in which case the procedure is recursively applied to one of the borders of the other subnetwork $N_2$, or does not find such a cut, in which case we say that $N$ is *unbreakable* from the border $b$ from where the search started, and we should then start a search from another border to see if a cut can be found from there. Should $N$ be *unbreakable* from all borders, it is *non-decomposable*.

Actually, it has been proved in [11] that any well-formed network[3] can be decomposed into a set of elementary networks: this property is used in that context to immediately verify safety properties *without model-checking*. Indeed, since elementary networks are pre-verified to be safe, a network made of only elementary networks is also safe (by the compositionality theorem of [17]). It is hence enough to verify well-formedness conditions on the network topology.

The decomposition procedure has been implemented at the Technical University of Denmark both giving an executable formal RSL specification and translating the same specification in C++ [16]. In this work we use this implementation for the decomposition task.

## 4 Reliability Evaluation

The decomposition framework reviewed in the previous section was designed and validated exclusively for *qualitative* safety properties; we now show how the same structural representation of an interlocking can be exploited for *quantitative* reliability evaluation.

In this section, we present two automated workflows – one monolithic, one compositional—that both take the RobustRailS XML as input and produce an exact path reliability curve as output. The key challenge both workflows must address is the correct handling of physical components shared between consecutive routes; the two approaches solve it by different means, and we prove that they yield identical results.

Before presenting the two workflows in detail, we introduce the component failure model and the formal definitions of route and path reliability on which both workflows rely.

### 4.1 Reliability of Components

The interlocking network contains three families of physical components, each modelled with a failure distribution (here exponential).

- **Track circuits** are modelled as single-failure-mode components with constant failure rate $\lambda_{tc}$. A failure renders the section unavailable for route allocation.
- **Signals** are modelled as single-failure-mode components with constant failure rate $\lambda_{sig}$. A signal failure prevents the interlocking from displaying a movement authority at that location.

[3] Well-formedness conditions regard the correct orientation and connection of the network elements and the absence of loops [11].

- **Points** are modelled with two independent failure modes: *blocked*, in which the point cannot be moved from its current position (rate $\lambda_{pt,b}$), and *loss of control*, in which the point moves to an unintended position (rate $\lambda_{pt,l}$). Either failure mode renders the point unavailable for route allocation. The combined failure rate is $\lambda_{pt} = \lambda_{pt,b} + \lambda_{pt,l}$.

The specific values of $\lambda_{tc}$, $\lambda_{sig}$, $\lambda_{pt,b}$, and $\lambda_{pt,l}$ used in both case studies are extracted from [30].

### 4.2 Reliability of Routes and Paths

The reliability of a station is investigated as the probability that no failure prevents a train to enter the station on an assigned platform, or to depart from the station, or to pass the station without stopping there. In this case every element of the network can independently fail, and we assume that they have a fail-safe behaviour, that is, a failure of an element is understood by the interlocking system as preventing the use of such element to set-up a safe route, hence resulting in negating the related movement authority to trains.

This assumption is actually more nuanced. We adopt a liberal fail-safe policy that allows maximal availability of routes. Indeed, three different degrees of fail-safe behaviour could be adopted, listed from the most liberal to the most conservative one:

1. For each route (or path) $r$, we consider $r$ available when all the elements (tracks, points, signals) that are physically on $r$ are not failed; in this policy we are not concerned with failures of points and signals which are external to the route, even if they are commanded a determined position or aspect to protect $r$. The hypothesis is that the interlocking itself and operational rules guarantee that the fail-safe state of such external signals or points does not allow to set a route in conflict with $r$ (for example, when operational directives equates a signal with no light - its fail-safe state - to a red signal);
2. We consider a route (or path) $r$ available when all the elements whose state is queried and commanded by the interlocking to set $r$, including elements not belonging to $r$: in this case the fail-safe policy imposes that also the failure of such external elements brings the path in a fail-safe state, not allowing $r$ to be set;
3. The failure of any track, point, signal brings the whole system in a fail-safe state.

The adoption of the first policy in this paper is motivated on one side by the interest for maximal availability, and on the other side by the direct applicability of decomposition in elementary networks. The second, more conservative, policy indeed requires to rethink decomposition: decomposition in elementary networks does not preserve side protection, since protection elements external to the route are discarded [10]. The latter policy, in which also a fault of a distant element does not allow to set any route, is not suitable to exploit decomposition in elementary networks.

We define *Route reliability* as the probability that all physical components required for the route allocation in the route table are functional. We define *Path Reliability* as the joint reliability of the component routes.

*Route reliability* can be evaluated by a Fault Tree model that expresses the route failure as the disjunction of all the primary failure events of the physical components. *Path reliability*, however, cannot be evaluated by a mere disjunction of the component route failures: routes of a path share some common elements, and this would violate the assumption of independence between primary events in a Fault Tree. Hence, the Fault Tree model of a path shall exclude duplicate events in one of the component routes.

### 4.3 Monolithic Modelling

The monolithic workflow constructs an exact fault tree for a given path directly from the route table. It proceeds as follows.

1. **Path enumeration.** Starting from $s_{in}$, the workflow traverses the route table to identify the sequence of routes $r_1, r_2, \ldots, r_n$ connecting $s_{in}$ to $s_{out}$. If multiple paths exist, the workflow will separately evaluate their reliability.
2. **Condition extraction.** For each route $r_i$, the allocation conditions are extracted from the route table, yielding the set of physical components[4] whose failure would prevent movement authority on $r_i$.
3. **Duplicates removal.** The union of all conditions across the routes of the path is computed. Components shared between consecutive routes appear exactly once in the result.
4. **Fault tree serialisation and analysis.** The set of resulting required physical components is serialised as a JSON fault tree and submitted to FaultFlow [4].

The output is a reliability curve $R_{mono}(t)$ representing the path reliability. A significant challenge in modeling large-scale interlocking systems is the exponential growth of the state space when analyzing a global Fault Tree [30].

### 4.4 Exploiting Elementary Networks to Evaluate Reliability

The compositional workflow evaluates path reliability by: i) considering the network decomposed in a set of elementary networks, ii) projecting the path on elementary networks to obtain on a sub-path, one for each elementary network, iii) separately evaluating each subpath, iv) composing the results in a final reliability curve. The approach is based on the following principles about the reliability of elementary networks:

[4] Either according to policy 1 or to policy 2 above.

1. Elementary networks can be trivially classified in two main types: in reference to Fig. 3, $a$ and $b$ are of type *Platform*, $c$ and $d$ are of type *Switch*. While the former provide only one route in one direction, the latter support two routes, each using one of the branches of its point.
2. The reliability of an EN is defined as the probability that a functioning path exists between its entry and exit boundaries. In particular, we differentiate on the type of EN:
   - **Platform EN:** Reliability $R_{EN\_platform}$ is the series reliability of all internal components (track sections and signals). Note that, even if the railway traffic is considered as bidirectional, a single-direction evaluation is sufficient as it covers the complete set of physical assets.
   - **Switch EN:** reliability is considered route-wise: if its point has a stem $S$ and branches $P$ (Plus) and $M$ (Minus) we associate to the EN a reliability vector: $\mathbf{R}_{EN\_switch} = [R_{path\_P}, R_{path\_M}]$, that represents the reliability of the path $S \rightarrow P$ (resp. $\rightarrow M$) given the point is commanded in Plus (resp. Minus) position.
3. Given the above classification of elementary networks in two types, and assuming to use the same reliability parameters for each component of the same kind, we can pre-evaluate once for all the reliability of the elementary networks on the basis of their type and of the involved number of the employed components. The evaluation is made applying the monolithic approach.
4. In each elementary network we will distinguish between virtual and physical elements; the former will be assigned a full reliability ($R = 1$) while the latter ones will be assigned their actual probability density functions. In particular:
   - **Topological Boundaries:** Any linear track section added by the decomposition algorithm or serving as an external network border is marked as virtual.
   - **Interface Signals:** Signals mounted on virtual track sections, or those created at cut-boundaries during decomposition, are marked as virtual.
   - **Functional Integrity:** Every EN must contain at least one non-virtual track section (linear or point) to ensure the physical reliability of the infrastructure is preserved.

The decomposition strategy described in Sect. 3.4 is then applied to a well-formed network, producing a set of elementary networks. The reliability of a route of the original network is evaluated by composing the reliability of traversed elementary networks, properly considering shared and virtual elements, and focusing, inside each elementary network, on the branch that belongs to the route. For example, decomposing the network of Fig. 1, we obtain two elementary networks, each containing one point. The reliability of an end-to-end path (such as `mb10` $\rightarrow$ `mb14`) is computed as a proper composition of the reliability of the two elementary networks by means of a high-level Fault Tree.

This composition shall take into account shared and virtual elements. The latter, which do not contribute to reliability, constitute a large part of the overall number of elements in a decomposed network. For example, in Fig. 5 we see virtual and physical elements in the elementary networks obtained after the decomposition of Lvr1 (for the original layout see Fig. 4). The components highlighted in orange are virtual.

### 4.5 Correspondence Between the Monolithic and Compositional Evaluation

We give here a proof sketch that the two approaches defined above produce the same reliability curve. The statement to prove is:

**Proposition 1.** *For any path and any well-formed interlocking layout:*

$$R_{\text{comp}}(t) = R_{\text{mono}}(t)$$

*Proof. (Proof sketch).* We consider the case in which reliability of a path is computed as a combinatorial composition of the reliability of its elements. A similar proof can be done in the case of evaluation through Fault Tree modeling.

Let $TPS(p)$ denote the set of physical elements (tracks, points and signals) of a path $p$, and $Elem(p)$ the set of sub-paths of $p$, each sub-path being a projection of path $p$ on a different elementary network.

For the monolithic approach we can define for a path $p$:
$R_{mono}(t) = \prod_{i \in TPS(p)} R_i(t)$

For the compositional approach, we can define:
$R_{comp}(t) = \prod_{s \in Elem(p)} R_s(t)$, and:
$\forall s \in Elem(p) : R_s(t) = \prod_{j \in TPS(s)} R_j(t)$
Adopting fail-safe policy 1, since the sub-paths of $p$ form a partition of $TPS(p)$ in the various $TPS(s)$, we have that:
$R_{comp}(t) = \prod_{s \in Elem(p)} \prod_{j \in TPS(s)} R_j(t) = \prod_{s \in Elem(p)} R_s(t) = R_{mono}(t)$

Note that adopting a different fail-safe policy, the partition is not possible.

### 4.6 A Library of Pre-computed Reliability Patterns

The primary computational advantage of the compositional approach lies in the observation that railway interlocking layouts, regardless of their size, are composed of recurring topological structures. By applying the virtualization rule described in Sect. 4.4, we can abstract these structures into a finite library of Elementary Network Patterns.

A further efficiency gain is then available when component failure rates are uniform within each component family. In this case, the reliability of an elementary network depends only on its topological pattern and the number of real physical components of each type in the path, not on its position in the layout. Each EN (and consequently each path) always contains at least a physical component (a linear or a point), furthermore on the basis of the decomposition algorithm we can assume that the number of physical signals in a path contained in a EN varies from 0 to 4. If we also assume a limited number of real linear track circuits (1 for a path in a *Platform* EN and at most 2 for each path in a *Switch* EN) we have a library of 9 different path reliability functions that can be pre-computed once using FaultFlow and reused across all paths and layouts. This assumption is valid for all the layouts analysed in [16].

The workflow for evaluating a large interlocking is thus transformed from a monolithic Fault Tree Analysis (FTA) into a modular lookup process:

1. **Decomposition:** The target path is mapped on the interlocking decomposed into its constituent ENs.
2. **Matching:** Each EN is mapped to one of the pre-computed patterns in the library.
3. **Retrieval:** The corresponding reliability function $R_i(t)$ in CSV, pre-calculated using *FaultFlow*, is retrieved.
4. **Composition:** The path reliability $R_{path}(t)$ is calculated as the product of the retrieved functions using `rbdEngine`.

This modularity allows for $O(n)$ evaluation time relative to the path length, as opposed to the exponential growth associated with the state-space of monolithic models. Modularity also allows for reusing reliability figures of unchanged components in cases in which a few components have their reliability parameters changed.

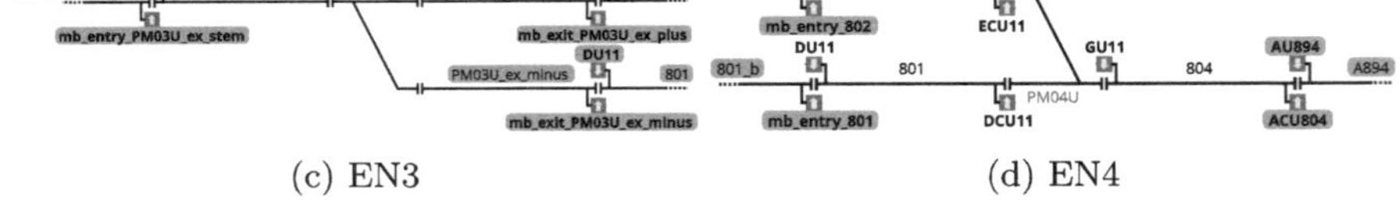


(a) EN1 (b) EN2

(c) EN3 (d) EN4

**Fig. 5.** Elementary Networks obtained decomposing Lvr1. Highlighted components are virtual.

## 5 Results and Discussion

This section presents the results of applying the proposed two workflows to the two case studies. The evaluation proceeds in two stages. First, the reliability of each elementary network type is computed independently using FaultFlow, establishing the building blocks of the composition. Second, we select four representative paths across the two case studies and evaluate path reliability using the monolithic and compositional workflow. The agreement of the results is then discussed. All experiments were conducted on a machine with an AMD Ryzen 5 PRO 3500U and 14.2 GB of RAM.

### 5.1 Reliability of Elementary Networks

The FaultFlow evaluation of both types of elementary networks shown in Fig. 3 was performed for an analysis time of 8000 h[5]. The computation times for the reliability functions are reported in Table 1.

**Table 1.** FaultFlow evaluation metrics for the two elementary network types. Note that for the Switch type the reported computation time is the sum of the two possible paths.

| Elementary network | Computation time (ms) |
|---|---|
| Platform | 6241 |
| Switch | 26710 |

### 5.2 Path Reliability Evaluation

The monolithic and compositional workflows were applied to determine path reliability in two layouts. We chose

- three representative paths of the Lvr1 interlocking: AXU594-ACU803, AU593-DU11-ACU804, and AU593-EU11-ACU804.
- the longest path in the tramway interlocking: uT1S-uVACS.

The monolithic evaluation serves as reference ground-truth: agreement between the two methods validates correctness of the compositional workflow.

**Reliability Agreement.** For all the paths, the compositional and monolithic methods yielded the same reliability values. This result provides empirical confirmation of Proposition 1: the virtualisation rule correctly partitions physical components across elementary networks, satisfying the independence assumption. Figure 6 shows the obtained reliability curves for the analysed paths in the

[5] We have chosen a time interval close to one year, under the realistic assumption that a periodic maintenance will anyway occur within one year. On the other hand, Fig. 6 shows that a longer time interval is not informative, since the diagram will only show a long tail in which reliability is low and slowly decreasing.

Lvr1 (3 paths) and tramway (1 path) case studies. The strong similarity of two paths of Lvr1 makes their curves exactly overlapped. Notice that the reliability of the path uT1S-uVACS is much lower than the one of the shorter paths in Lvr1. This is due to the high number of involved points. Since the scope of this paper was to evaluate the compositional method, we have used a rather basic modelling for point reliability. A more sophisticated failure model would consider the fact that a point machine is not continuously commanded, so the failure probability should be rather evaluated with respect to the number of operations instead of the number of operation hours.

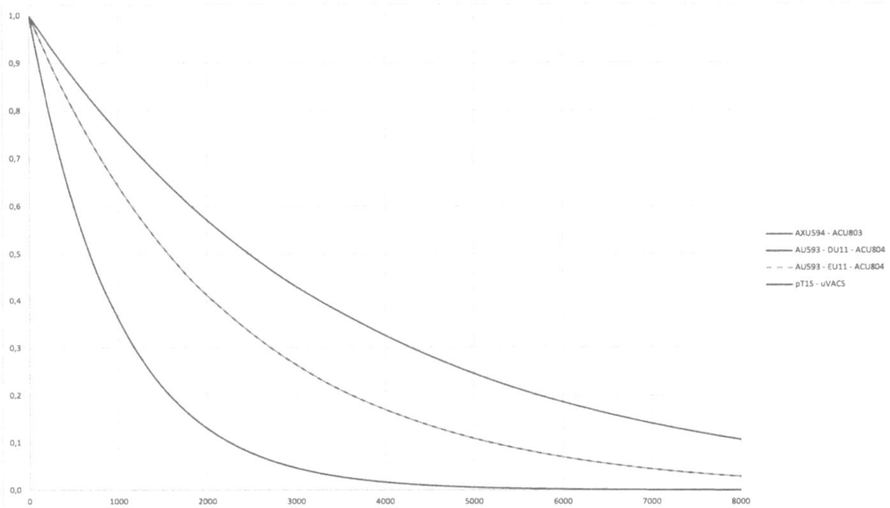


**Fig. 6.** Reliability functions of the three paths in Lvr1 and of the one in the tramway case study, over the mission time horizon.

**Table 2.** Computation time comparison between monolithic and compositional Fault-Flow evaluation for the four paths. The relative speed-up is defined as $t_{\text{mono}}/t_{\text{comp}}$.

| Path | Time (ms) | | Speed-up | #EN |
|---|---|---|---|---|
| | Monolithic | Compositional | | |
| AXU594-ACU803 | 15052 | 10596 | 1.42 | 2 |
| AU593-DU11-ACU804 | 16147 | 8254 | 1.96 | 4 |
| AU593-EU11-ACU804 | 17541 | 9188 | 1.91 | 4 |
| uT1S-uVACS | 23947 | 14468 | 1.66 | 11 |

**Computation Time.** Table 2 compares the computation times of the monolithic and compositional workflows for each path. The results show that the compositional workflow reduces computation time on all evaluated paths, with speed-up generally increasing with path length. The speed-up arises both because elementary network models are smaller than the monolithic interlocking model and because their analysis has been parallelized on a 4-core CPU. Notably, uT1S-uVACS shows a lower speed-up than two of the other tests. This happens because it contains a larger number of elementary network paths to parallelize, and it hits a performance bottleneck on the 4-core CPU used in this analysis; ideally, a CPU with a matching core count would provide a greater speed-up. The FaultFlow state-space complexity grows super-linearly with model size [3], so decomposition yields disproportionate reductions in evaluation time. A notable consequence of parallelisation is that the total compositional evaluation time is bounded by the slowest elementary network rather than by their sum, making it nearly constant ($\approx$ 11 s evaluated as average of Table 2 values) regardless of path length. The decomposition step itself adds only 1 s of overhead [16], which is negligible relative to the FaultFlow evaluation time. This contrasts with the monolithic workflow, whose evaluation time grows with the number of components in the path.

When the pre-computed library of Sect. 4.6 is used instead of invoking FaultFlow at evaluation time, the composition step via rbdEngine completes in 23–46 ms regardless of path length, reducing total compositional time to well under one second.

**Discussion.** The agreement between compositional and monolithic reliability values confirms that the virtualisation rule correctly partitions physical components across elementary networks, satisfying the independence assumption of Proposition 1, and that the product-form composition introduces no approximation error.

The computation time results suggest that the methodology scales favourably with path length: the compositional time grows approximately linearly in the number of elementary networks comprising the path, whereas monolithic evaluation time grows at a higher rate. This is consistent with the theoretical complexity analysis in Sect. 4 and supports the practical applicability of the approach for online or repeated reliability assessments during the RAMS lifecycle, as required by EN 50126 [7]. The larger the interlocking and longer the path is, the more convenient the compositional approach is over the monolithic one.

## 6 Conclusion

This paper has presented a framework for path-level reliability evaluation in railway interlocking systems, that includes two alternative procedures, namely a monolithic combination procedure that takes into account an entire station layout and its elements, and a compositional procedure obtained by repurposing an established network decomposition technique originally developed for qualitative safety verification by model checking. The latter decomposes a given interlocking layout into elementary networks, evaluates their reliability independently and composes the results into an exact path reliability function via a product-form composition rule. The key enabler of correctness is the virtualization rule: considering only once shared elements and identifying virtual elements that do not contribute to reliability computation, the independence assumption underlying fault tree composition is satisfied. The correctness of the composition rule rests on the well-formedness of the interlocking and on the correctness of the decomposition algorithm, and holds under the liberal fail-safe policy adopted in Sect. 4.2: we provided a proof sketch of the equivalence of monolithic and compositional evaluation.

The framework was validated on two different interlocking layouts, evaluating a total of four representative paths of increasing length by both the monolithic and the compositional procedure. The two workflows produced identical reliability functions across the full 8000-hour analysis horizon, and the compositional evaluation was faster on every tested path, with speedup growing with path length until parallelism saturates the available CPU cores. When the pre-computed library of Sect. 4.6 is used in place of on-the-fly FaultFlow invocations, the composition step completes in under one second regardless of path length.

*Future Work.* Several directions extend the present work naturally. First, the gain in computation time of the compositional approach w.r.t. the monolithic one has been measured on interlockings of a rather limited size. We observed that the gain grows with station size: we plan a more extensive test campaign to quantify this scaling behaviour more precisely. Also, the case study assumes exponential failure distributions for all three component families, consistent with the standard EN 50126 parametrisation; FaultFlow supports non-Markovian distributions as well, so relaxing this assumption is technically feasible but has not been investigated yet. Given the flexibility of our approach, a more sophisticated model for point reliability could also be accommodated.

Second, the framework targets reliability, but availability, the long-term proportion of time in which a path is operational, is the metric most directly required by EN 50126 for infrastructure planning and maintenance scheduling; extending the composition rule to steady-state availability is a near-term priority.

Third, the framework evaluates a single path at a time and does not address alternative paths sharing the same source and destination. Combining their reliabilities is not straightforward, since shared components introduce stochastic dependence between paths; handling this case is an important next step toward station-level dependability assessment. The addition of extra safety mechanisms, such as *flank protection*, is common in the design of interlocking systems to enforce safety also in the case in which trains do not strictly respect signals, due to a driver's misbehaviour or accidental inability to brake [25]. These mechanisms assume a maximum pre-determined distance to be travelled by the offending train, and are based on conditioning the movement authority for a route to the availability of a sufficient buffer area after a signal. The area is protected by (extra) signals or points that are external to the protected route.

These mechanisms are not considered in this paper, but their presence would impact on the reliability of a route (or a path), since they add other physical elements that may fail, and they are not compatible with the liberal fail-safe policy assumed in this paper. Extending the methodology to flank-protected networks is a natural next step, building on the compositional safety verification results of [16].

**Acknowledgements.** This study was carried out within the MUR PRIN 2022 PNRR P2022A492B project ADVENTURE (ADVancEd iNtegraTed evalUation of Railway systEms) and received funding from the European Union NextGeneration-EU (PIANO NAZIONALE DI RIPRESA E RESILIENZA (PNRR) – MISSIONE 4, COMPONENTE 2, INVESTIMENTO 1.4 – D.D. 1033 17/06/2022, CN00000023. This manuscript reflects only the authors' views and opinions, neither the European Union nor the European Commission can be considered responsible for them.

## References

1. Arnold, F., Belinfante, A., Van der Berg, F., Guck, D., Stoelinga, M.: DFTCalc: A Tool for Efficient Fault Tree Analysis. In: Bitsch, F., Guiochet, J., Kaâniche, M. (eds.) SAFECOMP 2013. LNCS, vol. 8153, pp. 293–301. Springer, Heidelberg (2013). https://doi.org/10.1007/978-3-642-40793-2_27
2. Budde, C.E., Ruijters, E., Stoelinga, M.: The Dynamic Fault Tree Rare Event Simulator. In: Gribaudo, M., Jansen, D.N., Remke, A. (eds.) QEST 2020. LNCS, vol. 12289, pp. 233–238. Springer, Cham (2020). https://doi.org/10.1007/978-3-030-59854-9_17
3. Carnevali, L., Cerboni, S., Montecchi, L., Vicario, E.: Faultflow: an MDE library for dependability evaluation of component-based systems. IEEE Trans. Dependable Sec. Comput. 1–18 (2025). https://doi.org/10.1109/TDSC.2025.3532340
4. Carnevali, L., Cerboni, S., Picano, B., Scommegna, L., Vicario, E.: An observation metamodel for dependability tools. In: 2024 19th European Dependable Computing Conference (EDCC), pp. 169–172. IEEE (2024)
5. Carnevali, L., et al.: Data-driven synthesis of stochastic fault trees for proactive maintenance of railway vehicles. In: International Conference on Formal Methods for Industrial Critical Systems, pp. 162–181. Springer, Cham (2025). https://doi.org/10.1007/978-3-032-00942-5_9
6. Carnevali, L., Giandomenico, F.D., Fantechi, A., Gnesi, S., Gori, G.: Quantitative dependability evaluation of train control systems in presence of uncertainty: A systematic literature review. IEEE Trans. Intell. Transp. Syst. **26**(4), 4298–4314 (2025). https://doi.org/10.1109/TITS.2025.3530112
7. CENELEC: EN 50126-1: Railway Applications – The Specification and Demonstration of Reliability, Availability, Maintainability and Safety (RAMS) - Part 1: Generic RAMS Process (2017)
8. Chiacchio, F., Aizpurua, J.I., Compagno, L., D'Urso, D.: SHyFTOO, an object-oriented monte carlo simulation library for the modeling of stochastic hybrid fault tree automaton. Expert Syst. Appl. **146**, 113139 (2020)

9. Cimatti, A., Giunchiglia, F., Mongardi, G., Romano, D., Torielli, F., Traverso, P.: Model Checking Safety Critical Software with SPIN: an Application to a Railway Interlocking System. In: Ehrenberger, W. (ed.) SAFECOMP 1998. LNCS, vol. 1516, pp. 284–293. Springer, Heidelberg (1998). https://doi.org/10.1007/3-540-49646-7_22
10. Fantechi, A., Gori, G., Haxthausen, A.E.: Compositional Model Checking of Railway Interlocking Systems Featuring Flank Protection. In: ter Beek, M.H., Dutilleul, S.C., Lecomte, T. (eds.) Proceedings of the 6th International Conference on Reliability, Safety, and Security of Railway Systems: Modelling, Analysis, Verification, and Certification (RSSRail'25), Pisa, Italy, November 26–28, 2025. Lecture Notes in Computer Science, vol. 16236. Springer, Cham (2025). https://doi.org/10.1007/978-3-032-10762-6_21
11. Haxthausen, A.E., Fantechi, A., Gori, G., Petersen, S.A., Mikkelsen, Ó.K.: Scaling model checking of railway interlocking systems by safe automated decomposition. European Transport Research Review **18**(1), 38 (2026). https://doi.org/10.1186/s12544-026-00798-1
12. Ferrari, A., Magnani, G., Grasso, D., Fantechi, A.: Model Checking Interlocking Control Tables. In: FORMS/FORMAT 2010 - Formal Methods for Automation and Safety in Railway and Automotive Systems, pp. 107–115. Springer, Cham (2010). https://doi.org/10.1007/978-3-642-14261-1_11
13. Gori, G., Papini, M., Fantechi, A.: Efficient Reliability Block Diagram Evaluation Through Improved Algorithms and Parallel Computing. Appl. Sci. **15**(21), 11397 (2025)
14. Haxthausen, A.E., Le Bliguet, M., Kjær, A.A.: Modelling and Verification of Relay Interlocking Systems. In: Choppy, C., Sokolsky, O. (eds.) Monterey Workshop 2008. LNCS, vol. 6028, pp. 141–153. Springer, Heidelberg (2010). https://doi.org/10.1007/978-3-642-12566-9_8
15. Haxthausen, A.E., Fantechi, A., Gori, G.: Decomposing the verification of interlocking system. In: Haxthausen, A.E., Huang, W., Roggenbach, M. (eds.) Applicable Formal Methods for Safe Industrial Products - Essays Dedicated to Jan Peleska on the Occasion of His 65th Birthday. Lecture Notes in Computer Science, vol. 14165. https://doi.org/10.1007/978-3-031-40132-9_7
16. Haxthausen, A.E., Fantechi, A., Gori, G., Mikkelsen, Ó.K., Petersen, S.: Automated compositional verification of interlocking systems. In: Milius, B., Dutilleul, S.C., Lecomte, T. (eds.) Proceedings of the 5th International Conference on Reliability, Safety, and Security of Railway Systems: Modelling, Analysis, Verification, and Certification (RSSRail'23). Lecture Notes in Computer Science, vol. 14198, pp. 146–164. Springer, Cham (2023). https://doi.org/10.1007/978-3-031-43366-5_9
17. Haxthausen, A.E., Fantechi, A.: Compositional verification of railway interlocking systems. Form. Asp. Comput. **35**(1) (2023). https://doi.org/10.1145/3549736
18. Hidirov, S., Guler, H.: Reliability, availability and maintainability analyses for railway infrastructure management. Struct. Infrastruct. Eng. **15**(9), 1221–1233 (2019)
19. James, P., Möller, F., Nguyen, H.N., Roggenbach, M., Schneider, S., Treharne, H.: Decomposing scheme plans to manage verification complexity. In: FORMS/FORMAT 2014 - 10th Symposium on Formal Methods for Automation and Safety in Railway and Automotive Systems, pp. 210–220. Institute for Traffic Safety and Automation Engineering, Technische Universität Braunschweig (2014)
20. Limbrée, C., Cappart, Q., Pecheur, C., Tonetta, S.: Verification of Railway Interlocking - Compositional Approach with OCRA. In: Lecomte, T., Pinger, R., Romanovsky, A. (eds.) RSSRail 2016. LNCS, vol. 9707, pp. 134–149. Springer, Cham (2016). https://doi.org/10.1007/978-3-319-33951-1_10

21. Macchi, M., Garetti, M., Centrone, D., Fumagalli, L., Pavirani, G.P.: Maintenance management of railway infrastructures based on reliability analysis. Reliab. Eng. Syst. Safety **104**, 71–83 (2012)
22. Macedo, H.D., Fantechi, A., Haxthausen, A.E.: Compositional Verification of Multi-station Interlocking Systems. In: Margaria, T., Steffen, B. (eds.) ISoLA 2016. LNCS, vol. 9953, pp. 279–293. Springer, Cham (2016). https://doi.org/10.1007/978-3-319-47169-3_20
23. Macedo, H.D., Fantechi, A., Haxthausen, A.E.: Compositional Model Checking of Interlocking Systems for Lines with Multiple Stations. In: Barrett, C., Davies, M., Kahsai, T. (eds.) NFM 2017. LNCS, vol. 10227, pp. 146–162. Springer, Cham (2017). https://doi.org/10.1007/978-3-319-57288-8_11
24. Meier-Hirmer, C., Riboulet, G., Sourget, F., Roussignol, M.: Maintenance optimization for a system with a gamma deterioration process and intervention delay: application to track maintenance. Proc. Inst. Mech. Eng. Part O J. Risk Reliab. **223**(3), 189–198 (2009)
25. Pachl, J.: Railway Operation and Control, VTD Rail Publishing (2002)
26. Ruijters, E., Stoelinga, M.: Fault tree analysis: A survey of the state-of-the-art in modeling, analysis and tools. Comput. Sci. Rev. **15**, 29–62 (2015)
27. Trivedi, K.S., Sahner, R.: SHARPE at the age of twenty two. ACM SIGMETRICS Perf. Eval. Rev. **36**(4), 52–57 (2009)
28. Volk, M., Sher, F., Katoen, J.P., Stoelinga, M.: SAFEST: Fault tree analysis via probabilistic model checking. In: Annual Reliability and Maintainability Symposium (RAMS), pp. 1–7. IEEE (2024)
29. Vu, L.H., Haxthausen, A.E., Peleska, J.: A Domain-Specific Language for Railway Interlocking Systems. In: Schnieder, E., Tarnai, G. (eds.) FORMS/FORMAT 2014–10th Symposium on Formal Methods for Automation and Safety in Railway and Automotive Systems, pp. 200–209. Technische Universität Braunschweig, Institute for Traffic Safety and Automation Engineering (2014)
30. Weik, N., Volk, M., Katoen, J.P., Nießen, N.: DFT modeling approach for operational risk assessment of railway infrastructure. Int. J. Softw. Tools Technol. Transfer **24**(3), 331–350 (2022)
31. Winter, K.: Symbolic Model Checking for Interlocking Systems. In: Flammini, F. (ed.) Railway safety, reliability, and security: technologies and systems engineering, IGI Global (2012)

# Lazy Three-Way Model Merging in Cinco Cloud: A Lattice-Theoretic Approach

Jonas Schürmann(✉) and Bernhard Steffen

Chair for Programming Systems, TU Dortmund University, Dortmund, Germany
jonas.schuermann@cs.tu-dortmund.de, steffen@cs.tu-dortmund.de

**Abstract.** In this paper, we transfer our operation-based lazy merging approach to the snapshot-based three-way merge setting of Git. Central to this transfer is the introduction of conflicts as first-class citizens, enabling an elegant lattice-theoretic modeling framework in which merges are defined as suprema. Our extension makes Git's traditional text-based merging approach syntax-sensitive, thereby extending its applicability to the versioning of graphical models. Cinco Cloud, our Git-powered collaborative workbench for graphical modeling, produces merges with strong mathematical guarantees, while conflicts are visualized, shared, and then resolved collaboratively.

**Keywords:** Lattice Theory · Version Control Systems · Conflict Tolerance · Model-Driven Development

## 1 Introduction

In model-driven engineering, as in traditional software engineering, complex projects and large-team collaboration are commonplace. This leads to a need for advanced version control features: Participants want to develop features and improvements in parallel without restrictions on when or where they can edit model files. They also want to work in isolation to avoid constant interruptions from peers. As we seek to include non-technical domain experts directly into the development process [21], the usability and comprehensibility of such features is particularly important to us.

### 1.1 The Git Version Control System

Git[1] and similar version control systems (VCSs) provide these collaboration capabilities with branching & merging workflows. Developers can branch off their own version of the software at any point, bring in their own changes step by step, and later integrate their contribution back into the mainline. While this enables unrestricted parallel work in isolation of others, it creates the difficult problem of software merging: As divergent versions evolve, contradicting

[1] https://git-scm.com/


P. Gorm Larsen and K. Y. Rozier (Eds.): FMICS 2026, LNCS 16967, pp. 118–136, 2027.
https://doi.org/10.1007/978-3-032-36849-2_7

changes can accumulate on the different branches, resulting in merge conflicts when branches are integrated [3]. The resolution of these conflicts poses a major challenge in VCSs [13], sometimes characterized as an "integration hell" [17], which limits the feasibility of the approach and leads to the exclusion of non-technical participants.

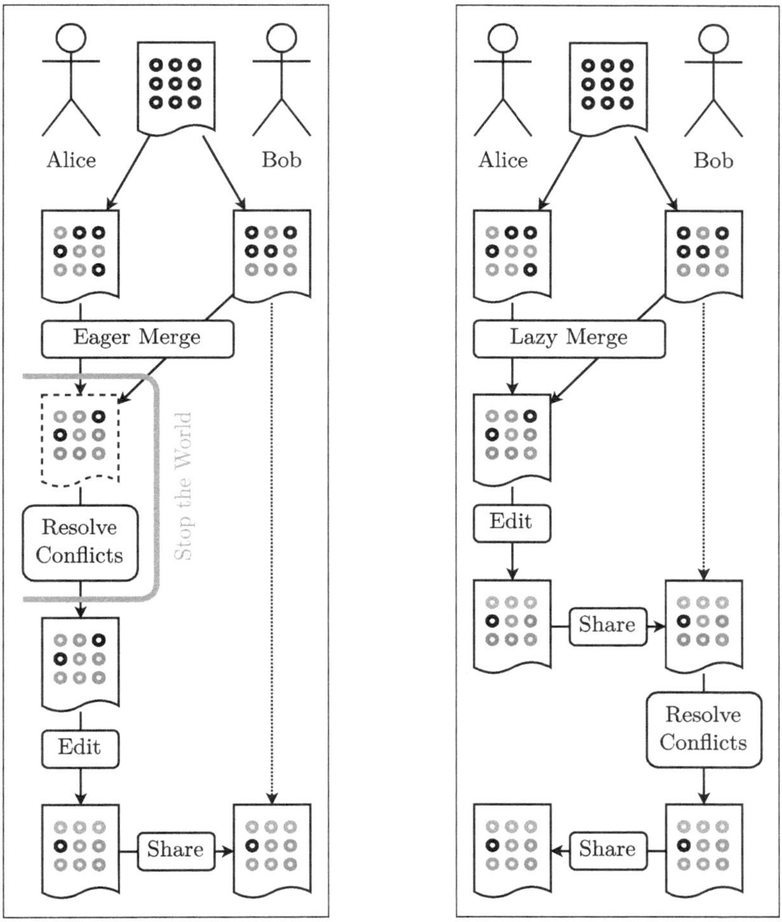


(a) Eager merging concept (b) Lazy merging concept

**Fig. 1.** Eager merging requires immediate conflict resolution; lazy merging defers the decision

One major limitation of Git is what we call the eager merging strategy (cf. Fig. 1a). As Git cannot represent conflicts within the repository, every merge conflict that arises must be resolved immediately, by whichever participant first encounters it. Git marks conflicts with textual conflict markers that break the language syntax, and will only continue to operate when they are all resolved [7]. This behavior enforces conflict-free versions, but it also interrupts participants in their work, forcing a mental context switch between development and integration. Worse, participants are completely isolated during conflict resolution, leading to unilateral decisions that misinterpret and dismiss the other participants' work.

Another limitation is Git's unstructured merging approach: It is entirely unaware of language syntax, treating all files as lists of text lines — compatible with any plaintext syntax, but at the cost of merge accuracy. Since text lines have no persistent identity, code movement must be inferred via error-prone heuristics. Moreover, line-level granularity cannot disambiguate concurrent changes within the same line, producing false-positive conflicts and verbose conflict markers [7]. In our context of model-driven engineering, the unstructured approach is particularly concerning: Participants edit models in an intuitive graphical DSL, but merge conflicts force them to suddenly work in the plaintext serialization. While this shift is already challenging for technical experts, it cannot be expected of non-technical stakeholders.

Finally, Git's conceptual design lacks a stringent formal model. Merge algorithms like `diff3` apply text-based matching in a best-effort approach, in which formal analysis has already uncovered a number of problems [9]. Generally, it is difficult to establish strong correctness properties for Git's merge algorithm, and the behavior in complex edge cases is hard to predict or understand.

### 1.2 The Cinco Cloud Graphical Language Workbench

Cinco Cloud [2] (formerly Cinco) is our open-source[2] language workbench for the rapid development of domain-specific languages, editors, and code generators [16]. Over its evolution, it has cycled through several collaboration models: plain Git with plaintext conflict resolution [16], the Model Compare and Merge (MCaM) framework with syntax-aware graphical merging [23], and Pyro's live collaboration workspace which traded versioning power for effortless always-online collaboration [25]. With the recent migration to Eclipse Theia[3] and Eclipse GLSP[4], Git was reinstated for versioning [2] — but without further integration, merging and conflict resolution remained painful, just as they were at the outset.

### 1.3 Contribution

Our main contribution is the transfer of the existing lazy merge algorithm [18] from a fine-grained operation-based data model into Git's three-way merge setting, which only exposes snapshots of the three input revisions. This yields the *lazy three-way merge* algorithm, which is included with the current mainline version of Cinco Cloud. We pursue a lattice-theoretic approach where every merge

2 https://gitlab.com/scce/cinco-projects/cinco-editor/
3 https://theia-ide.org/
4 https://eclipse.dev/glsp/

is a supremum — complete, minimal, and unique with regard to the contributions that are included. This requires conflicts to be represented explicitly. A supremum is complete and must retain every contribution, whereas resolving a conflict discards all but the chosen one. A resolved merge would therefore no longer be the supremum of its inputs. We therefore make conflicts first-class citizens in the Git repository, where they are preserved, shared, and collaboratively resolved rather than forcing developers to resolve them immediately in isolation. On this foundation, our structured merge algorithm matches changes to their precise structural position — and delivers the full lattice guarantees: Git merges become associative, commutative, and idempotent, making merge order irrelevant and repeated merges harmless. Additionally, our lattice-theoretic approach guarantees a robust conflict representation within graphical models: Complex conflicts involving more than two edits are properly aggregated, and if concurrent resolutions contradict each other, they are folded back into a regular conflict. First-class conflicts only deliver value if the entire development environment recognizes them — we therefore present a *conflict-tolerant architecture* for Cinco Cloud that propagates lazy merging's in-repository conflict representation through the entire toolchain, from the VCS to the graphical editor.

Section 2 describes the conflict-tolerant workbench architecture. Section 3 introduces the lazy merging concept and its formal foundations. Section 4 develops the lazy three-way merge algorithm. Section 5 discusses related work before Section 6 concludes the paper.

## 2 Conflict-Tolerant Workbench Architecture

The following conflict-tolerant architecture lays the foundation for lazy merging, ensuring conflicts are consistently addressed throughout the development environment. The entire architecture is implemented generically so that it applies automatically to any domain-specific graphical language built with Cinco Cloud. Fig. 2 shows how we extended Cinco Cloud to:

1. visualize and interact with conflicts in the graphical editor,
2. add a conflict representation to the abstract syntax of graphical languages,
3. render and manipulate conflicts in a projection, and
4. integrate lazy merging as a custom merge driver in Git.

① First, we created conflict visualizations in the graphical Cinco languages. We developed a syntax extension that adds conflict marker nodes, additional edge connectors, and control elements for conflict resolution. Fig. 3 shows a screenshot of the conflict visualization in action. The example shows a scenario in the WebStory language, a graphical Cinco DSL for modeling point-and-click adventures that generates playable web applications. Players navigate between screens by clicking on designated areas; transitions connect these clickable areas to the next screen and to other logical elements such as variable assignments and conditionals.

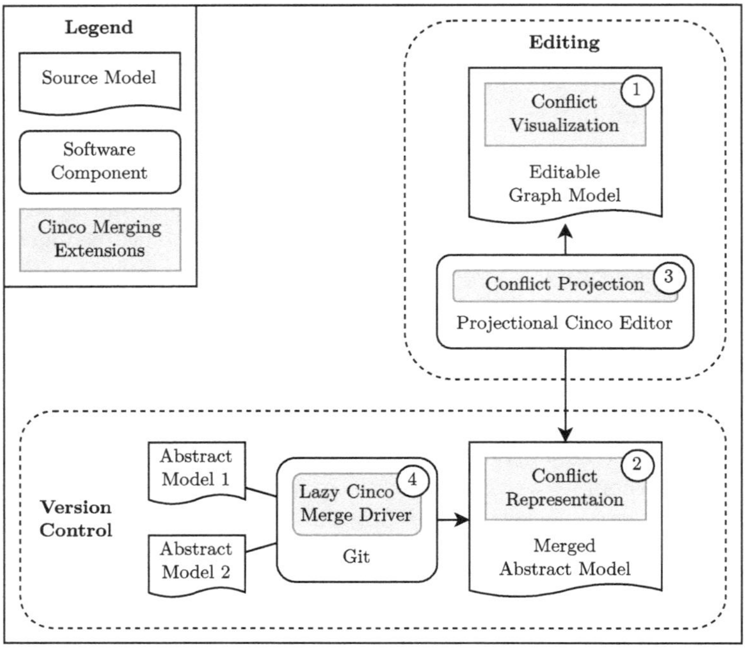


**Fig. 2.** Cinco Cloud's conflict-tolerant architecture

The conflict marker on the top transition $t_1$ indicates a three-way edit conflict in the transition's target screen. Three participants each moved the target to a different screen concurrently; after merging all contributions, the conflict encompasses all three options. The conflict marker connects $t_1$ to each candidate screen and offers a checkmark button per option to resolve the conflict by selection. Alternatively, the edge endpoint can be dragged to an entirely different screen to resolve with a new target.

The ghost icon on the bottom transition $t_2$ indicates that one participant edited the transition (e.g., by reconnecting it) while another deleted it concurrently. Within the conflict marker, two buttons allow the participant to either restore the transition to keep the edit or finalize the deletion.

These graphical visualizations and resolution proposals are produced by the Cinco editor interpreting the property-level conflicts in the abstract syntax. For each conflict, the editor selects a suitable rendering and the interactions that resolve it: An abstract conflict in a transition's target-ID property turns into selectable edge candidates, while an edit/delete marker becomes a ghost indicator proposing to restore or delete the transition. The same mechanism yields custom-tailored visualizations and interactions for any representable conflict type, fostering understanding and facilitating conflict resolution.

② Next, we added structured conflict representations to the abstract syntax of graphical languages to recognize conflicts programmatically and store them

**Fig. 3.** The Cinco editor visualizes conflicts: a three-way edit conflict in the top transition $t_1$ and an edit/delete conflict in bottom transition $t_2$

on-disk. Listing 1.1 shows the abstract representation of the conflicts visualized in Fig. 3; comments annotate the candidate screens with the names $s_3$, $s_4$, and $s_5$, under which Fig. 3 traces the evolution of this conflict. While the conflict-free `sourceID` property of $t_1$ is a plain string, the `choice` object in `targetID` represents a three-way edit conflict with its available options, and `isGhost` set to true on $t_2$ marks an edit/delete conflict. Since the abstract syntax captures structure rather than visual display, a simple representation best supports programmatic access and mergeability. We chose a fine-grained representation that breaks down conflicts to the atomic properties of syntax elements. The syntax extension is purely additive: conflict-free model files remain unchanged.

③ The projectional Cinco editor is then extended for conflict editing, connecting the abstract conflict representations to graphical visualizations. First, the render pipeline translates the abstract conflict representations into graph-based visualizations with the aforementioned graphical syntax extension. Second, we developed additional event handlers for the Cinco editor to process conflict resolution actions such as choosing a conflict option or restoring/deleting a ghost element. Existing event handlers were adapted for compatibility with conflicts, e.g., reconnecting an edge now resolves source or target conflicts. The conflict-tolerant editor allows participants to freely edit graph models independent of existing conflicts. Projectional editing is fundamental to lazy merging, as it allows for unique identifiers and easy programmatic access in the abstract syntax, while

**Listing 1.1.** Conflict representation in the abstract syntax

```
const t1 = {
    id: "59d7",
    type: "webstory:transition",
    sourceID: "24ef",
    targetID: {
        tag: "choice",
        options: [
            "22e9", // s3
            "dd9b", // s4
            "afb2"  // s5
        ]
    }
}

const t2 = {
    id: "e96c",
    type: "webstory:transition",
    sourceID: "24ef",
    targetID: "afb2", // s5
    isGhost: true
}
```

allowing for comprehensible visualizations and easy interactions in the graphical syntax.

④ Finally, we implemented a custom Git merge driver for lazy merging. Whenever Git performs a three-way merge — e.g., merging branches, rebasing, or reverting — it calls our lazy merge driver instead of its line-based heuristic. Our lazy merge driver can operate on the abstract syntax of model files, match syntax elements by their unique identifiers, and realize our merge semantics for value sets. It returns the lazily merged model file to Git and always indicates that no conflict occurred, regardless of whether new conflicts appeared in the abstract syntax. Git will therefore never abort merges for conflicts and happily commit the conflict representations to the repository. Thus, Git becomes conflict-tolerant: Conflicts are preserved, shared, and can be resolved collaboratively. As Git no longer reports conflicts in model files, the workbench takes over the responsibility of surfacing them: In addition to the visualization in the graphical editor, we plan to report outstanding conflicts through Cinco Cloud's model validation system.

The conflict-tolerant architecture is implemented end to end in the current mainline version of Cinco Cloud, presently restricted to a subset of the syntax of Cinco languages. We trialed the implementation in a hands-on workshop in which participants explored conflict-tolerant collaboration along a guided scenario, merging concurrent contributions to a shared WebStory model and resolving the resulting conflicts collaboratively. After introducing our existing lazy merging concept in Section 3, we will specify the exact algorithm for lazy three-way merging in Section 4.

## 3 The Lazy Merging Concept

To address the limitations of eager and unstructured merging, we previously developed lazy merging, an abstract versioning concept. Rooted in lattice theory, it performs accurate structured merging on the abstract syntax and introduces a robust language-integrated conflict representation.

Fig. 1b demonstrates how lazy merging, in contrast to the eager approach, allows participants to continue working in the presence of conflicts, share their progress, and resolve conflicts collaboratively. The conflict representation captures all concurrent contributions, ensuring every opinion is reflected in the merged documents. Participants are no longer interrupted by conflicts; instead, they can discuss the changes, wait for more information, and then deliberately choose when to resolve them. This prevents premature unilateral decisions, which tend to overlook others' contributions and introduce downstream errors. Additionally, conflicts are preserved in the version history, keeping decisions traceable and auditable at any point in the future [18].

The foundation of lazy merging is the causal order of edit operations, following the partial *happened-before* order of events within the distributed collaboration system [12]. This order is captured in two data structures: the full repository-wide causal order of operations, and the set of localized causal orders for each syntax element. Ordered by set inclusion — with set union as the join — both form a lattice, connected by a homomorphic projection [18]. The full repository-wide causality order is not relevant here, as we keep Git's conceptual model of version history. But the localized causality orders representing the current state of syntax elements are the foundation for lazy three-way merging, bringing conflict tolerance to Git.

Fig. 4 shows how the localized causality order for the target of $t_1$ evolves across four versions. Each version contains the partial order of all edit operations that were applied to the target of $t_1$ up to that point. Every new edit operation is appended at the bottom of the causal order and connected to all previously alive assignments, overwriting their values. An operation can thus only overwrite assignments already present in its own causal history; assignments made concurrently lie outside that history and remain untouched. The current valuation of the syntax element is determined by the values of the maximal elements of the causality order (i.e., the assignments that have not been overwritten). In the figure, these alive operations are highlighted white, while the overwritten, dead operations are grayed out. A single value indicates a conflict-free syntax element, while multiple values represent the different options of a conflict.

The evolution starts at the common ancestor $V_0$, which already contains a conflict: Two participants concurrently overwrote the initial target assignment, leaving two alive operations, so the target of $t_1$ ranges over the two values $s_2$

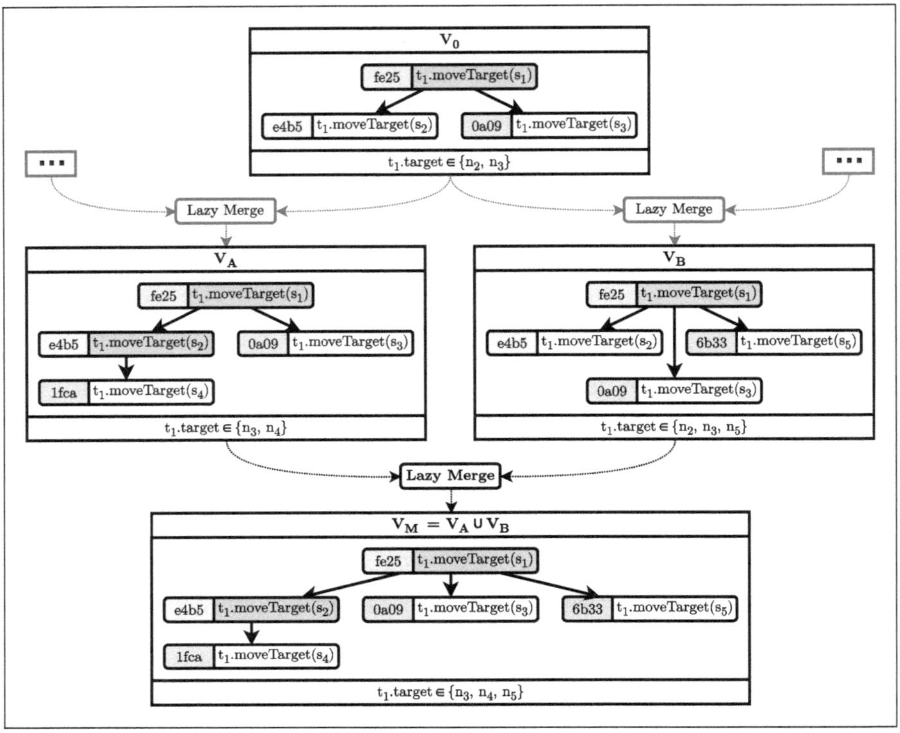


**Fig. 4.** Evolution of the localized causality order for the target of $t_1$, where white operations are alive and gray operations are dead

and $s_3$. From there, $V_A$ and $V_B$ each merge in edit operations from concurrent branches. $V_A$ incorporates an operation whose author had only seen the assignment of $s_2$; it therefore overwrites just that assignment, replacing the option $s_2$ with $s_4$. $V_B$ instead receives an operation that was created concurrently to both existing options and thus only overwrites the initial assignment, adding $s_5$ as a third option alongside $s_2$ and $s_3$.

Merging two versions simply means taking the union of their causality orders. The final lazy merge therefore combines all five operations into $V_M = V_A \cup V_B$, where the assignments of $s_3$, $s_4$, and $s_5$ remain maximal. The target of $t_1$ now carries a three-way conflict between these values — precisely the version that the conflict-tolerant editor visualizes in Fig. 3.

The key insight is that a merge, defined as the union of the causality orders, is precisely their supremum in this lattice. This immediately gives merges a number of strong correctness properties: Merges are unique by construction, complete, and minimal. They are efficiently and unambiguously computed, guaranteed to include all concurrent contributions and exclude any extraneous artifacts. Particularly, complex conflicts are properly aggregated in a minimal form. As resolution decisions are modeled with regular assignments, they are concurrency-safe as well: Contradicting resolution decisions result in a regular conflict when they are merged. Additionally, the algebraic properties of suprema hold, making merges associative, commutative, and idempotent. Thus, merge order is irrelevant and repeated merges pose no problem [18].

There are three main challenges for the practical adoption of lazy merging in collaborative development environments:

1. Almost none of the currently popular VCSs provide in-repository conflict representations. Eager merging is the norm, and the resolution of all conflicts during merging is expected.
2. The introduction of language-integrated conflict representation creates pervasive changes in the core language syntax. This necessitates conflict tolerance support within the whole development environment, from the VCS up to the editor.
3. While lazy merging follows an operation-based approach, current VCSs are usually built on a snapshot-based model and three-way merging. The operation-based approach provides direct access to the causality order of operations, whereas a snapshot-based approach requires inferring it by differencing versions.

Cinco Cloud's conflict-tolerant architecture (cf. Section 2) already addresses challenges one and two, and the next section will address challenge three.

## 4 Lazy Three-Way Merging

In this section, we describe the transfer of our operation-based lazy merging algorithm to Git's snapshot-based three-way merging. Our lazy merging approach offers direct access to the fine-grained causal history of edit operations, but Git presents a different setting: For every merge, it only provides three snapshots of a given file: version A, version B, and the greatest common ancestor. To apply lazy merging, we infer the operation causality by differencing these versions. This is a two-step process: First, versions are aligned to match syntax elements, then merging semantics select the appropriate values. We show that lazy merging naturally extends to this setting: The merge computed from the three snapshots alone coincides with the operation-based lazy merge of the underlying causality orders, thereby inheriting its strong formal guarantees.

Git's unstructured merge approach must first align the version snapshots to infer changes. It heuristically attempts to match unchanged text lines across the three snapshots, to then detect insertions and deletions between them [9]. Because text lines are not unique and can move anywhere, this content-based analysis is difficult and can only approximate the actual edits. Mismatched changes cannot be merged correctly in the next step; they will be applied in the wrong place and can mask merge conflicts.

Lazy merging's structured approach completely sidesteps the alignment problem. In Cinco languages, every syntax element carries a unique identifier that persists throughout its evolution. As lazy merging operates on the abstract syntax, it can perfectly match syntax elements with these identifiers across all three version snapshots. Change detection is accurate and efficient, and closely resembles the actual edits that have happened between the versions.

Turning to value selection, Git's approach is straightforward. Because version snapshots are conflict-free, there are at most three values that need to be compared. The values that are different from the greatest common ancestor are selected, and if both version A and B have changed the value, a conflict is detected.

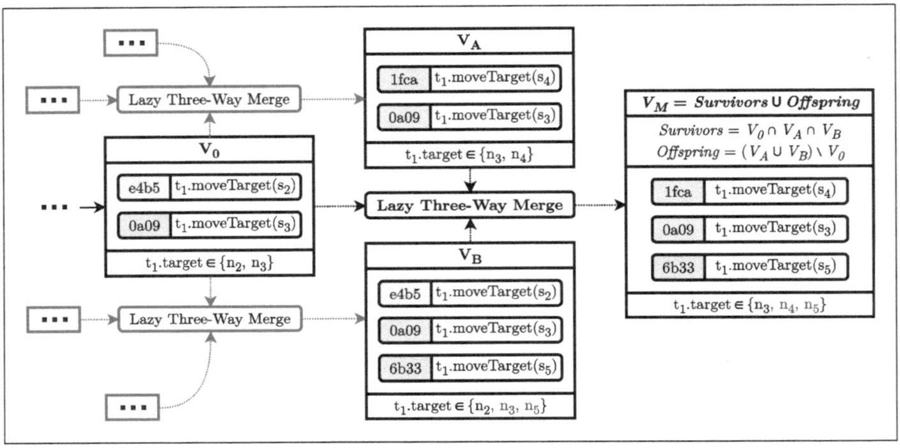


**Fig. 5.** Lazy three-way merge on snapshots showing only the current valuation

For lazy merging, the value selection from matched changes is more challenging. As all version snapshots can contain conflicts, each snapshot contributes a whole set of assignments from which a selection must be made. In the formal model, every assignment carries a unique identifier under which it is stored in the snapshot; concurrent assignments thus remain distinguishable even if they assign identical values. For readability, we refer to assignments by their assigned values $s_2, \ldots, s_5$, which are unique in our example; all set operations, however, compare assignments by their identifiers. Fig. 5 shows the previous operation-based merge of Fig. 4 in a three-way merge setting for all changes to the upper transition target. Compared to the operation-based merge, the causal history of edits is missing: Denoting the causality order underlying a version $V_X$ by $O_X$, every snapshot only shows its maximal assignments: $V_X = \max(O_X)$. From only $V_A$, $V_B$, and $V_0$, we must determine the maximal assignments of the hypothetical causal order underlying the merged snapshot $V_M$. A simple union of the value sets would be incorrect, as it would include edits that have already been overwritten.

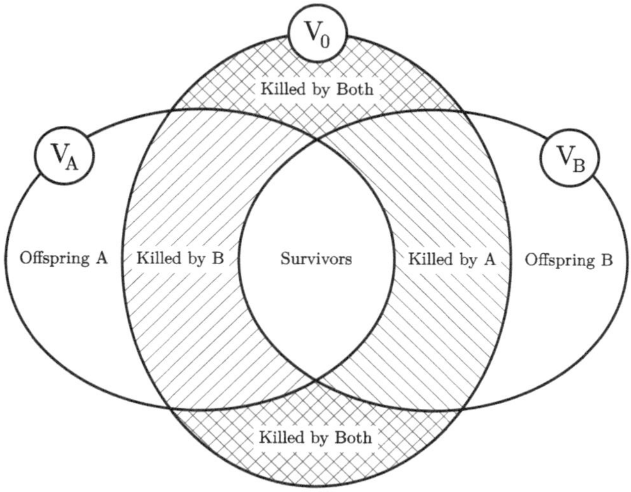


**Fig. 6.** Value selection in the lazy three-way merge: white areas are included in $V_M$; hatched areas are discarded

To merge two development lines, operation-based lazy merging forms the union of the two causality orders: $V_M = \max(O_A \cup O_B)$. A value can only be maximal in this union if it was already maximal in at least one of the two original orders — that is, if it appears in $V_A$ or $V_B$. Hence the merge result is a subset of $V_A \cup V_B$, determined by the greatest common ancestor $V_0$.

For values already present in $V_0$, there are two possibilities: If they were kept in both $V_A$ and $V_B$, they survive into the merge result.

$$\mathit{Survivors} = V_0 \cap V_A \cap V_B \tag{1}$$

But if either version is missing a value from $V_0$, that version must have overwritten it with a causally later assignment — otherwise the value would still be maximal. A value absent from either $V_A$ or $V_B$ is therefore not maximal in the merged order and is omitted.

$$\mathit{Killed} = V_0 \setminus (V_A \cap V_B) \tag{2}$$

Every value in $V_0$ falls into exactly one of these two categories. The remaining values in $V_A$ and $V_B$ were newly introduced and are selected as offspring.

$$\mathit{Offspring} = (V_A \cup V_B) \setminus V_0 \tag{3}$$

Since these values were absent from $V_0$, neither version could have overwritten them — a version can only supersede values it received from the common ancestor. Furthermore, $V_A \setminus V_0$ and $V_B \setminus V_0$ are disjoint: Since assignments are compared by their identifiers, the same fresh assignment cannot be independently introduced by both versions. The final merge result consists of *Survivors* and *Offspring*.

$$V_M = \mathit{Survivors} \cup \mathit{Offspring} = (V_0 \cap V_A \cap V_B) \cup ((V_A \cup V_B) \setminus V_0) \qquad (4)$$

Fig. 6 illustrates the intersections between the three versions in a Venn diagram. The following theorem casts this derivation into a formal statement:

**Theorem 1.** *Let $O_A$ and $O_B$ be the causality orders of a syntax element's property in two versions to be merged, such that their shared history is exactly the causality order of the greatest common ancestor: $O_0 = O_A \cap O_B$. Then the lazy three-way merge of the snapshots $V_X = \max(O_X)$ coincides with the operation-based lazy merge:*

$$V_M = \mathit{Survivors} \cup \mathit{Offspring} = \max(O_A \cup O_B)$$

*Proof.* Every assignment of $O_A \cup O_B$ lies in the shared history $O_0$, in $O_A \setminus O_0$, or in $O_B \setminus O_0$. An assignment of $O_0$ is maximal in $O_A \cup O_B$ if and only if it is overwritten in neither $O_A$ nor $O_B$, i.e., if and only if it lies in $V_A \cap V_B$; as $O_0 \subseteq O_A$, it then also lies in $V_0$. These assignments are exactly the *Survivors*. An assignment of $O_A \setminus O_0$ never occurs in $O_B$, and as operations only overwrite assignments of their own history, it remains unaffected by $O_B$: It is maximal in $O_A \cup O_B$ if and only if it lies in $V_A$ — and, being absent from $O_0$, it never lies in $V_0$. Together with the symmetric case for $O_B \setminus O_0$, these assignments are exactly the *Offspring*.

Lazy three-way merging therefore computes exactly the operation-based lazy merge of the underlying causality orders, and Theorem 6 of [18] carries over: Merges are complete, minimal, and unique, as well as associative, commutative, and idempotent.

Our implementation deviates from this formal account in one respect: Its snapshots store assignments by their values alone, without unique assignment identifiers — the `options` in Listing 1.1 contain the identifiers of the candidate screens themselves. An assignment identifier names a unique event in the causal history, but Git also constructs snapshots through operations that replay or invert changes, such as reverts, rebases, and cherry-picks. These operations cannot mint fresh identifiers and would instead duplicate or resurrect existing ones, silently embedding a false history in the snapshot. To avoid this problem, we keep assignment identifiers out of the persisted representation and compare assignments by value. The price is that concurrent assignments of identical values collapse into a single assignment, which can lead to edits being silently discarded without a conflict. Theorem 1 hence carries over to the implementation only under the additional assumption that concurrent assignments to the same property assign distinct values.

## 5 Related Work

In this section, we will first survey existing VCS implementations that introduce a structured model for first-class conflicts and subsequently present approaches that model merges as mathematical operations. There are five VCSs that introduce conflict tolerance but lack the rigor of a mathematical foundation. Then there are the lattice-theoretic conflict-free replicated data types (CRDTs), which model merges as suprema but do not consider first-class conflicts. To our knowledge, only the Pijul VCS combines a foundation from category theory with first-class conflicts, yet it is limited by an unstructured merging approach.

### 5.1 Conflict-Tolerant Versioning

Wieland et al. implemented a conflict-tolerant model VCS to uncover disagreements and align team members' intentions by embedding conflicts directly in the model. This in-model representation defers the resolution decision, and a structured process guides the collaborative resolution of conflicts. Their empirical study evaluated the practical impact and examined the role of human behavior in resolving merge conflicts [22]. However, conflicts are represented textually within annotation nodes rather than as first-class model objects, which complicates the aggregation of complex conflicts. Completeness and minimality of the conflict representation are only discussed informally, supported by empirical interviews. Furthermore, it is unclear how the system handles concurrency for conflict resolution decisions, i.e. what happens if participants concurrently select contradictory resolutions.

The Jujutsu VCS[5] introduces conflict-tolerant merging by storing all involved file trees with the merge commit, from which conflicts are computed on-the-fly rather than stored as first-class objects. Deferred resolution means merging is always possible and conflicts can be shared. Conflict tolerance is vital for the expressive history editing capabilities that Jujutsu provides, as it prevents recursive merge conflicts during rebasing. After repeated merges, the list of file trees is minimized by algebraic simplification. The conflict algebra can represent complex merges that result in multi-value conflicts [24]. Like Git, Jujutsu is limited by its unstructured merge approach that performs line-based differencing on plaintext files. Its content-based heuristic matching algorithm can produce inaccurate results and mismatched changes.

Exelmans et al. propose an operation-based versioning approach for blended modeling that records not only edits but also the bi-directional change propagations between concrete and abstract syntax. The operation deltas are arranged in a partial order that captures causal and contextual dependencies. The version history is conflict-tolerant by allowing conflicting deltas to coexist. Conflicts are resolved by generating maximal conflict-free subsets of the history and selecting the correct resolution from a side-by-side comparison. Thus, conflicts do not block ongoing work and can be resolved collaboratively [8]. However, conflicts

[5] https://www.jj-vcs.dev/

are not first-class objects in the models themselves, so it is unclear which version of the model the editor presents and whether editing can continue in the presence of conflicts. Furthermore, the paper only demonstrates resolution of a single conflict; as the number of possible resolutions grows exponentially with the number of conflicts, side-by-side comparison becomes infeasible at scale.

Brosch et al. represent and visualize conflicts with UML profiles, a standard extension mechanism supported by regular UML editors. Conflicts are first-class objects in the UML models, allowing for a comprehensible notation and deferred resolution. Their UML profile provides extensive visualizations for various conflict types and perspectives on the conflicted state [4,6]. However, the robustness of the conflict representation is unclear. It is not evident whether complex conflicts involving more than two overlapping changes at the same location can be aggregated, or whether they instead generate a conflict for every pair of overlapping changes. Similarly, the approach does not address what happens when concurrent conflict resolutions produce inconsistent results.

The AMOR model VCS [1] features a synchronous protocol for collaborative conflict resolution. During merging, a collaborative conflict resolver allows participants to cooperatively edit the merge result. Edits are immediately replicated to everyone else, and once all participants accept the result, the model can be committed [5]. Their approach avoids unilateral decision making, but conflicts do not become first-class objects. Particularly, conflicts still need to be resolved eagerly during merging and cannot be deferred.

### 5.2 Lattice-Theoretic Approaches

The concept of conflict-free replicated data types (CRDTs) leverages lattice theory to build a formal framework for a wide selection of eventually consistent data structures. They operate in a decentralized manner without coordination, and by modeling their evolution as a monotonic semilattice, merges are established as suprema to prove eventual consistency [20]. They are commonly used to realize distributed collaboration systems that exhibit implicit branching from working offline, such as local-first software [11]. While their use of a lattice structure and supremum-as-merge is similar to our approach, our goals differ. CRDTs provide general-purpose building blocks for any domain where eventual consistency is beneficial, while our approach focuses on what lattice theory means for versioning and conflict resolution. Since we showed that operation-based lazy merging forms a CRDT [18], it follows that through lazy three-way merging, Git itself becomes a state-based CRDT as well. The Patchwork project[6] is currently developing a prototype that explores CRDT-based versioning. Although Patchwork inherently realizes a structured merging approach, they have no support for conflict tolerance or collaborative conflict resolution — lattice theory is used solely to guarantee eventual consistency.

[6] https://www.inkandswitch.com/project/patchwork/

### 5.3 Category-Theoretic Approaches

Pijul[7] is a distributed VCS for plaintext files that derives its internal representation and merge algorithm from a categorical theory of patches that makes an argument analogous to ours. Instead of suprema in lattices they use pushouts in categories, but they arrive at the same conclusion that conflict tolerance is the key enabler for complete, minimal, and unique merges [15]. Thus, Pijul integrates a robust conflict representation and theoretically guarantees the same mathematical properties [14]. However, their approach is limited by an unstructured, character-level merging approach that necessitates the same content-based change matching heuristics as in standard Git and inherits the same problems of mismatched edits. Furthermore, while the in-repository representation of conflicts is formally sound and robust, the serialization into plaintext files cannot faithfully represent it.

## 6 Conclusion

We addressed the challenge of bringing high-quality, collaborative merging to graphical model-driven development built on Git. Git's merging approach leaves developers in a difficult position: conflicts interrupt their work, force immediate decisions without the full picture, and cannot be shared or discussed with peers. For graphical modeling tools, the situation is even worse, as conflicts surface in raw text rather than the familiar visual representation. We closed this gap with two contributions.

First, we developed the lazy three-way merge algorithm, which transfers lazy merging into Git's snapshot-based three-way merge model. Lazy merging's strong formal properties were previously established for operation-based VCSs: merges are complete, minimal, and unique by construction, and as suprema they are also associative, commutative, and idempotent — meaning merge order is irrelevant and repeated merges pose no problem. A robust conflict representation aggregates complex conflicts and makes conflict resolution concurrency-safe. We show that these properties carry over to the three-way merge setting, without access to the full operation history. Furthermore, by replacing Git's line-based heuristics with structured, syntax-aware merging on unique persistent identifiers, changes are accurately matched across snapshots, eliminating false-positive conflicts and misapplied edits.

Second, we presented a conflict-tolerant workbench architecture for Cinco Cloud that supports collaborative work throughout the entire development process, enabling conflicts to be resolved just-in-time as needed. Rather than forcing an immediate resolution, conflicts are preserved in the repository, visualized in the graphical editor, and available to the whole team. Participants can continue working, discuss the conflicting changes with their peers, and resolve them deliberately when the time is right. Together, these contributions establish formally

[7] https://pijul.org/

grounded, collaborative model-driven development on Git — with strong correctness guarantees and a workflow that treats conflicts as transparent, shared artifacts rather than hard blockers.

Conflict-tolerant merging and editing, as presented in this paper, form the foundation of a broader approach to conflict management. Building on this, we have developed a concept for the lazy interpretation of conflicted programs, enabling a test-driven approach to conflict resolution. Lazy interpretation lets developers inspect runtime behavior prior to committing to resolution decisions, and enables continuous integration in the presence of unresolved conflicts [19]. Beyond interpretation, conflict tolerance can be extended to further development tools — such as build systems, static analyzers, and type checkers — enabling a fully conflict-tolerant toolchain in which conflicts do not interrupt any stage of the development process.

For future work, we envision replacing Git with a custom VCS based on conflict-free replicated data types (CRDTs) such as Automerge[8] [10]. CRDTs provide formally grounded, eventually consistent data structures and naturally support lazy merging, as their join operation aligns with our merge semantics. By combining state- and operation-based replication, they enable both expressive versioning and real-time collaboration without the mismatch of Git's snapshot model. This overcomes limitations of Git, where merge anomalies can silently drop edits due to the absence of unique operation identifiers. In fact, by assigning identifiers to each edit, CRDTs (i) reliably distinguish concurrent edits even if they yield identical values, preventing accidental loss of changes, (ii) preserve a complete and traceable history of operations, strengthening correctness guarantees, and (iii) enable fine-grained conflict analysis by making causal relationships between edits explicit. Overall, this foundation supports a simpler and more transparent system for collaborative workflows.

## References

1. Altmanninger, K., Kappel, G., Kusel, A., Retschitzegger, W., Seidl, M., Schwinger, W., Wimmer, M.: AMOR – Towards adaptable model versioning. In: 1st Int. Workshop on Model Co-Evolution and Consistency Management, in conjunction with Models'08 (2008), http://hdl.handle.net/20.500.12708/52277
2. Bainczyk, A., Busch, D., Krumrey, M., Mitwalli, D.S., Schürmann, J., Tagoukeng Dongmo, J., Steffen, B.: CINCO Cloud: A holistic approach for web-based language-driven engineering. In: Margaria, T., Steffen, B. (eds.) Leveraging Applications of Formal Methods, Verification and Validation. Software Engineering. pp. 407–425. Springer Nature Switzerland, Cham (2022). https://doi.org/10.1007/978-3-031-19756-7_23
3. Barr, E.T., Bird, C., Rigby, P.C., Hindle, A., German, D.M., Devanbu, P.: Cohesive and isolated development with branches. In: de Lara, J., Zisman, A. (eds.) Fundamental Approaches to Software Engineering. pp. 316–331. Springer Berlin Heidelberg, Berlin, Heidelberg (2012). https://doi.org/10.1007/978-3-642-28872-2_22

[8] https://automerge.org/

4. Brosch, P., Kargl, H., Langer, P., Seidl, M., Wieland, K., Wimmer, M., Kappel, G.: Conflicts as first-class entities: A UML profile for model versioning. In: Models in Software Engineering, pp. 184–193. Springer Berlin Heidelberg (2011). https://doi.org/10.1007/978-3-642-21210-9_18
5. Brosch, P., Seidl, M., Wieland, K., Wimmer, M., Langer, P.: We can work it out: Collaborative conflict resolution in model versioning. In: Wagner, I., Tellioğlu, H., Balka, E., Simone, C., Ciolfi, L. (eds.) ECSCW 2009. pp. 207–214. Springer London, London (2009). https://doi.org/10.1007/978-1-84882-854-4_12
6. Brosch, P., Seidl, M., Wimmer, M., Kappel, G.: Conflict visualization for evolving UML models. The Journal of Object Technology **11**(3), 2:1 (2012). https://doi.org/10.5381/jot.2012.11.3.a2
7. Chacon, S., Straub, B.: Pro Git. The expert's voice, Apress (2014), https://git-scm.com/book/en/v2
8. Exelmans, J., Pietron, J., Raschke, A., Vangheluwe, H., Tichy, M.: Optimistic versioning for conflict-tolerant collaborative blended modeling. In: FPVM 2022: 2nd International Workshop on Foundations and Practice of Visual Modeling, July 4–8, 2022, Nantes, France. vol. 3250, pp. 1–12 (2022), https://hdl.handle.net/10067/1935730151162165141
9. Khanna, S., Kunal, K., Pierce, B.C.: A formal investigation of diff3. In: Arvind, V., Prasad, S. (eds.) FSTTCS 2007: Foundations of Software Technology and Theoretical Computer Science. pp. 485–496. Springer Berlin Heidelberg, Berlin, Heidelberg (2007). https://doi.org/10.1007/978-3-540-77050-3_40
10. Kleppmann, M., Beresford, A.R.: A conflict-free replicated JSON datatype. IEEE Transactions on Parallel and Distributed Systems **28**(10), 2733–2746 (Oct 2017). https://doi.org/10.1109/TPDS.2017.2697382
11. Kleppmann, M., Wiggins, A., van Hardenberg, P., McGranaghan, M.: Local-first software: You own your data, in spite of the cloud. In: Proceedings of the 2019 ACM SIGPLAN International Symposium on New Ideas, New Paradigms, and Reflections on Programming and Software. p. 154–178. Onward! 2019, Association for Computing Machinery, New York, NY, USA (2019). https://doi.org/10.1145/3359591.3359737
12. Lamport, L.: Time, clocks, and the ordering of events in a distributed system. Commun. ACM **21**(7), 558–565 (Jul 1978). https://doi.org/10.1145/359545.359563
13. Mens, T.: A state-of-the-art survey on software merging. Software Engineering, IEEE Transactions on **28**, 449–462 (Jun 2002). https://doi.org/10.1109/TSE.2002.1000449
14. Meunier, P.É.: Pijul — model. https://pijul.org/model/
15. Mimram, S., Giusto, C.D.: A categorical theory of patches. Electronic Notes in Theoretical Computer Science **298**, 283–307 (Nov 2013). https://doi.org/10.1016/j.entcs.2013.09.018
16. Naujokat, S., Lybecait, M., Kopetzki, D., Steffen, B.: CINCO: A simplicity-driven approach to full generation of domain-specific graphical modeling tools. Software Tools for Technology Transfer **20**(3), 327–354 (2017). https://doi.org/10.1007/s10009-017-0453-6
17. Phillips, S., Sillito, J., Walker, R.: Branching and merging: An investigation into current version control practices. In: Proceedings of the 4th International Workshop on Cooperative and Human Aspects of Software Engineering. ACM (May 2011). https://doi.org/10.1145/1984642.1984645
18. Schürmann, J., Steffen, B.: Lazy merging: From a potential of universes to a universe of potentials. Electronic Communications of the EASST **Volume 82: 11th**

**International Symposium on Leveraging Applications of Formal Methods** (2023). https://doi.org/10.14279/tuj.eceasst.82.1226
19. Schürmann, J., Steffen, B.: Towards test-driven conflict resolution. Electronic Communications of the EASST **84** (Nov 2025). https://doi.org/10.14279/eceasst.v84.2677, https://eceasst.org/index.php/eceasst/article/view/2677
20. Shapiro, M., Preguiça, N., Baquero, C., Zawirski, M.: A comprehensive study of convergent and commutative replicated data types. Research Report RR-7506, Inria – Centre Paris-Rocquencourt ; INRIA (Jan 2011), https://hal.inria.fr/inria-00555588
21. Steffen, B., Gossen, F., Naujokat, S., Margaria, T.: Language-driven engineering: From general-purpose to purpose-specific languages. In: Steffen, B., Woeginger, G. (eds.) Computing and Software Science: State of the Art and Perspectives, Lecture Notes in Computer Science, vol. 10000. Springer (2019). https://doi.org/10.1007/978-3-319-91908-9_17
22. Wieland, K., Langer, P., Seidl, M., Wimmer, M., Kappel, G.: Turning conflicts into collaboration. Computer Supported Cooperative Work (CSCW) **22**(2-3), 181–240 (Sep 2012). https://doi.org/10.1007/s10606-012-9172-4
23. Wirkner, D.: Merge-Strategien für Graphmodelle am Beispiel von jABC und Git. Diploma thesis, TU Dortmund (Feb 2015), [Unpublished manuscript]
24. von Zweigbergk, M., et al.: Conflicts - Jujutsu docs. https://docs.jj-vcs.dev/v0.13.0/technical/conflicts/
25. Zweihoff, P., Naujokat, S., Steffen, B.: Pyro: Generating domain-specific collaborative online modeling environments. In: Proc. of the 22nd Int. Conf. on Fundamental Approaches to Software Engineering (FASE 2019) (2019). https://doi.org/10.1007/978-3-030-16722-6_6

# Domain-Specific 3D Visualization of Formal Models

Max Richter(✉) and Fabian Vu(✉)

Faculty of Mathematics and Natural Science, Institute of Computer Science, Heinrich Heine University Düsseldorf, Universitätsstr. 1, 40225 Düsseldorf, Germany
maric118@uni-duesseldorf.de, fabian.vu@hhu.de

**Abstract.** Visualization plays a crucial role in making formal models accessible and comprehensible. While existing tools such as VisB enable 2D visualizations of formal models in ProB, many application domains involve behaviors that are difficult to express adequately in two dimensions. This paper presents VisB-3D, an extension of VisB for ProB2-UI, which introduces interactive three-dimensional visualizations for state-based formal models. The approach integrates a Unity-based WebGL visualization with ProB2-UI. A 3D glue file format specifies how the state of a formal model is mapped to 3D models, materials, transformations, and camera placement. This feature enables domain experts to explore and manipulate model states directly through intuitive 3D scenes. Finally, we demonstrate how 3D visualizations can enhance understanding, validation, and debugging of formal specifications through case studies, highlighting their main advantages over 2D visualizations.

**Keywords:** Visualization · 3D · Formal Methods · Validation · Unity · WebGL

## 1 Introduction and Motivation

Formal methods provide rigorous techniques for specifying, verifying and validating complex systems. State-based formal methods, such as Classical B [1], Event-B [2], Z [25], and TLA$^+$ [16,17], enable the precise description of system states and transitions. Tools like ProB [18] provide model checking and animation of formal models, allowing users to explore and reason about the system behaviors.

However, the complexity of formal models can make them challenging to understand, especially for domain experts who may not be familiar with formal notations. Domain-specific visualizations tools like VisB [32] in ProB can bridge this gap, making systems created with formal methods more accessible and comprehensible for domain experts. VisB allows users to create 2D visualizations using a glue file format that maps a model's state to a scalable vector graphics (SVG) image [32]. VisB [32] has been successfully applied in various domains, including railway [10,11,20], automotive [19,27] and aviation [9,28].


P. Gorm Larsen and K. Y. Rozier (Eds.): FMICS 2026, LNCS 16967, pp. 137–153, 2027.
https://doi.org/10.1007/978-3-032-36849-2_8

The majority of existing visualization tools for formal methods focus on 2D representations, such as PVSio-Web [31], JeB [33], and Brama [24]. These tools can be applied effectively to certain domains, but may fall short in adequately expressing behaviors and structures that are inherently three-dimensional (3D). For instance, interactions with landscape characteristics, volumetric phenomena and flight trajectories often involve spatial relationships and movements that are better captured in 3D [6]. In industrial applications, many case studies require 3D visualizations to represent the real world more precisely. For instance, 3D visualizations are used to create virtual prototypes, i.e., digital twins in different domains, such as aviation [22], automotive [5,34], and production [7]. Furthermore, physical AI, including autonomous systems such as self-driving vehicles and drones, is playing an increasingly important role. These systems interact in a real-world 3D environment, making 3D representation particularly crucial for their analysis. For such systems, the Robot Operating System (ROS) [23] provides 3D visualization capabilities with Gazebo[1], enabling developers to interact and monitor with complex robotic environments. While ROS operates independently of formal methods, there is a need to apply formal methods to robotic systems and visualize the system and its environment in 3D [4,8,28]. More generally, 3D visualizations can provide a more realistic and intuitive understanding of the system's dynamics and help identify potential issues that may not be apparent in 2D views.

This paper introduces VisB-3D, an extension of the VisB visualization tool for ProB2-UI [3], which enables dynamic *interactive* 3D visualizations of state-based formal models. To achieve this, VisB-3D uses the Unity Engine [2] to render and transform 3D objects based on the 3D model hierarchy defined in a glTF [12] format file. VisB-3D is synchronized with the current state of the formal model loaded in ProB2-UI and is available via a web browser. As a result, the 3D visualization represents the current state of the formal model, while interactions with the formal model are possible via both the 3D visualization in the web browser and ProB2-UI. We present VisB-3D's core concepts based on a 3D traffic light visualization. To demonstrate the importance of 3D visualization features, we consider a drone case study in a 3D environment.

The goals while developing VisB-3D are:

1. *Improve the comprehensibility of formal models with three-dimensional components.* VisB-3D aims to provide domain experts and developers with intuitive 3D visual representations that facilitate understanding of system states and behaviors without requiring detailed knowledge of the underlying formal notation.
2. *Support validation of systems operating in three-dimensional environments.* In particular, the approach aims to represent spatial relationships, movements, and interactions that are difficult to express adequately in traditional 2D visualizations. As a result, VisB-3D aims to help users inspect model behavior,

[1] Website of Gazebo: https://gazebosim.org.
[2] Website of the Unity Engine: https://unity.com/.

identify inconsistencies, and better understand the consequences of modelling decisions.
3. *Preserve the flexibility and language independence of* VisB. The visualization should remain separated from the formal model, enabling domain-specific visualizations without modifying the underlying specification and without restricting the approach to a specific formalism.

*Background.* ProB [18] is an animator, constraint solver, and model checker for formal models that are developed with various formalisms, including Classical B, Event-B, Z, TLA$^{+}$, and Alloy. ProB supports various validation techniques, including animation, trace replay, simulation [30], and visualization [15,21,32]. In particular, there are many types of visualizations in ProB, such as visualization of state spaces [15,21] and visualization of formal models from a domain-specific view with VisB [32]. This work focuses on VisB [32], which supports a *model-view controller pattern*, i.e., the formal model and visualization work independently from each other and are linked through a *glue file*. Yet VisB only supports 2D visualizations with SVG. Almost all validation and verification features in ProB are available through ProB2-UI [3], which is a graphical user interface (GUI) built on top of ProB.

## 2 Principles and Architecture

This section presents the design and implementation of VisB-3D. Figure 1 shows an overview of VisB-3D's architecture, which builds on VisB's [32] existing architecture for 2D visualizations in SVG.

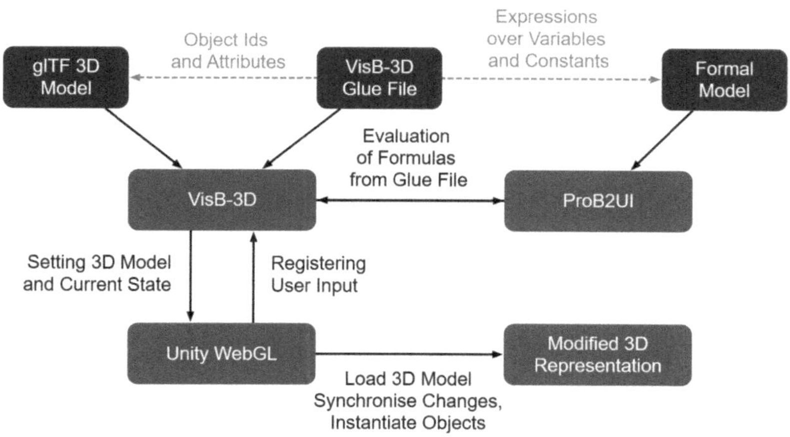


**Fig. 1.** Architecture of VisB-3D, adopting the existing architecture of VisB [32] for 2D Visualizations

The architecture of VisB-3D follows the Model-View-Controller (MVC) pattern, ensuring a clear separation of concerns between the formal model, the visualization, and the interaction logic. The formal model loaded in ProB2-UI defines the system state and behavior. The Unity WebGL-based 3D representation acts as the *view*, rendering the current state of the formal model as an interactive scene. The *controller* is realized through the glue file and the VisB-3D logic, which links the 3D visualization to the formal model by forwarding user interactions and causing the appearance of the 3D objects to change based on the machine's current state.

Similar to VisB visualizations in 2D, the user needs to load a formal model in ProB, and a visualization in the newly implemented VisB-3D component. As for VisB 2D visualizations, VisB-3D separates the formal model from its visual representation, allowing domain experts to create and modify visualizations without altering the underlying formal model. The user can also interact with the formal model via the animator or the 3D visualization. Within our implementation, events are registered and accordingly performed in both the formal model and the visualization.

More precisely, the 3D visualization is loaded in a web browser using Unity WebGL. Instead of a 3D library like three.js [3] or Babylon.js [4], we use a 3D engine because it significantly simplifies the development process and provides a wide range of built-in features for 3D rendering and handling user interactions.

We use the glTF 3D format to represent 3D visualizations (replacing 2D visualizations in SVG in the existing architecture). glTF is a widely adopted standard for efficient transmission and runtime loading of 3D content, supporting features, such as meshes, materials, texture images and most importantly for our use case, node hierarchies. Due to the preservation of node hierarchies, runtime transformations can be applied to individual parts of a model, enabling complex animations and interactions. Furthermore, glTF is optimized for web applications, making it suitable for integration in a WebGL-based visualization. Furthermore, glTF models can be created and exported using most 3D modeling software, such as Blender [5], Autodesk Maya [6], and Substance 3D Painter [7].

### 2.1 Synchronizing Formal Model and 3D Visualization

The communication between the VisB-3D backend and the Unity WebGL visualization is depicted in Fig. 2. The Unity WebGL application is hosted on a web server and communicates with the backend through WebSockets. Since Unity cannot directly communicate with WebSockets, we use a JavaScript WebSocket client that runs in the browser and relays messages using a custom JavaScript plug-in.

This implementation provides real-time visualization updates in response to changes in the formal model. When the state of the formal model changes, the

[3] Website of three.js: https://threejs.org/.
[4] Website of Babylon.js: https://www.babylonjs.com/.
[5] Website of Blender: https://www.blender.org/.
[6] Website of Autodesk Maya: https://www.autodesk.com/products/maya/overview.
[7] Website of Substance 3D Painter: https://www.adobe.com/de/products/substance3d/apps/painter.html.

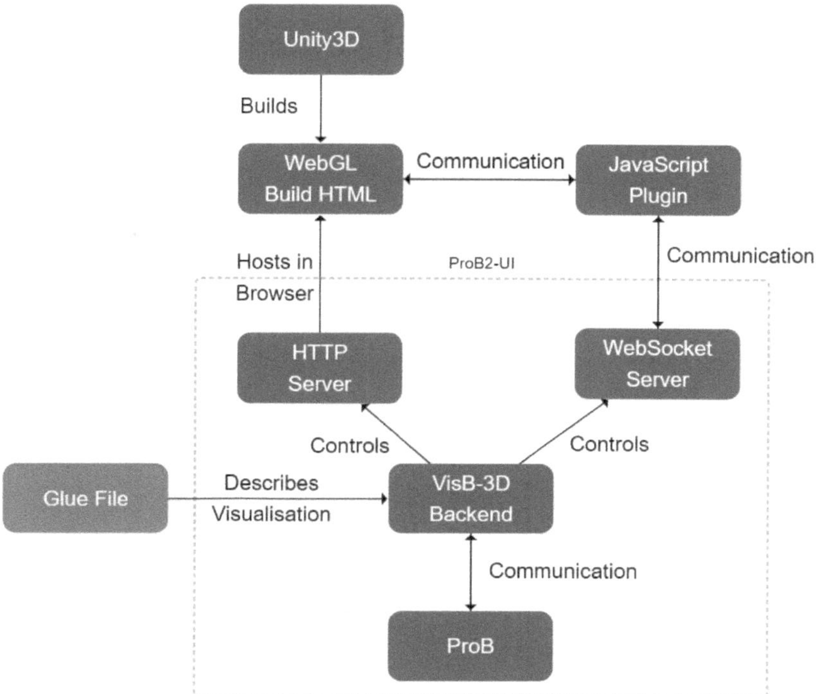


**Fig. 2.** The technical stack of VisB-3D, which facilitates the integration of a Unity WebGL visualization with the ProB2-UI backend. The WebGL build is hosted on a web server and communicates with the backend through WebSockets. The backend evaluates the glue file to update the visualization based on the state of the formal model.

backend evaluates the relevant B expressions defined in the glue file and sends the updated state information to the Unity application. The Unity application then processes this information to update the 3D scene accordingly, ensuring synchronization between the visualization and the underlying formal model. Similarly, user interactions in the Unity application can be sent back to the backend to trigger updates in the formal model, creating a bidirectional communication channel. As a result, domain experts can interact with the visualization and the formal model while seeing the effects of their interactions in real time.

Since the visualization is implemented in Unity, which has robust support for WebGL, it was more straightforward to deploy the visualization as a web application. However, this also means that the visualization cannot be directly embedded in the JavaFX-based ProB2-UI interface, due to the JavaFX WebKit's restrictions. Instead, we opted for a separate web application that is accessible via a web browser. This approach allows us to leverage the full capabilities of Unity for 3D rendering while still maintaining a connection to the ProB2-UI backend through WebSockets. Additionally, hosting the visualization as a web application makes it more accessible and easier to share with others, as it does not require users to install additional software beyond a web browser.

# 3 Linking 3D Visualization and Formal Model

This section presents how to link the 3D visualization in glTF and the formal model. There are three main aspects: (1) the update of the graphical 3D objects' appearances based on the state of the formal model, (2) the camera in the 3D visualization (which is also treated as a graphical 3D object), and (3) events performed through the 3D visualization.

**Fig. 3.** 3D Visualization for Traffic Light model with cars' traffic light in green and pedestrians' traffic light in red. Traffic Light 3D Model (https://skfb.ly/ovzFT) by Alt is licensed under CC BY 4.0 Attribution. City 3D Model (https://skfb.ly/py6HO) by golukumar is licensed under CC BY 4.0 Attribution.

## 3.1 Appearances of Graphical 3D Objects

The 3D glue file works similarly to the 2D glue file [32]. To describe the appearances of 3D graphical objects, one can define B expressions, which are then evaluated on the formal model by ProB. Afterward, the appearances change based on the evaluated results. Furthermore, it uses new attributes that inherently accommodate the additional properties of 3D objects, e.g. 3D transformations, materials and lighting. The 3D glue file also includes attributes for the instantiation of simple shapes, such as cubes and spheres, which one can use, e.g., to represent an arbitrary number of objects at runtime.

```
1 {"id":"traffic_light_cars_right",
2 "attr":"material-color",
3 "attr":"fill"
4 "value":"IF tl_cars=green THEN \"green\" ELSE \"black\"
     END"}
```

**Listing 1.** Example of VisB-3D item JSON format (line 3 in gray shows the difference of VisB in 2D compared to line 2)

Listing 1 shows an example of a VisB-3D item in the glue file in JSON format. Each VisB has three fields: the `id` field specifies the identifier of the graphical 3D object, the `attr` field indicates the attribute to be changed, and the `value` field contains an expression that evaluates to a value based on the current state of the formal model. Figure 3 shows a screenshot of the 3D visualization. Alternatively, VisB-3D also supports writing the 3D glue file in the `DEFINITIONS`. Instead of Listing 1, one could also write Listing 2 for the same effect.

```
VISB_SVG_UPDATES ==
  {rec('id': ''traffic_light_cars_right'',
       'material-color':
        IF tl_cars = green THEN ''green'' ELSE ''black''
           END)};
```

**Listing 2.** Example for VisB-3D DEF glue file

(a) First-person view from a car's perspective at the traffic light (b) First-person view from a pedestrian's perspective at the traffic light

**Fig. 4.** 3D visualization for Traffic Light model showing two different camera views. Same license as Fig. 3.

### 3.2 Camera in 3D Visualization

Using cameras, a user can view the 3D visualization from different angles and perspectives in VisB-3D. Technically, one can create multiple cameras as 3D objects using the 3D modelling software. Each camera can be configured with a specific position, rotation, and field of view to provide different views of the visualization. VisB-3D loads and manages all cameras and allows the user to switch between them using the user interface. For example, VisB-3D can provide a top-down view for an overview of the model, and a first-person view for a more realistic experience, as in Fig. 4, where the left image shows a first-person view from a car's perspective, and the right image shows a first-person view from a pedestrian's perspective at a traffic light. One can also set up a freely movable camera that a user can control using the mouse and keyboard to inspect the visualization from anywhere in real time. To accommodate models without predefined cameras, VisB-3D sets up a default camera when loading a 3D model. In the glue file, one can specify camera attributes, such as position and rotation. Listings 3 and 4 show examples of glue files setting the position of the default camera and another camera from the car's perspective in a 3D model.

```
{"id":"Camera", "attr":"x", "value":"10"},
{"id":"car_camera", "attr":"x", "value":"car_x"}
```

**Listing 3.** A VisB-3D JSON glue file whose contents describe the following: The x position of the default camera `Camera` and `car_camera` - a camera in the 3D model - is linked to the constant value 10 and the variable `car_x`, respectively.

```
VISB_SVG_UPDATES ==
    {rec('id': "Camera", x: 10, y: 12, z: 5),
     rec('id': "car_camera", x: car_x, y: car_y, z: car_z)
        };
```

**Listing 4.** A VisB-3D DEF glue file describing two cameras: Position of default camera `Camera` is linked to constant values (10, 12, 5), position of `car_camera` is linked to variables `car_x`, `car_y`, `car_z` in formal model.

### 3.3 Performing Events through 3D Visualization

Similar to VisB (in 2D), VisB-3D supports performing events in the formal model by interacting with the corresponding graphical 3D object. In particular, one can associate each 3D object with a specific event in the formal model, referred to as a VisB event. When a user clicks on such an object, ProB executes the corresponding event in the animator. All VisB events contain two fields: the `id` field specifying the identifier of the graphical 3D object, and the `event` field specifying the event to be executed on a click. An example of a VisB event for changing the cars' traffic light to green is shown in Listing 5.

```
{"id":"cars_green",
"event":"cars_g"}
```

**Listing 5.** Example of VisB-3D event in JSON format

The execution of events through the 3D visualization is tightly integrated with the synchronization mechanism described in Sect. 2.1. When a user triggers an event in the 3D scene, it is transmitted to the ProB2-UI backend via the established WebSocket connection. The backend executes the event on the formal model and computes the resulting state, which is then sent to the visualization to update the scene. This bidirectional communication ensures that interactions, event execution, and visualization updates remain fully synchronized.

## 4 Demonstration

This section demonstrates the capabilities of VisB-3D on the traffic light model introduced in Sect. 2 and a case study of a drone model. The traffic light model serves as a simple example to demonstrate how VisB-3D visualizes system states in 3D compared with 2D visualizations. In contrast, the drone model showcases the advantages of 3D visualizations for systems operating in 3D spaces. Furthermore, the drone case study demonstrates how 3D visualizations enhance understanding of formal models by providing intuitive, interactive representations of system behaviors.

### 4.1 Traffic Light

Section 3 already presented a traffic light case study from a technical perspective. Now, we demonstrate the advantages of 3D compared to 2D. Figure 5 shows the 3D visualization of the traffic light model using a simple glTF model. The visualization shows all possible states of the traffic light model, with the lights changing based on the formal model's current state. As a result, the traffic light's appearance changes dynamically as the formal model transitions between states.

Initially, the car and the pedestrian traffic lights are red, as shown in Fig. 5a. By clicking on the pedestrian traffic light in VisB-3D, the light changes from red to green, as shown in Fig. 5b. Clicking the pedestrian traffic light one more time changes it back to red (Fig. 5a). From Fig. 5a, one could also click on the car traffic light, where after the lights change from red to red and yellow (Fig. 5c), then to green (Fig. 5d), then to yellow (Fig. 5e), and finally to red again (Fig. 5a). This dynamic visualization allows users to easily understand the different states of the traffic light model and how they relate to one another.

A 2D visualization of a traffic light was already created in VisB using SVG (see Fig. 6). However, the 3D visualization in Fig. 5 provides a more realistic and intuitive representation of the traffic light model, showing the traffic light in a realistic street scene and better capturing that the formal model represents a real-world system consisting of two distinct traffic lights, one for car traffic and one for pedestrian traffic. For instance, Fig. 6 only shows the car and pedestrian traffic lights side by side, while Fig. 5 presents more clearly that the traffic lights

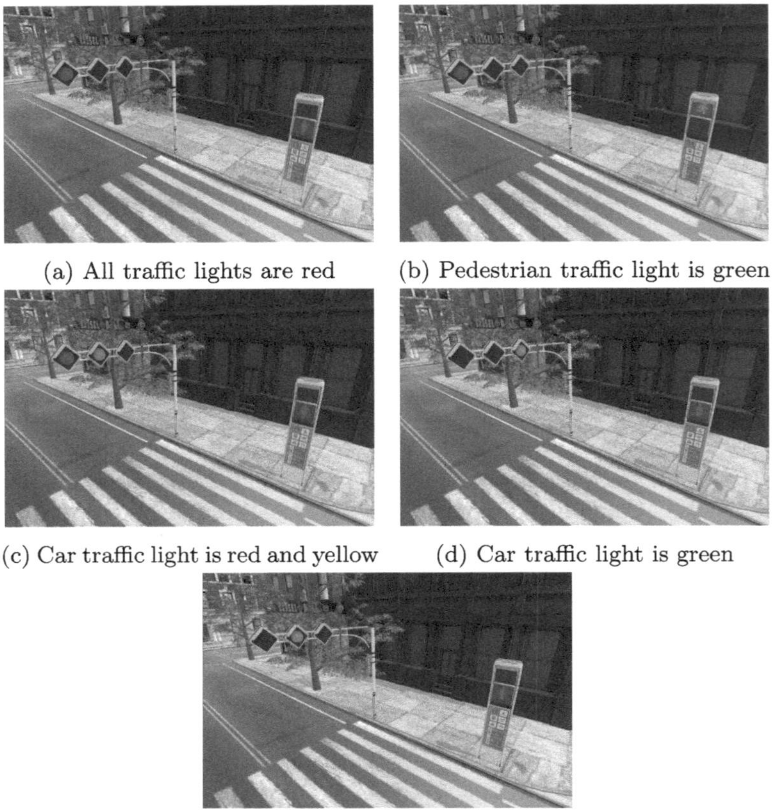

(a) All traffic lights are red

(b) Pedestrian traffic light is green

(c) Car traffic light is red and yellow

(d) Car traffic light is green

(e) Car traffic light is yellow

**Fig. 5.** 3D Visualization of Traffic Light model showing all possible allowed states using a simple glTF model of a traffic light in a street scene. The lights change based on the state of the formal model. Same license as Fig. 3.

are located on the same section of the road, meaning that cars and pedestrians might collide in case of an error.

While this example demonstrates the advantages of 3D visualizations over 2D, VisB-3D's strengths are more efficiently showcased with an inherently three-dimensional model.

### 4.2 Drone

The second case study is about a drone flying in a 3D room and avoiding obstacles. The formal model of the drone includes variables and constants representing the drone's current 3D position, detected obstacles, and the drone's size and sensor capabilities. Furthermore, the formal model includes events for changing

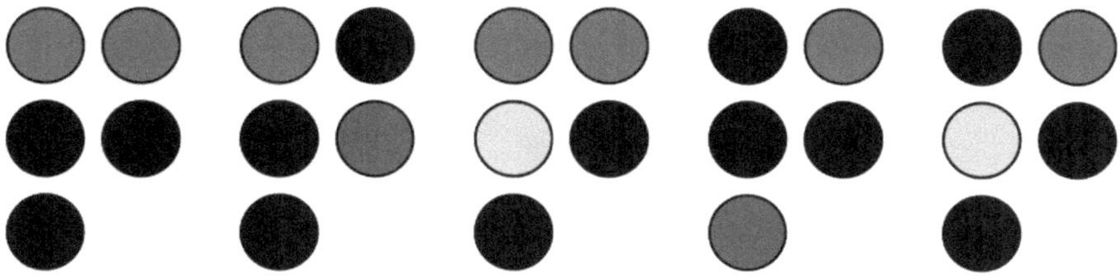

(a) All traffic lights are red (b) Pedestrian traffic light is green (c) Car traffic light is red and yellow (d) Car traffic light is green (e) Car traffic light is yellow

**Fig. 6.** 2D Visualization of Traffic Light Model showing all possible allowed states using a simple SVG model of a traffic light in a street scene.

the drone's position and detecting obstacles around it, while ensuring collision avoidance.

The drone operates in a 3D room, making it challenging to represent its position and orientation using traditional 2D visualizations. The 3D visualization in Fig. 7 allows users to see the drone's movements and interactions with its perceived environment. In the presented scenario, the drone first takes off (see Fig. 7a) and then observes its environment. When the drone observes its environment, as shown in Fig. 7b, it detects an obstacle. Afterward, the drone flies over the obstacle (see Fig. 7c). The camera in Figs. 7a to 7c is set up from the drone's third-person perspective. This scenario would be more complicated to represent and comprehend in a 2D visualization.

The camera perspective can be switched between multiple preset perspectives. The drone's first-person view shows what the drone *sees* through its sensors. The bounded view provides an external view of the drone and its surroundings nearby. Lastly, a freely movable camera, as described in Sect. 3.2, allows the user to move freely inside the scene. The visualizations from this perspective are shown in Fig. 7d to Figure 7f. In particular, the states in Fig. 7d to Fig. 7f correspond to Fig. 7a to Fig. 7c, respectively. These different perspectives allow users to understand the drone's behavior more easily and can, for example, help reason about why a collision occurs by showing the drone's perspective and what it perceives as an obstacle, in contrast to the actual surroundings.

In contrast, an outside view can help to understand the spatial relations between the drone and its surroundings. This can be especially useful for debugging the formal model of the drone, as it allows users to see the consequences of their modeling decisions in an intuitive and safe way without the danger of damaging the actual drone or its surroundings. A comparison between the first-person view and the bounded view is depicted in Fig. 8.

(a) Drone taking off as seen by drone camera

(b) Drone discovering an obstacle (orange) as seen by drone camera

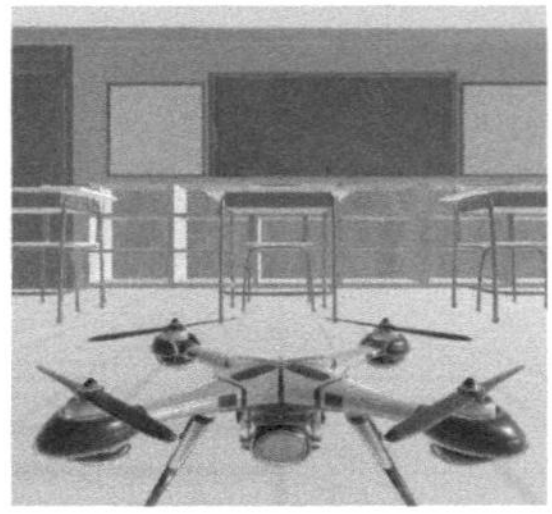

(c) Drone flying over an obstacle as seen by drone camera

(d) Drone taking off as seen by free camera

(e) Drone discovering an obstacle (orange) as seen by free camera

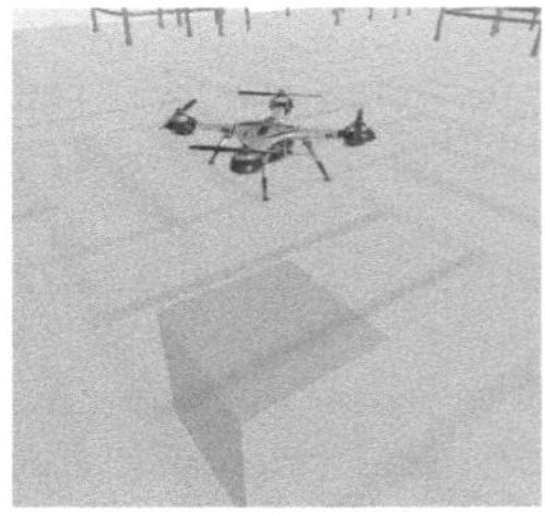

(f) Drone flying over an obstacle (orange) as seen by free camera

**Fig. 7.** 3D visualization of the drone model showing a drone in a classroom near a discovered obstacle. Figures. 7a–7c show the drone's perspective, while Figs. 7d–7f show a free camera perspective. Drone 3D Model (https://skfb.ly/6UGIq) by Mateus Schwaab is licensed under CC BY 4.0 Attribution. Japanese Classroom 3D Model (https://skfb.ly/6UGIq) by T I A N is licensed under CC BY 4.0 Attribution.

## 5 Discussion

The case studies presented in Sect. 4 provide an initial assessment of the goals introduced in Sect. 1.

1. *Improve the comprehensibility of formal models.* The traffic light and drone examples suggest that VisB-3D improves the accessibility of formal models by presenting model states in a domain-specific representation. In particular, the traffic light visualization places the formal model into a realistic street environment, making the represented system easier to understand than a 2D or code-based representation.
2. *Support validation of systems operating in three-dimensional environments.* The drone case study demonstrates the evidence for this goal. The drone's position, obstacle detection, and movement are inherently three-dimensional concepts that are difficult to represent using 2D visualizations. VisB-3D supports exploration and debugging of formal models through interaction

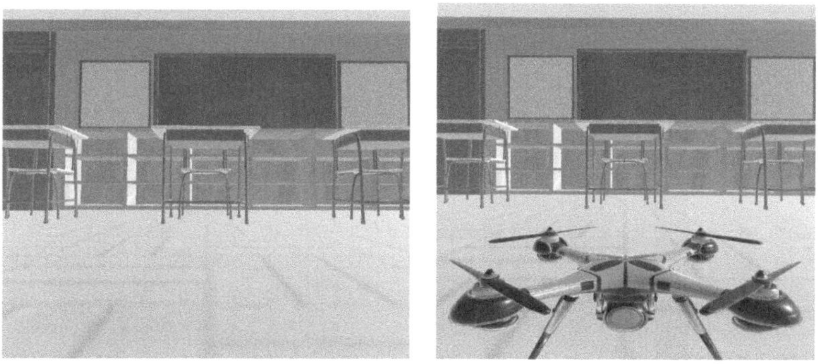

(a) Drone flying as seen by a first person view (b) Drone flying as seen by a camera behind the drone

**Fig. 8.** 3D visualizations of the drone model showing a drone in a classroom. The subfigures visualize the difference between the drone's (ego) perspective, and a camera placed behind the drone. License similar to Fig. 7

with graphical objects and synchronized execution of linked formal events. In the drone example, switching between cameras can help explain unexpected behavior and support debugging by exposing the drone's perception and the actual spatial situation.

3. *Preserve the flexibility and language independence of* VisB. The implementation maintains the separation between the formal model and visualization inherited from VisB. The use of glue files allows domain-specific visualizations to be created independently of the underlying specification. Furthermore, the solution remains compatible with the state-based formalisms supported by ProB.

The presented case studies indicate that VisB-3D successfully achieves its design goals. However, the current evaluation remains qualitative. A systematic user study involving developers and domain experts would be required to quantify the extent to which the prepended goals are met. Future work could, for example, compare validation activities with traditional 2D visualizations and VisB-3D. Such studies are planned as future work.

The main motivation of this paper is to improve the validation of systems operating in three-dimensional environments. Although this cannot be verified without a systematic user study involving developers and domain experts, existing work that utilizes VisB has shown that domain-specific visualizations can support communication between formal methods experts and domain experts during validation activities [29]. In these settings, visualizations help bridge the gap between formal specifications and domain experts who are often unfamiliar with formal notation. VisB-3D builds on this idea and extends it to systems with inherently three-dimensional behavior.

Validation through domain-specific visualizations using VisB is already an established workflow in the ProB ecosystem that is used extensively on a wide variety of domains [9,10,19,20,27].

## 6 Related Work

Visualization support for formal methods has been investigated extensively, with most existing tools focusing on 2D representations, including PVSio-Web [31], JeB [33], and Brama [24]. These visualization tools provide graphical views or animations of formal models and can be effective for viewing certain formal models, but may fall short in adequately expressing behaviors and structures that contain spatial relationships and movements that are better captured in 3D [6].

A 3D visualization approach is presented in [26], where a prototype tool, called ReqViZ3D, is used to support the validation of system requirements. In this work, formal specifications written in Z are translated into an executable form and visualized in an interactive 3D environment using Java3D. This allows users to explore a system's behavior through animated 3D scenarios, trying to improve communication between developers and domain experts. While this early approach demonstrates the potential of combining formal methods with 3D visualization, it focuses primarily on the validation of system requirements while also relying on the Z specification language and transformation pipeline. In contrast, VisB-3D provides a more flexible solution by directly linking state-based formal models to domain-specific 3D visualizations via a glue file, without requiring a transformation pipeline or restricting the approach to a single specification language.

Within the broader area of formal methods for computer-aided design (FMCAD), several approaches have explored visualization techniques. For example, Krauß and Nonnengart [14] demonstrated the feasibility of linking formal models to 3D representations using XML3D. Other 3D visualization approaches like [13] have been proposed for visualizing Petri nets. These approaches focus on visualizing the formalism itself rather than providing domain-specific visualizations of arbitrary state-based models.

In contrast, VisB-3D is integrated in ProB2-UI and supports multiple state-based formalisms while remaining independent of a specific modeling language. By using modern 3D standards (glTF) and a 3D engine, it provides a flexible and extensible foundation for long-term support and further extension.

## 7 Conclusion and Future Work

This paper presented VisB-3D, an extension of the VisB visualization tool for the animator, constraint solver, and model checker ProB. VisB-3D enables domain-specific 3D visualizations of state-based formal models. By replacing the traditional 2D SVG-based feature with a 3D visualization engine based on Unity WebGL and glTF, VisB-3D allows formal models to be explored and manipulated in intuitive 3D scenes. Equivalent to VisB, the strict separation between formal model and visualization is preserved through a 3D glue file, enabling domain experts to design visualizations without modifying the underlying specification. We demonstrated the techniques on two case studies, namely a traffic light model and a drone case study, where we outline the advantages of 3D visualizations compared to 2D. 3D visualization is particularly important when a system interacts in a 3D environment that acts as a digital twin of the real world, as we demonstrated in the drone case study. Another advantage of our implementation is the ability to view a system from various camera perspectives in 3D. As a result, VisB-3D also enables the user to view a system from the perspective of a specific object, as demonstrated in the case studies.

All examples are available at:

https://gitlab.cs.uni-duesseldorf.de/general/stups/visb-3d-examples

The ProB2-UI extension is available at:

https://github.com/DerHyper/ProB2-UI-VisB-3D

The Unity 3D visualization is available at:

https://github.com/DerHyper/VisB-3D-Unity-Visualization

In the future, one could improve animation support in the visualization, such as linear interpolation between state changes instead of discrete jumps, or explicit transition animations between states. Additional interaction techniques, e.g., hover for clickable surfaces and in-scene texts, could improve usability and feedback during model exploration. Furthermore, enhanced lighting control, configurable brightness levels, and time-of-day settings would allow visualizations to better adapt to different domains and scenarios. Other improvements in the field of user experience include the execution of events by input methods like keyboard button presses or interaction with custom UI elements. Besides extending the technical capabilities of VisB-3D, a systematic study involving developers and domain experts would be required in the future. In particular, one could investigate whether three-dimensional representations, digital twins, and game-like prototypes can further improve communication between formal methods engineers and domain experts. Additionally, a systematic study might help identify and implement features that are not supported yet.

## References


1. Abrial, J.R.: The B-Book: Assigning Programs to Meanings. Cambridge University Press (2005). https://doi.org/10.1017/CBO9780511624162
2. Abrial, J.R.: Modeling in Event-B: System and Software Engineering. Cambridge University Press (2010). https://doi.org/10.1017/CBO9781139195881
3. Bendisposto, J., et al.: ProB2-UI: A Java-Based User Interface for ProB. In: Proceedings of the FMICS, pp. 193–201. LNCS 12863, Springer (2021). https://doi.org/10.1007/978-3-030-85248-1_12

4. Cardoso, R.C., Farrell, M., Luckcuck, M., Ferrando, A., Fisher, M.: Heterogeneous Verification of an Autonomous Curiosity Rover. In: Proceedings of the NFM, pp. 353–360. LNCS 12229, Springer (2020). https://doi.org/10.1007/978-3-030-55754-6_20
5. Dosovitskiy, A., Ros, G., Codevilla, F., Lopez, A., Koltun, V.: CARLA: an open urban driving simulator. In: Proceedings of the Conference on robot learning, pp. 1–16. PMLR (2017)
6. Dübel, S., Röhlig, M., Schumann, H., Trapp, M.: 2D and 3D presentation of spatial data: a systematic review. In: 2014 IEEE VIS International Workshop on 3DVis (3DVis), pp. 11–18 (2014). https://doi.org/10.1109/3DVis.2014.7160094
7. Fan, Y., et al.: A digital-twin visualized architecture for Flexible Manufacturing System. J. Manuf. Syst. **60**, 176–201 (2021). https://doi.org/10.1016/j.jmsy.2021.05.010
8. Ferrando, A., et al.: ROSMonitoring: a runtime verification framework for ROS. In: Proceedings of the TAROS, pp. 387–399. LNAI 12228, Springer (2020). https://doi.org/10.1007/978-3-030-63486-5_40
9. Geleßus, D., Stock, S., Vu, F., Leuschel, M., Mashkoor, A.: Development and validation of a formal model and prototype for an air traffic control system. Formal Aspects Comput. **38**(7), 1–37 (2025). https://doi.org/10.1145/3774647
10. Gruteser, J., Leuschel, M.: Validation of railML Using ProB. In: Engineering of Complex Computer Systems., pp. 245–256. Springer (2025). https://doi.org/10.1007/978-3-031-66456-4_13
11. Gruteser, J., Roßbach, J., Vu, F., Leuschel, M.: Using formal models, safety shields and certified control to validate AI-based train systems. Electr. Proc. Theor. Comput. Sci. **411**, 151–159 (2024). https://doi.org/10.4204/eptcs.411.10
12. The Khronos®3D Formats Working Group: glTF™2.0 Specification (2021), version 2.0.1, 2021-10-11 23:01:57Z: from git branch: main commit: 8e798b02d254cea97659a333cfcb20875b62bdd4
13. Kindler, E., Páles, C.: 3D-Visualization of petri net models: concept and realization. In: Applications and Theory of Petri Nets 2004, pp. 464–473. Springer (2004). https://doi.org/10.1007/978-3-540-27793-4_27
14. Krauß, C., Nonnengart, A.: Formal analysis meets 3D-visualization. In: Concurrent Engineering Approaches for Sustainable Product Development in a Multi-Disciplinary Environment, pp. 145–156. Springer (2013). https://doi.org/10.1007/978-1-4471-4426-7_13
15. Ladenberger, L., Leuschel, M.: Mastering the visualization of larger state spaces with projection diagrams. In: Proceedings of the ICFEM, pp. 153–169. LNCS 9407, Springer (2015). https://doi.org/10.1007/978-3-319-25423-4_10
16. Lamport, L.: The temporal logic of actions. ACM Trans. Program. Lang. Syst. (TOPLAS) **16**(3), 872–923 (1994). https://doi.org/10.1145/177492.177726
17. Lamport, L.: Specifying systems. Addison-Wesley Boston (2002)
18. Leuschel, M., Butler, M.: ProB: an automated analysis toolset for the B method. Int. J. Softw. Tools Technol. Transfer **10**(2), 185–203 (2008). https://doi.org/10.1007/s10009-007-0063-9
19. Leuschel, M., Mutz, M., Werth, M.: Modelling and validating an automotive system in classical B and event-B. In: Proceedings of the ABZ, pp. 335–350. Springer (2020). https://doi.org/10.1007/978-3-030-48077-6_27
20. Leuschel, M., Nayeri, N.: Modelling, visualisation and proof of an ETCS level 3 moving block system. In: Proceedings of the RSSRail, pp. 193–210. Springer (2023). https://doi.org/10.1007/978-3-031-43366-5_12

21. Leuschel, M., Turner, E.: Visualising larger state spaces in ProB. In: ZB 2005: Formal Specification and Development in Z and B, pp. 6–23. LNCS 3455, Springer (2005). https://doi.org/10.1007/11415787_2
22. Masci, P., Muñoz, C.A.: A graphical toolkit for the validation of requirements for detect and avoid systems. In: Ahrendt, W., Wehrheim, H. (eds.) TAP 2020. LNCS, vol. 12165, pp. 155–166. Springer, Cham (2020). https://doi.org/10.1007/978-3-030-50995-8_9
23. Quigley, M., et al.: ROS: an open-source Robot Operating System. In: Workshop on Open Source Software at the International Conference on Robotics and Automation. IEEE (2009)
24. Servat, T.: BRAMA: a new graphic animation tool for B models. In: B 2007: Formal Specification and Development in B, pp. 274–276. Springer (2006). https://doi.org/10.1007/11955757_28
25. Spivey, J.M.: The Z notation: A Reference Manual. Prentice Hall Hemel Hempstead (1992)
26. Teyseyre, A.R.: A 3D visualization approach to validate requirements (2002)
27. Vu, F., Dunkelau, J., Leuschel, M.: Validation of Reinforcement Learning Agents and Safety Shields with ProB. In: Proceedings of the NFM, pp. 279–297. LNCS 14627, Springer (2024). https://doi.org/10.1007/978-3-031-60698-4_16
28. Vu, F., et al.: Hardware-in-the-loop validation of formal models: an application to AI-controlled drones. In: Proceedings of the NFM, pp. 120–141. LNCS 16622, Springer (2026). https://doi.org/10.1007/978-3-032-28079-4_6
29. Vu, F., Happe, C., Leuschel, M.: Generating interactive documents for domain-specific validation of formal models. Int. J. Softw. Tools Technol. Transfer **26**(2), 147–168 (2024). https://doi.org/10.1007/s10009-024-00739-0
30. Vu, F., Leuschel, M., Mashkoor, A.: Validation of formal models by timed probabilistic simulation. In: Proceedings of the ABZ, pp. 81–96. LNCS 12709, Springer (2021). https://doi.org/10.1007/978-3-030-77543-8_6
31. Watson, N., Reeves, S., Masci, P.: Integrating user design and formal models within PVSio-web. Electr. Proc. Theor. Comput. Sci. **284**, 95–104 (2018). https://doi.org/10.4204/eptcs.284.8
32. Werth, M., Leuschel, M.: VisB: A lightweight tool to visualize formal models with SVG graphics. In: Proceedings of the ABZ, pp. 260–265. LNCS 12071, Springer (2020). https://doi.org/10.1007/978-3-030-48077-6_21
33. Yang, F., Jacquot, J.P., Souquières, J.: JeB: safe simulation of event-b models in JavaScript. In: 2013 20th Asia-Pacific Software Engineering Conference (APSEC), vol. 1, pp. 571–576 (2013). https://doi.org/10.1109/APSEC.2013.83
34. Zapridou, E., Bartocci, E., Katsaros, P.: Runtime verification of autonomous driving systems in CARLA. In: Proceedings of the Runtime Verification, pp. 172–183. LNCS 12399, Springer (2020). https://doi.org/10.1007/978-3-030-60508-7_9

# Author Index





P. Gorm Larsen and K. Y. Rozier (Eds.): FMICS 2026, LNCS 16967, p. 155, 2027.
https://doi.org/10.1007/978-3-032-36849-2

FSC
www.fsc.org
MIX
Papier | Fördert
gute Waldnutzung
FSC® C083411

Kolibri 360 GmbH
Ferdinand-Jühlke-Straße 7
99095 Erfurt, Deutschland
produktsicherheit@kolibri360.de